110846

Stephen Castles
and
Wiebke Wüstenberg

The Education of the Future
An Introduction to the Theory and Practice of Socialist Education

Pluto  Press

First published 1979 by Pluto Press Limited
Unit 10, Spencer Court
7 Chalcot Road, London NW1 8LH

Copyright © Pluto Press 1979

ISBN paperback 0 86104 070 8
ISBN hardback 0 86104 070 6

Cover designed by Richard Hollis GrR

Map on p. 176 reproduced by permission of
Tvind Schools, Denmark

Printed in Great Britain by
Latimer Trend & Company Ltd Plymouth

Contents

1.
Introduction

1. The Importance of Education for Socialist Strategy

The transition from capitalism to socialism is not just a matter of changing economic and political structures. It also involves changing the way people think about work, social relationships and society in general. Social consciousness is above all a product of economic and social conditions; but it is not only that – it is also a factor which itself helps to shape the development of economic and social conditions. In other words: there is a dialectical relationship between consciousness and material conditions. Backward consciousness can hinder changes in material conditions and vice versa. Education is the name we give to the planned and systematic shaping of consciousness. Socialists have always understood the importance of education as an instrument of social transformation, and have given it great priority in their strategies.

Before the Socialist Revolution

Each historical form of society has developed its own ways of raising children and preparing them to take an appropriate part in production and social life. In less developed societies these tasks are carried out in the course of daily life by parents and the community. In more complex societies special institutions such as schools, universities and apprenticeships have been devised. In class societies there is no single education system, but rather a whole range: the education of a slave is different from that of a slave-owner, that of a serf different from the lord of the manor. To understand the class-specific forms of education it is necessary to analyse the way in which society produces and distributes food and other necessary goods, and the social and political structures which arise from this mode of production. Education is controlled by the class which controls the means of production, and has two main functions: first, to provide the general capabilities and vocational training necessary for a member of a specific social class to carry out his or her appointed tasks; second, to pass on the dominant religious or political ideology which legitimates the existing form of class domination.

When a specific mode of production reaches the limits of its development, a process of transition to a new mode of production begins. Such periods of transition – like the transition from feudalism to capitalism, or from capitalism to socialism – are historical epochs of social crisis. Changes in the mode of production lead to changes in social and political structures. The old forms of education are no longer adequate and have to change as well. The old ruling class tries to maintain or reform the old education system, and the new classes which are rising to power develop new forms of education. It is in such periods that revolutionary theories of education can arise. The suppressed and exploited classes realise that they need new ways of shaping consciousness to achieve their emancipation, and the breakdown of the old forms of education gives them the chance to introduce innovations.

But what sort of education is needed to serve the emancipation of the suppressed and exploited classes? That is the basic question which this book tries to answer. Here is a preliminary pointer: the interest of the ruling class is to prevent the lower classes from understanding the real structures of production and of society. The more ignorant the workers are, the better for the ruling class. In pre-industrial societies, education is therefore mainly restricted to religious indoctrination which proves that the current state of society is the will of God. But as the mode of production and the social structure get more complicated, this no longer suffices. Basic education becomes the pre-condition for being able to work and live in society. Now the interest of the ruling class is to make learning as abstract and compartmentalised as possible: workers should learn only what is necessary for their jobs, and as little as possible about technology, economics and politics. The more specialised their training, the easier it is to keep them under control.

Obviously, the interest of workers is the opposite: the more they understand about the technological, economic and political relationships which govern society and production, the better they can fight against class domination. Education for emancipation means getting away from narrow specialisation and fighting for a high level of scientific, political and cultural education for everybody. We shall go into this in more detail below, and discuss what it means for the contents and methods of schooling.

The working-class movement has always understood the key role of education. In many countries, the first institutions of the working-class movement were workers' education groups, and free education for everybody has always been one of its main demands. In the course of the nineteenth century the bourgeoisie of most Western capitalist countries had to give way on this point, but it turned out to be an empty victory for the labour movement. By introducing compulsory state education the bourgeoisie was able to regain control of the content and form of schooling, and to undermine seriously working-class influence in education. The school in capitalism is not an instrument of emancipation, but a potent instrument of ideological control.

So education remains a major problem of socialist strategy in capitalist countries: how can socialist parents and teachers work to change education, to make it an instrument for social transformation rather than a tool for preserving class domination?

After the Socialist Revolution

But education will not cease to be a problem after a successful workers' revolution. The conquest of state power is only the first step towards building a new society. The revolutionary government is then faced with the task of transforming the political, economic and social structures which it has inherited from the old society. As long as this task has not been achieved the risk of a restoration of capitalism, in one form or another, persists. Again, this is not just a problem of changing material conditions, but also one of altering social consciousness. People's cultural level and the way in which they see society has been shaped by capitalism. Values such as individualism, profit-seeking, competitiveness, and belief in the superiority of mental work over manual work are unsuitable for building socialism. In addition, the low level of technological and political education received by workers in capitalism makes it extremely difficult for them to run and develop production and society. That is why socialist revolutionaries have always regarded a 'cultural revolution' as vital for the victory of socialism.[1]

The transformation of social consciousness is necessary not only in itself, as the basis of new forms of socialist morality and ethics,[2] but also as a vital factor in changing the material structures of society. This applies particularly in the case of revolutions in backward countries like Russia and China. Faced with under-developed economic structures and strong pressure from the capitalist countries, revolutionaries have been compelled to develop the means of production at break-neck speed and to attempt the leap from peasant agriculture to modern industry in one generation. But, before the revolution, education was as backward as the economy. 'You know that a communist society cannot be built in an illiterate country', Lenin told the youth organisations of the Soviet Union in 1920.[3] Raising the educational level of the population is a vital precondition for developing the means of production.

The cultural revolution is also vital for maintaining workers' rule and preventing the degeneration of the revolution. Upon gaining state power, revolutionaries have always found that they lacked the trained people necessary for running the economy and for administering social affairs. This is not surprising: under capitalism, there is a division between manual and mental work. Mental workers are often privileged compared with manual workers. Some mental workers actually serve the ruling class in helping to dominate other workers. Manual workers are deliberately denied the knowledge they would need to control production and society. That is why both the Russian and Chinese communists had to rely on bourgeois specialists immediately after their respective revolutions. These specialists had to be given material rewards to induce them to work. This is dangerous both because it brings back class privilege, and because the specialists may try to sabotage the construction of socialism. The cultural revolution therefore has two pressing tasks: firstly, the rapid training of 'red specialists' of working-class origin to replace the bourgeois specialists; secondly, raising the cultural level of the masses to allow them to control the specialists (both bourgeois and red) through democratic organs such as workers' and peasants' councils. Failure to achieve these aims may lead to the degeneration of the revolution: the old ruling class of landowners and capitalists may be replaced by a new bureaucratic bourgeoisie which holds the key posts in party, state and economic hierarchies.[4]

To put the problem in a nutshell: to build socialism you need people who possess socialist consciousness and culture, but such people can only be produced by socialist society itself. Socialism has to be built with the 'men and women who grew up under capitalism, were depraved and corrupted by capitalism, but steeled for the struggle by capitalism . . .'[5] The resolution of this dilemma has been an important theme of socialist theory. It is one reason why marxists have never envisaged a direct transition from capitalism to communism, but have always seen the need for an intermediary stage, generally known as socialism.[6] Marx described the transitional stage as follows:

> We are dealing here with a communist society, not as it has *developed* on its own foundations, but on the contrary, just as it *emerges* from capitalist society. In every respect, economically, morally, intellectually, it is thus stamped with the birth-marks of the old society from whose womb it has emerged.[7]

Under socialism commodity production, unequal incomes, classes and class struggle still persist. But it is not a permanent state of society: it is a transitional stage, in which the control of the means of production by the working class allows the planned transformation of political, economic, and social structures, in order to create the conditions necessary for communist society. Since the old privileged classes are certain to fight against these changes, a strong workers' state – the dictatorship of the proletariat – remains necessary under socialism.[8] As the capitalist forms of production and distribution are overcome, the old classes disappear. The state, as an instrument of class repression becomes unnecessary and withers away.

> In a more advanced phase of communist society, when the enslaving subjugation of individuals to the division of labour, and thereby the antithesis between intellectual and physical labour have disappeared; when labour is no longer just a means of keeping alive but has itself become a vital need; when the all-round development of individuals has also increased their productive powers and all the springs of co-operative wealth flow more abundantly – only then can society wholly cross the narrow horizon of bourgeois right and inscribe on its banner: From each according to his abilities, to each according to his needs![9]

The implication here is that one of the major tasks of transitional society is to create the conditions necessary for overcoming the distinction between mental and manual work. Obviously, education has a major role to play in this. It must help to make all citizens capable not only of doing productive work, but also of planning and organising this work – not individually, but collectively with their workmates. However, the workers' horizon must not be restricted to the place of work. They can only control production in their own interest and in the interest of society in general if they all have a full grasp of the technological, economic and political relationships between their own workplace and the whole system of social production.

2. Polytechnic Education

What we have written so far should be sufficient to show the importance of education for socialist strategy, and to indicate some of the tasks of education in social transformation. In this book, we set out to examine how the theory and practice of socialist education has developed in response to these challenges. We will not attempt to present a systematic and comprehensive history of socialist education, but rather to concentrate on important turning points in the development of the theory and in its application. Our starting-point is the transition to industrial capitalism in nineteenth-century Britain and its effects on mass education. The early socialist response to the new problems is illustrated by an examination of one of the most important educational models of the age: Robert Owen's New Lanark schools.

Marx leaned on Owen's experience when he came to set out his theory of a new type of education, which he regarded as both a necessary product of modern industry and a vital precondition for further human progress. This new form of education has generally been referred to, particularly by German and Russian marxists, as 'polytechnic education' and we use this term here. We shall look at the marxist theory of education in detail in chapter two, but it is necessary to mention a few basic principles at this point.

> As Robert Owen has shown us in detail, the germ of the education of the future is present in the factory system; this education will, in the case of every child over a given age, combine productive labour with instruction and gymnastics, not only as one of the methods of adding to the efficiency of production, but as the only method of producing fully developed human beings.[10]

Linking education with productive work is a basic element of the marxist theory of education. Indeed, in some Eastern European countries, there has been a tendency to reduce marxist education theory to this principle. Polytechnic education really means much more than this. Its aim is to produce 'fully developed human beings', which means people who are capable not only of doing productive work, but also of controlling production and running society. Every person must be capable of mastering the aims, technology and concrete methods of production processes, and understanding their relationship with society in general. This does not mean that specialisation can be completely avoided, but rather that everybody must possess sufficient basic knowledge and capabilities to be able to learn any occupation as needed. The preconditions for this are:

- a high level of education for everybody;
- overcoming the division between manual and mental work: polytechnic education is pointless if one person spends a lifetime doing purely mental work, another only manual labour; all workers must have the chance of doing both;
- removal of the distinction between working and learning, between school and work; every child should take part in socially necessary production from an early age; every adult should have the chance to go on learning, both at work and elsewhere;
- everybody must participate in planning and decision-making; once polytechnic education has given everybody an understanding of social aims and technological problems, there can be no justification for excluding anybody from the organs of planning and decision-making: a society with polytechnic education cannot but be a democratic society.

Now the last point might be taken to mean that polytechnic education is only relevant once communist society has been achieved. Marx meant it differently. He saw the struggle for the 'education of the future' as part of the struggle for a new society. Polytechnic education may only be partly realisable under capitalism, but by fighting for new forms of mass education it is possible to change existing forms of schooling which hinder the development of class consciousness. And every step towards the realisation of polytechnic principles will help to change mass consciousness in the future. That is why Marx calls the new form of education 'revolutionary ferments' which 'stand in diametrical contradiction with the capitalist form of production, and economic situation of workers which corresponds to that form'.[11]

Marx's theory of polytechnic education was taken up by Lenin and Krupskaya and adapted to the conditions of backward Russia. Krupskaya – herself a former teacher – made an important contribution in showing that not only the content, but also the form of teaching is important in shaping personality. Rigid curricula and authoritarian drill cannot educate socialists capable of running society in their own interests. Krupskaya took over the best ideas of progressive bourgeois educationalists and combined them with the principles of polytechnic education, to form the basis of the new school system of revolutionary Russia.

Having described the theory of polytechnic education, our main concern is to examine the way it has been applied in various countries as part of the transition to socialism. We look at the Soviet Union from 1917 to 1931, at China from 1949 to 1976, and at the German Democratic Republic. In all these cases, attempts have been made to realise the marxist principles of polytechnic education. Methods have varied considerably – due partly to political differences and partly to varying social and economic conditions in the countries concerned. It is only possible to understand educational developments by showing their close relationship with the economic, social and political problems and changes in the countries concerned. We shall try to show how and why the leadership of all three countries has, at a certain stage, started retreating from polytechnic education. This is most obvious in the case of the Stalinist era in the Soviet Union after 1931. Socialist education, designed to produce critical and versatile people, had no place in a rigid development dictatorship. After the demise of Stalin, polytechnic education was re-introduced in the Soviet Union and throughout Eastern Europe. We examine this new version by looking at the case of the German Democratic Republic – which appears to be representative of educational developments throughout the Soviet bloc at the present time. Developments in China have followed a different course. The priority given to education has been even greater than elsewhere. In fact, in the 'Great Proletarian Cultural Revolution' of the mid-1960s, the changing of consciousness through new forms of education appeared for a while as the crucial lever of social transformation.

Finally, we look at recent tendencies in the education systems of advanced capitalist countries. Attempts are being made to introduce productive work at school, and to relate learning to pupils' future occupational roles. Such trends appear to have gone furthest in West Germany, where there is actually a new school subject called *Polytechnik*. Although this subject is designed to Foster the adaptability and social integration of workers, rather than to further their political emancipation, it does reflect important changes in technology, work organisation and the problems of maintaining the legitimacy of capitalist domination. These changes – as we shall try to show – provide an opportunity for socialist educators to fight for the introduction of genuine polytechnic education in schools, nurseries, youth work and similar fields. Here is a new chance to make education a 'revolutionary ferment' for capitalist society.

2.

Owen and Marx: Polytechnic Education During the Ascendancy of British Industrial Capitalism

1. Early Ideas on Mass Education

In feudal society the vast majority of the peasants and urban labourers received no formal schooling. They learnt to work by watching and helping their parents. Social norms and behaviour patterns were passed on by the family and the local community. The only special institution concerned with creating and controlling consciousness was the Catholic Church, which provided compulsory ideological indoctrination on the benefits of the prevailing 'divine order'. The ruling aristocracy had its own educational system, and, in the late middle ages, the up and coming classes of merchant capitalists and urban master craftsmen started developing their own schools and vocational training systems. But the majority of the population remained illiterate and ignorant. The ruling class wanted to keep things that way, regarding knowledge as a dangerous weapon in the hands of the poor.

The social upheavals associated with the transition from feudalism to capitalism began to change this situation. The turning point in the process was the early sixteenth century (in the case of Britain). The move to capitalist agriculture was marked by the enclosure of arable land for sheep farming. This in turn led to mass evictions, poverty, vagabondage and crime. The typical response of the ruling class to this social crisis of 'primitive accumulation'[1] was the introduction of draconian laws to punish the poor for their destitution and to keep them under control. But some early bourgeois thinkers realised that the impending changes in the mode of production also heralded a transformation of society. They put forward plans for a new rational form of society, in which mass education appeared as a new means of securing social stability and integration.

An important early example of this type of theory is to be

found in Sir Thomas More's *Utopia*, written in 1515. *Utopia*[2] is a blueprint for an ideal society in which there are no idle rich or starving poor. All members of society take part in agricultural and handicraft production, and live communally. All children receive a high level of general education and learn useful trades. The pursuit of knowledge through study and research is regarded as the noblest occupation. More's ideas have often been regarded as a sort of 'primitive communism'. Indeed in some respects – for instance the linking of learning with productive work – they do foreshadow socialist theory. But More's ideas are basically elitist. The new social order was to be introduced from above, by wise rulers. The citizens who distinguished themselves in intellectual activities were to form a 'meritocracy' who would rule over the masses. Ordinary workers were not regarded as capable of understanding or representing their own interests. They needed a special class of scholars to decide what was good for them. There is no place in More's *Utopia* for the workers as the subject of educational and social change. Education is not designed to equip workers to run society, but rather to make them work efficiently and loyally in a framework determined from above. More's work may be regarded as the beginning of a tradition of educational reform theory which calls for mass education as a means of integrating workers into capitalist society, rather than emancipating them from it.

But the earliest stirrings of popular revolt against the new forms of social inequality were to bring forward a quite different tradition of educational change. One of its first representatives was Gerrard Winstanley, a leading spokesman of the Diggers, who tried to set up revolutionary agricultural communes in the mid-seventeenth century, immediately after the English Civil War. Winstanley set down the Diggers' blueprint for a new egalitarian society in a political manifesto entitled 'The Law of Freedom in a Platform', written in 1652.[3] Education was to play a vital part in the 'true commonwealth'. Its citizens were to receive a good general education, including not only basic abilities like reading, writing and arithmetic, but also history, politics, law, and the basic elements of the natural sciences. They were all to learn useful trades and to go on learning throughout their working lives through observation and experiment. Regular discussion and study of the laws of nature and the problems of society was to be an essential aspect of life for all citizens of the 'true commonwealth'. A comprehensive information service was to ensure that everybody was well informed about public affairs. And all this acquisition of knowledge was not to be just for its own sake. Scientific and technical information was to be used to improve the means of production; knowledge of history, politics and law was to help every citizen to take an active part in the political life of the commonwealth. Education was for Winstanley primarily political education. By becoming the subject of a life-long learning process, the worker was to become the subject of political and economic transformation. The citizen of the 'true commonwealth' would have come close to what Marx was later to call the 'totally developed individual'.

The difference between the ideas of More and of Winstanley on society and education is not accidental, but a result of differing class perspectives. More was a leading member of the English ruling class, and was later to become Lord Chancellor under Henry VIII. Winstanley was a ruined tailor, living in a revolutionary period and himself an active revolutionary. But in fact neither of their plans was to have much effect on the development of mass education in the sixteenth and seventeenth centuries. Workers and farmers remained uneducated, for their rulers preferred to keep them ignorant. Large profits and rapid capital accumulation – the preconditions for the industrial revolution of the eighteenth and nineteenth centuries – were most easily achieved with downtrodden and impoverished workers, who lacked the knowledge necessary for political organisation.

None the less, the period leading up to the great political and economic changes of the late eighteenth century was marked by considerable discussion on the problems of mass education. The ideas of the Czech educationalist Jan Amos Komensky (known as Comenius) were influential throughout the seventeenth century. The English philosopher John Locke,[4] as well as the early political economists John Bellers and William Petty, published educational schemes.[5] The French philosophers, whose work was to make an important contribution to the ideas of the bourgeois revolution of 1789, paid great attention to education. In their struggle against the privileges of the nobility, they denied that any man was born with qualities better than another. The 'Encyclopaedist' Helvetius emphasised that the ideas, capabilities and character of a person were the product of their environment and could therefore be shaped by education, which was one of the most important tasks of society. Jean-Jacques Rousseau's educational novel *Emile* (1762) set out to show how character could be moulded to produce a 'natural' and 'reasoning' person. In the early years of the French Revolution there were several attempts to put such ideas into practice in a new educational system. Plans were put forward first by Mirabeau (in 1791) and then by Condorcet (1792). Under Robespierre the Jacobin Convention discussed a plan for free, compulsory, state education for all children; however, it was not adopted.

We cannot describe any of these important educational theories here. It is important to realise that the new rationalism of the ascendent and still revolutionary bourgeoisie, with its emphasis on man as a product of his environment, was a vital precondition for the development of socialist ideas on education in the nine-teenth century. The other vital precondition was the industrial revolution with its inherent contradiction: on the one hand new oppression and misery for the working masses; on the other hand the potential for the emancipation of the workers and for the transformation of society. Large-scale industry and the growth of the industrial working class were to remove the utopian character of polytechnic education theories and to make them a real possi-bility – indeed, a necessity for the future progress of society.

It is impossible to put forward a coherent socialist theory without trying to explain how people are to be educated for the transition to a new society. Virtually all socialist thinkers of the early nineteenth century made proposals for mass education. Most were based on the linking of learning with productive work, and on making general, scientific and political education available to everybody. Examples are the work of the French socialists Henri de Saint-Simon and Charles Fourier, and of Wilhelm Weitling in Germany. Our analysis here will deal only with Robert Owen and Marx and Engels: Owen, because he not only wrote about educa-tion, but actually put his ideas into practice in one of the most interesting school experiments in history; Marx and Engels, be-cause their ideas represent a new level in the theory of the re-lationship between mode of production and education, and because their theory of polytechnic education became the basis of the new educational systems of the Soviet Union and other countries where attempts were made to construct socialism.

2. Production and Society

From the sixteenth century onwards, the growth of merchant capital and the effects it had on agriculture began to create the conditions necessary for the transition to industrial capitalism: on the one hand, the concentration of large amounts of capital in the hands of a relatively small class; on the other hand, exclusion of the great majority of the population from ownership of the means of production, so that they were forced to become wage labourers. Between the sixteenth century and the mid-eighteenth century, the move from merchant capital to industrial capital took various transitory forms:

– domestic industry, or the putting-out system, in which merchant capitalists tried to break the power of the craft guilds by putting out work to rural workers, working in their own homes; the materials and the finished product belonged to the capitalist, who paid the dependent worker a piece rate;

– co-operation, in which large numbers of craftsmen were employed in one workshop by a capitalist, who might himself be either a merchant capitalist or a master craftsman; the form of working and division of labour remained as in traditional handicrafts, with each labourer working in all stages of production; the tools (generally), the workshop, materials and the finished commodity belonged to the capitalist, who paid the workers a piece rate or an hourly wage; although the workers were dependent, they did have a fairly strong bargaining position, for they had to be fully qualified craftsmen;

– manufacture – a logical further development of co-operation; once many workers were employed together in one workshop, it was an obvious step to change the division of labour between them, so that each performed only one operation in the production of a particular commodity, then passing it on to his or her neighbour, who performed the next operation and so on.

We cannot go into any detail on these forms of production here. They are described with a wealth of historical examples by Marx in *Capital*.[6] In the Appendix (see pages 195–201) we attempt a schematic summary of the relationship between the various forms of production and education. Manufacture is the real break-through for capitalism in non-agricultural production. It is highly advantageous to the employer: he saves on costs because each worker requires relatively few tools; work becomes much faster because each worker becomes highly proficient in one restricted task; labour becomes cheaper, for the worker does not require a lengthy craft training; old, slow, sick or rebellious workers can easily be replaced. For the workers, manufacture means new sub-jections: deskilling – the knowledge of the trained craftsman be-comes worthless; physical and mental degeneration – the constant repetition of one single simple operation is monotonous and stupefying, and certain parts of the body become overdeveloped while others wither; wage-cuts – because anybody can work in a manufactory there is growing competition between the workers, so that the capitalist can push wages down to or even below the subsistence minimum. (When one considers that around a third of the population were without fixed employment in eighteenth-century London, then the catastrophic effects of manufacture for the craftsmen become evident.)

The Scottish economist Adam Smith regarded improved division of labour as the main cause of increased productivity. He described how the production of a simple needle was divided up into eighteen operations, with the result that ten workers could produce 48,000 needles per day.[7] This great improvement in productivity compared with traditional craft production took place in many sectors before the industrial revolution. Although manufacture then only made up a minor part of total commodity production, it was vital in paving the way for the factory system. Many of the earliest manufactories were started in workhouses. This applied particularly in countries where the guilds were still strong enough to prevent the employment of free wage workers – like Prussia. Industrial schools (of which more below) were often primarily manufactories, where schooling took a very poor second place. It is part of the dialectic of industrialisation (and not only of the private capitalist variety, as Stalin's labour camps were to show two centuries later) that a system which requires and creates the free wage worker needs unfree workers to get started.

By the mid-eighteenth century primitive accumulation and the development of manufacture had created conditions favourable to the invention and use of new machines. The spinning Jenny, invented by the weaver James Hargreaves of Blackburn in 1764, spun on sixteen spindles simultaneously, instead of just one, like the traditional spinning-wheel. At first turned by hand, it led to an economic and social upheaval in the textile trade. It was rapidly followed by a whole series of inventions, which completely changed the form of production for textiles.

As Marx points out: 'All fully developed machinery consists of three essentially different parts, the motor mechanism, the transmitting mechanism and finally the tool or working machine.'[8] The machines which started the industrial revolution belonged to the last category – they were working machines, moved at first by hand and then by water power (which is one reason why industry sprang up along the rivers of Lancashire, and not in the old cities). But it was only the liberation from these natural forces, brought about by the steam engine, which made large-scale industry really possible. James Watt's improvements to the steam engine between 1762 and 1775 made it a suitable motor-mechanism for textile working machines. Large-scale industry meant the final victory of the capitalist mode of production. All other forms of production were condemned to death, to be replaced by the factory system.

> An organised system of machines to which motion is communicated by the transmitting mechanism from an automatic centre is the most developed form of production by machinery. Here we have, in place of the isolated machine, a mechanical monster whose body fills whole factories, and whose demonic power, at first hidden by the slow and measured motions of its gigantic members, finally bursts forth in the fast and feverish whirl of its countless working organs.[9]

Marx showed the revolution in productivity by following up Adam Smith's example of the needle manufacture: where ten men had, in Smith's time, made 48,000 needles per day, one woman or girl supervising four machines was now producing *600,000* needles in a day.[10]

The enormous increase in commodity production, the reduction in prices for manufactured goods and the reduction of the physical effort required for production – all these great changes were no blessing for most of the population. Inventions which could have reduced the drudgery of work and improved living conditions were, under the prevailing economic system, a new means for the enslavement of the workers. Existing ways of living and working were destroyed overnight; ruined artisans were forced to migrate to the new industrial areas, where living conditions were appalling and social and hygienic facilities often nonexistent. Working conditions in the new factories were equally abysmal: poor ventilation, no safety regulations or devices, long working hours and wages even below subsistence level. But perhaps the worst thing for the former handweavers and spinners was that they came up against new competitors in the factories, who worked for less pay and took away their jobs. These competitors were their own wives and children.

The introduction of machinery continued the deskilling process which had started with the manufacture system. By dividing the production process up into several unskilled repetitive tasks, manufacture had deskilled the former craftsmen. Industry went a step further by removing the need for physical strength. Women and children could serve the working machines as well – or even better – than men: the employers were full of praise for the 'little nimble hands'. The employment of women and children became general; working days of twelve, fourteen or even sixteen hours for nine-year-old children, under the worst possible conditions, were not unusual. The father, who often could not find work, had to stay home in the meantime and look after the smallest children – a task for which his own socialisation had not prepared him at all. One result was the custom of giving babies gin or opium (in the shape of the well-known patent medicine 'Godfrey's Cordial') to keep them quiet.[11]

It goes without saying that such conditions led to an appalling degeneration in the health of the industrial working class. Illness, epidemics and greatly reduced life-expectancy were the results. Grinding poverty, constant toil from an early age, a complete lack of economic and social security – that was the lot of the worker. At first, cheap alcohol was the only available escape.

Under these circumstances, it is not surprising that one of the first effects of industrialisation was the collapse of the family. To start with it lost the function it had fulfilled in agriculture, handicraft production and domestic industry as the basic unit of production. But the industrial working-class family was not even capable of keeping the worker in a fit state to sell his or her labour power, nor of caring adequately for the children. Since there were no public nurseries or schools for working-class children, the upshot was their complete neglect. The moral and mental level of children in the industrial areas was indescribably low. Illiteracy and complete ignorance of all public affairs was the rule.

At first, this situation did not bother Britain's rulers much. The poverty of the working class appeared to them as the necessary price for Britain's development as 'the workshop of the world' – and for keeping their own profits high. If the inhabitants of Lancashire died off too quickly to keep the mills going, then they could easily get new workers from rural counties. If these sources dried up, there was always the Irish, just a few sailing-hours away.[12] Nor did the ignorance and degeneration of working-class children seem a problem to the employing class: the machines of the industrial revolution required of their servants neither vocational training nor the ability to read and write.

But about half a century after the beginning of the industrial revolution new factors began to change the attitude of the ruling class towards the social conditions of the workers:

1. The ruling class found itself unable to stifle the growing workingclass movement through laws like the Combination Acts (which forbade working class organisations) or through military force (like the Peterloo Massacre of 1819). The beginnings of a trade-union movement, the Owenite co-operatives, and above all the Chartist movement of the 1830s and 1840s, forced the ruling class to make concessions.

2. It became apparent that such extreme exploitation was endangering the sheer physical existence of the working class. Since it was becoming increasingly difficult to recruit new workers from other areas, and since the bourgeoisie could not manage without workers, certain measures for the protection of workers and their children had to be taken.[13]

3. The 'first technological revolution'[14] led to a reversal of the previous historical tendency to deskilling. The new engineering industry required workers who were capable of working precisely and methodically according to a blue-print, and who possessed knowledge of materials, machines and working methods; in other words – skilled workers. The training of skilled workers required basic cultural capabilities like reading, writing and numeracy.

For all these reasons, the first effective factory legislation was introduced in Britain in 1833. It restricted the employment of women and children and contained certain educational provisions. 'Paltry as the education clauses of the Act appear on the whole'; wrote Marx thirty years later, 'they do proclaim that elementary education is a compulsory precondition for the employment of children.'[15] This legislation, which will be dealt with in more detail below, was a breakthrough, both for the development of public education and for the marxist theory of polytechnic education.

3. The Beginnings of Public Education

In pre-industrial Britain there had been no schools for most members of the poorer classes. In the villages, 'dame schools' had taught a few children the rudiments of reading and writing, but their main concern was to keep younger children out of mischief. Schools kept by parish clerks had been mainly devoted to teaching the catechism. In the towns, 'charity schools' had given certain poorer children enough basic education to enable them to become apprentices. But the overwhelming majority of the children of the rural and urban poor had received no general education.

There was a special school for the very poorest: the school of industry, usually attached to a workhouse. These institutions were an attempt by the ruling class to deal with the mass poverty resulting from primitive accumulation. It is estimated that about every fifth family was receiving poor relief in 1700.[16] The General Workhouse Act of 1723 tried to reduce the costs of relief by confining the poor, the unemployed and the sick in institutions where they were to carry out 'useful work'. The workhouse was planned as a 'house of terror'.[17] Children learned to spin, weave and knit in the schools of industry, and, if they were lucky, the rudiments of reading and writing. The main purpose was to get children used to strict discipline by means of hard work, beating and religious indoctrination. As soon as possible, the children were apprenticed to pedlars, chimney sweeps, etc, who could treat them like slaves.[18] Towards the end of the eighteenth century, such 'parish apprentices' were sent in batches to the new factories, where 'the transformation of children's blood into capital'[19] played an important part in the development of the textile industry.

By the end of the eighteenth century, the social crisis caused by the rise of industry had made all these old educational forms totally inadequate. The better-off felt threatened, at first by rising criminality and by Luddism (machine-breaking), then by the spread of epidemics in the industrial towns, and later by the danger of a reduction of the labour power of the working class as a result of bad living conditions. Early attempts to start schools for working-class children were often motivated by the desire to keep them off the streets and to discipline them through religion. The first step was the Sunday-school movement of the 1780s: both evangelicals within the Church of England and Methodists set up Sunday-schools 'to train up the lower classes in habits of industry and piety' as Hannah More, one of the leaders of the movement, put it.[20] Children were taught to read religious texts, but writing was regarded as superfluous for the poor. Sunday-schools had considerable success, spreading throughout the country and remaining important until the introduction of general elementary education after 1870.

The next step was the 'monitorial school' devised more or less simultaneously at the turn of the century by the Quaker, Joseph Lancaster, and the Church of England clergyman, Andrew Bell. The system was propagated by the nondenominational British and Foreign School Society and the Church of England-controlled National Society. The monitorial system was a true child of the industrial revolution, based on the principles of division of labour, hierarchy and standardisation. Anything up to a thousand children were collected together in a vast school-room, under the supervision of a single teacher. The more advanced children (the 'monitors') received instruction from the teacher and then passed it on to groups of smaller children. All words and movements took place according to a rigid timetable. The teacher gave orders through bells and signals. The main method was learning by heart, the teaching material usually consisting of theological texts which were quite incomprehensible to the children.[21] Apart from religion, reading, writing and arithmetic were taught, and sewing for girls. The children were kept in order through a system of rewards (medals, small sums of money) and punishments (confinement in a closet, suspension in a basket, the pillory, handcuffing, being washed in public, wearing a fool's cap, and expulsion).[22] The effectiveness of monitorial schools was very low: the small children received highly inadequate instruction from the monitors, who were only a little older than themselves, while the monitors were prevented from learning much by their teaching duties. About all that can be said for the system is that it was cheap and that it was better than nothing at all. The monitorial schools dominated popular education in Britain until the middle of the nineteenth century. But most working-class children still received no schooling.

A new type of school for working-class children resulted from the 1833 Factory Act, which prohibited the employment of children under nine years old in the main branches of the textile industry. The work of those between nine and thirteen was restricted to nine hours per day on six days per week. Two hours' schooling per day was made a condition for the employment of these children. Factory inspectors were appointed to make sure that the law was carried out, although their number was far too small for effective surveillance.[23] Factory schools varied greatly in quality: some employers had special school-rooms built and engaged capable teachers for the education of the young workers. Far more commonly, however, the children were taught in some corner of the noisy workshop by a completely unqualified person. One factory inspector reported that it was 'not at all an unusual thing to have certificates presented to us subscribed by the teacher with his or her mark',[24] because the 'teacher' was illiterate. Even the better factory schools can have had little success in teaching anything to children who still had to do fifty-four hours hard work each week. The Factory Act of 1844 increased school hours to three per day or in some cases to five hours every second day. The factory school did not completely disappear until 1918.

Another important measure taken in 1833 was the granting of the first state subsidy for education: £20,000 divided between the National and the British and Foreign Schools Societies. Initially the subsidies were at the free disposal of the Societies, but in 1839 the Committee of the Privy Council on Education was appointed, with the tasks of appointing school inspectors and supervising the use of the subsidies, which had been greatly increased in the meantime. The Committee encouraged the spread of elementary schools, set up teacher training colleges and laid down minimum qualifications for teachers. But the religious societies still controlled the content of school instruction, which was, accordingly, mainly religious indoctrination. A school inspector wrote: 'The "classics" of the poor in a Protestant country must ever, indeed, be the Scriptures: they contain the most useful of all knowledge.'[25] Both the voluntary agencies and the state education officials regarded elementary schooling as a means of combating Chartist and socialist ideas, and efforts were made to set up schools in areas where there had been social unrest.

Education, however, also played a big part in the struggles of the working-class movement. The Owenite co-operative movement of the 1830s set up schools for working-class children and 'halls of science' for adult education. Later, Chartist meeting halls took on a similar role, and often had their own libraries. The newspapers and pamphlets of working-class organisations provided a strong impetus for literacy. The ruling class made efforts to get ideological control of workers' education by setting up 'mechanics' institutes', which gave opportunities of vocational training, but kept dangerous thoughts and books out of courses and libraries.[26] During the transition to the trade-union movement of the 1860s, the self-education measures of the workers declined somewhat, although they did not disappear altogether. Now the demand for free, general, state education came to the fore.

Although economic and social conditions were more advanced in Britain than anywhere else, compulsory education came later than in some other countries. For instance, school became compulsory throughout Prussia in 1825, with strict penalties for parents who did not conform. The express purpose of this was ideological control over the workers. But the first big step in this direction in England was the Elementary Education Act of 1870. Where provision of schooling by voluntary efforts (i.e. church schools) was not sufficient, school boards were to be elected to build and run new schools with public finance. This Act finally led to the general introduction of basic education for working-class children. However, many schools remained under Church control, school fees were charged (though often remitted for poorer children), and elementary education did not become compulsory until 1880. The public elementary schools were one part of a class system: they were meant for the children of the poor, while the ruling class and the middle classes maintained their own private schools. A pamphlet of the National Union of Teachers published at the beginning of the twentieth century could still state: 'Six million children are in the Public Elementary Schools of England and Wales. They are the children of the workers, to be themselves England's workers a few years hence.'[27] The poorly equipped and often overcrowded elementary schools confined themselves to keeping children out of mischief until they could start work at thirteen, and to teaching them discipline through religion and drill; only the rudiments of reading, writing and arithmetic were taught. There was no trace of information about nature or society, which might help future wage workers to understand and improve their class position. Opportunities for gaining any form of intellectual training were very small for those destined to become manual workers. Towards the end of the nineteenth century, a small number of scholarships from elementary schools to technical schools or even to grammar schools did become available. As a rule, these could only be attained by a relatively small stratum of children of the lower middle class or of the 'labour aristocracy' of skilled workers, whose parents were able to give them the necessary support. Apart from this exception, the division between preparation for manual and for mental work remained virtually complete until almost the middle of the twentieth century.

4. Robert Owen and the New Lanark Schools

Marx started his remarks on the 'education of the future' in *Capital* by referring to Robert Owen. This is not surprising, for Owen not only made an important contribution to the theory of socialist education but also, for the first time, tried to put this theory into practice. The schools set up by Owen next to his textile factories in New Lanark might be regarded as very advanced even today.

Robert Owen (1771–1858) owed his own rise to wealth to the industrial revolution. Yet he clearly understood the social misery caused by the new form of production. Owen was the son of a Welsh craftsman. Largely self-educated, he went to Manchester at the beginning of the 1790s. Here the development of the new technology was at its height. By the age of twenty-one Owen was manager of a cotton mill, where he made important contributions to improving production methods. At the same time, he played a leading part in the Manchester Literary and Philosophical Society, a circle of scholars and businessmen in the tradition of the eighteenth-century European Enlightenment. The ideas of Rousseau and Helvétius, and of the English philosopher, Godwin, helped shape Owen's belief in the potential of human reason and in the importance of systematic character training through education.[28] He regarded people as being entirely the product of social circumstances. Poverty and crime were the product of bad social circumstances and bad education. Through correct education it would be possible to give everybody a desirable character, and this would inevitably lead to a transformation of society.[29] The main principle of Owen's *A New View of Society*, written in 1812–13 and highly regarded by many of his contemporaries, was as follows:

> Any general character, from the best to the worst, from the most ignorant to the most enlightened, may be given to any community, even to the world at large, by the application of proper means; which means are to a great extent at the command and under the control of those who have influence in the affairs of men.[30]

Owen therefore criticised the existing form of society, which was bound to lead to a bad, or at best an irrational, character. All the world's governments were neglecting what should really be their most important task: the education of the people. Inequality, poverty and exploitation were, for Owen, caused merely by ignorance of the true interests of mankind: the happiness of self, 'which can only be attained by conduct that must promote the happiness of the community'.[31] Now that this true interest and the path to its attainment had been discovered and announced by Owen, a new society could be set up without revolution, war or bloodshed:

> These principles require only to be known in order to establish themselves: the outline of our future proceedings then becomes clear and defined, nor will they permit us henceforth to wander from the right path. They direct that the governing powers of all countries should establish rational plans for the education and general formation of the characters of their subjects. These plans must be devised to train children from their earliest infancy in good habits of every description (which will of course prevent them from acquiring those of falsehood and deception). They must afterwards be rationally educated, and their labour be usefully directed. Such habits and education will impress them with an active and ardent desire to promote the happiness of every individual, and that without the shadow of exception for sect, or party, or country, or climate. They will also insure, with the fewest possible exceptions, health, strength and vigour of body; for the happiness of man can be erected only on the foundations of health of body and peace of mind.[32]

Owen saw education as the solution to all social problems. It was just a matter of making this clear to those in power – then a peaceful transformation of society was sure to follow. The exploited workers had no part to play in this: they were the passive objects of the transformation and not its subjects. Owen addressed his pamphlets to kings and politicians, to employers and scientists. There was no place for class struggle in his theory of society; his political strategy was completely utopian.

In 1800 Owen became part-owner and manager of the New Lanark cotton mills in Scotland. He remained there until 1824. In this period Owen made his pioneering attempt at planned social transformation. (Not given to false modesty, he wrote of 'the most important experiment for the happiness of the human race that had yet been instituted at any time in any part of the world'.)[33] The remote site for New Lanark had been chosen in 1784 owing to the waterfalls, which provided power for the mills. Workers were recruited elsewhere. They were, according to Owen, 'persons destitute of friends, employment and character'.[34] In addition, about five hundred 'parish apprentices' aged between seven and twelve had been engaged. It was 'a very wretched society', where every vice and immorality prevailed. Crime, drunkenness, poverty and debt were rife. Dale, the former owner, had set up a school (which was unusual for the time), but insisted that the work of the children should meet the costs. They had to work from 6 a.m. to 7 p.m. and then go to school, where they were, of course, too tired to learn anything. 'Many of them became dwarfs in body and mind, and some of them were deformed.'[35] The one teacher (for 500 children!) could not achieve much.

Despite the mistrust of the Scottish workers for their new English employer, Owen began a programme of reforms. His first measure was to stop the recruitment of 'parish apprentices' and to cease employing children under ten in the factories. The houses were improved and new ones built, new streets were laid down. Food, clothes and fuel were purchased directly from the producers and sold to the workers at low prices. Owen tried to reduce drunkenness, theft, falsehood and deception and religious disputes, not through punishments but through reasoning, as well as through preventive measures, like reducing the number of public houses. As a result, Owen reports,

> Those employed became industrious, temperate, healthy; faithful to their employers, and kind to each other; while the employers were deriving services from their attachment, almost without inspection, far beyond those which could be obtained by any other means than those of mutual confidence and kindness.[36]

The reforms had to pay their way in terms of reduced labour turnover and higher productivity, for Owen's partners were not willing to tolerate any reduction in profits. The whole paternalistic experiment was made possible by the fact that New Lanark was a 'company town' where Owen's word was virtually law.

As Owen's ideas on the vital role of education would lead one to expect, school had a very important place in New Lanark. We describe Owen's educational system here in the developed form it took after 1816, when the new 'Institution for the Formation of Character' was set up. The very name Owen gave his school says a lot about his concept of education. The 'Institution' had three sections:

- the infant school, for children from eighteen months to five years;
- the day school, from six to ten years;
- the evening school, for children and young people aged ten to twenty, after working hours.

All three sections had certain common principles:

- no punishments or rewards;
- alternation of mental and physical activity;
- education based on the real environment and curiosity of the child, rather than on an abstract curriculum;
- learning from real objects, pictures, maps and similar material, rather than just from books.

We shall now examine each sector in turn.

The Infant School

Owen regarded working-class parents as quite unfit to educate their own children. In addition the houses and the neighbourhood were full of 'evil conditions', injurious to character development.[37] Realising the great importance of the earliest years in child development, Owen found it essential to educate children outside the family as soon as they could walk. The one-to-five-year-olds remained at the infant school all day, except for meal breaks, when they appear to have gone home. Half the time was used for simple instruction in small groups, the other half for free play (under supervision) on a special playground in front of the school. Owen described the form of instruction as follows:

> The children were not to be annoyed with books; but were to be taught the uses and nature or qualities of the common things

around them, by familiar conversation when the children's curiosity was excited so as to induce them to ask questions respecting them.[38]

Far ahead of his brutal times, Owen ordered his teachers that 'they were on no account ever to beat any one of the children, or to threaten them in any manner in word or action, or to use abusive terms'.[39] Solidarity among the children was an important aim: they were told that they: 'must on all occasions do all they could to make their playfellows happy, – and that the older ones, from four to six years of age, should take especial care of younger ones, and should assist them to make each other happy.'[40]

Owen soon found that existing teachers were not qualified to carry out such non-authoritarian education. He sought persons who had 'a great love and unlimited patience with infants, and who were thoroughly tractable and willing unreservedly to follow my instructions'.[41] The first teacher at the infant school was in fact 'a poor simple-hearted weaver, named James Buchanan, who had been previously trained by his wife to perfect submission to her will'.[42] The initial mistrust of the parents for this completely new institution was, Owen reports, quickly overcome, when they saw how healthy and happy the children were. Mothers could now go to work without worrying about their unsupervised children.

Owen's infant school was the first of its kind and became very famous. Attempts were made to imitate it – the resulting Infant School Movement seemed a solution to the appalling neglect of children during the period of industrialisation. Infant schools on Owen's model were set up, with varying success, in Scotland and England, in France, and in the Netherlands. The movement was bitterly attacked by the Church: Pope Gregory XVI condemned the Infant School as an irreligious institution, which was likely to undermine the very foundations of the family.[43]

The Day School

Unlike the infants, the six-to-ten-year-old boys and girls were taught in separate groups, usually in the same large school-room.[44] All children learned reading, writing, arithmetic, natural history, geography, and ancient and modern history. For the girls, there was also sewing. Dancing, singing and military exercises were practised as a change from mental work. Considering that all other schools for working-class children were based on copying out theological texts and learning them by heart, we can see how revolutionary Owen's curriculum was. The same applies to his teaching methods, as we shall see below.

Owen really did not want to start teaching children to read and write until they were seven or eight. He wanted to make the natural and social world the starting point of the education process. By explaining the nature and properties of familiar objects in subjects like natural history, geography, history, chemistry, and astronomy, the child's interest and curiosity could be developed. Only then should the 'artificial signs' (i.e. letters and numbers) which represent these objects be introduced. Owen criticised the practice of starting school by learning the 'artificial signs', and only later, if at all, going on to the real world.[45] This critique applies to school today as much as it did in Owen's times. But the pressure of the parents forced an early start with reading and writing. It was hard to find suitable books at the time, so in the main Owen used reports on voyages or simple geographical or historical texts. Usually a child or the teacher read out aloud, stopping after a few sentences to allow discussion of the content. The chief principle was that 'children should never be directed to read what they cannot understand'[46] – a far cry from the abstract theological texts of the monitorial schools.

Arithmetic was taught according to the method developed by the Swiss educationalist, Pestalozzi. The pupils were taught to understand what they were doing, and in what way it could be useful to them in later life. In the same way, usefulness was the main consideration in the girls' sewing lessons: they brought clothes in need of repair from their homes, so that learning and necessary productive work were combined. Cooking and housekeeping were learnt and practised in the public canteens.

Natural history, geography and history were regarded as being of the greatest importance and as closely related to each other. They were taught even to the youngest children, the usual method being short lectures by the teachers followed by questions and discussion. Various teaching aids were developed, including pictures, maps and chronological tables, hung on the schoolroom wall. Sometimes these were on long rolls of canvas, which could simply be turned back and forwards to the relevant illustrations. Owen regarded these subjects as particularly important for the development of character, for they could be used to combat narrow prejudice and nationalism: children who understood the origins of national peculiarities would no longer despise people with different customs. The children were called upon to ask themselves if they would not themselves have become Hindus or cannibals, if they had grown up under the appropriate conditions. 'A child who has once felt what the true answer to such a question must be, cannot remain uncharitable or intolerant.'[47]

The New Lanark schools had their own problems with the intolerance of the day. Owen rejected all religion as irrational, but it was impossible to exclude it completely from the schools. So he declared that true religion could be better learnt through understanding the works of the deity (i.e. through natural history and geography) than through bible-thumping. In this way reason should lead to belief. But Owen could not avoid teaching the children the catechism.[48] Dancing and singing, which Owen regarded as particularly important to prevent one-sided mental development, also came under attack from religious bigots, including Owen's Quaker partner, William Allen. The military exercises, consisting mainly of marching to music, were primarily intended to improve the children's health, although they did also have a political aspect: Owen regarded all war as irrational, but as long as there were still irrational people around, it was necessary even for rational beings to learn how to defend themselves. He even wanted to teach the boys how to use guns, although it is unclear whether this was actually done.[49]

There were no punishments or rewards here, as in the infant school. Social behaviour and solidarity were encouraged, and the competitivity which is characteristic for schools in capitalism was lacking:

> A sufficient degree of friendly emulation is excited amongst them, without any artificial stimulus; but it is an emulation, which induces them to prefer going forward with their companions, to leaving them behind. Their own improvement is not their only source of enjoyment. That of their companions they appear to witness with pleasure, unmixed with any envious feeling whatever; and to be eager to afford them any assistance they may require.[50]

The Evening School

The evening school was for children and young people who worked in Owen's factories. The minimum age for employment was ten, although Owen encouraged parents to keep their children in full-time education until the age of twelve. However, they usually could

B

not afford to. Working hours were also shorter than customary in the early nineteenth century: twelve hours per day (including an hour and a quarter for meal breaks), six days per week. We may doubt whether the children were capable of learning much after a long day in the factory. The subjects taught and the methods used in the evening school were much the same as in the day school. In addition there were lectures and meetings about topics of general interest.

The Importance of the New Lanark Experiment

In 1816 there were about three hundred children in the infant and day schools, and about four hundred attended the evening school. About ten teachers were employed during the day and two or three in the evening. (By comparison, a teacher in a monitorial school might be in charge of anything up to one thousand children.) The infant and the evening schools were free of charge. The parents of the day pupils had to pay three pennies a month, not to cover the costs of the school, which were much higher (about two pounds per year for each child, according to Owen), but so that it should not be regarded as a 'pauper school'.[51]

Were the New Lanark schools a model for polytechnic education in a society in transition to socialism? In many ways, they certainly foreshadowed later socialist education plans: the linking of learning with everyday experience, a high level of general education for everybody, alternation of mental and physical activity, and above all, a great emphasis on learning the economic and political relationships of society. At a time when most workers received no education at all, and those who did go to school were subjected to a stupefying religious indoctrination, Owen's schools were a great step forward. They showed the suppressed potential of the working class, and indicated the role to be played by education in its liberation.

However, two important principles were lacking in Owen's schools, in comparison with later socialist education models. The first concerns the linking of teaching with productive work. Apart from the girls' sewing and cookery classes (which were more concerned with individual reproduction than socially necessary production) no productive work appears to have been done in the schools. Nor do we find any attempt to link science teaching to improving and humanizing the means of production. On the other hand, it must be remembered that the New Lanark schools were a reaction to the evils of the exploitation of child labour. The children started working in the factory at the age of ten, and that was certainly too early. Moreover, this early phase of the textile industry was a period of extreme deskilling of labour power, so that it must have seemed unnecessary to put much emphasis on production technology, or on preparing children for their future work in the factory. In later works Owen did call for the abolition of the division between mental and physical work and for early participation of children in socially necessary production.[52]

The second principle is more important: Owen's paternalism makes it doubtful whether the workers of New Lanark had any part to play in the social transformation which was his aim. The mills were run as profitable capitalist enterprises under Owen's rule – there was not the least trace of workers' control. The schools were managed in the same way. Owen did not think much of the capabilities of parents and teachers – they merely had to follow his directions. The aims, contents and methods of education were decided upon by Owen alone. The children and their working-class parents had no say in the matter. But how can you educate people to be capable of running society, if you give them no say in the running of their daily lives while learning? There was no place for the worker as the subject of social transformation in Owen's New Lanark experiment. He called for social reforms from above by wise rulers, not for social revolution.

That is why Owen and his ideas were rejected by the leading radicals of his day – men like Cobbett and Hazlitt. When, in 1817, Owen put forward his proposal for 'Villages of Co-operation' as a solution for the poverty and mass unemployment of the period following the Napoleonic Wars,[53] Cobbett bitingly denounced the planned communities as 'parallelograms of paupers'.[54] The radicals were convinced that the execution of Owen's well-meant plans would merely lead to an extension of the appalling workhouse system. Sherwin wrote:

> Mr Owen's object appears to me to be to cover the face of the country with workhouses, to rear up a community of slaves, and consequently to render the labouring part of the People absolutely dependent upon the men of property.[55]

Owen himself saw New Lanark as a model for the whole world, yet, despite his appeals, the politicians and employers were not willing to adopt the system. So, in 1824, Owen left New Lanark, bought land in the USA and set up his own utopian community, New Harmony. This collapsed after a few years, and Owen lost a lot of money and some illusions. Upon returning to England in 1829, he discovered that a co-operative movement was springing up that owed a lot to his ideas. He devoted the rest of his life to working with this movement, but that story cannot be told here.[56]

5. The Marxist Theory of Polytechnic Education

The many volumes of the collected works of Marx and Engels contain few texts concerned primarily with education, yet education plays a vital part in the marxist theory of society. This apparent contradiction arises because Marx and Engels never dealt with education in isolation from other economic, social and political phenomena. They regarded education not as something standing above social reality, but as a living part of the totality of social structure, with a dialectical relationship to the mode of production and distribution of material products, as well as to social consciousness. Here they differed from utopians like Owen, who thought that society could be transformed by introducing a new form of education. In the 'Theses on Feuerbach', written in 1845, Marx criticised this point of view:

> The materialist doctrine that men are products of circumstances and upbringing and that, therefore, changed men are products of other circumstances and changed upbringing, forgets that it is men that change circumstances and that the educator himself needs educating. Hence, this doctrine necessarily arrives at dividing society into two parts, of which one is superior to society (in Robert Owen, for example).[57]

Marx emphasised that the ruling bourgeoisie, whose vast profits arose from the prevailing conditions, would certainly never transform society from above. Only the class which suffered most from the exploitation and alienation of labour in capitalism – the working class – could, through revolutionary practice, bring about a new form of society (and therefore also of education).

Ideas on the possibility and necessity of a new form of education are therefore to be found pervading the whole theory of Marx and Engels. Their analyses of society always take educational conditions into account. This applies particularly to the marxist theory of personality, which is developed in the early works, and to the theory of technology which is to be found above all in *Capital*. Important ideas on education are also to be found in the analysis of child labour and in the context of proposals for the political strategy of the labour movement. The costs of education and vocational training play an important part in determining the value of labour power, and are therefore very important for Marx's labour theory of value. This consideration is the basis for modern marxist economics of education, but is not relevant for our present discussion.

The core of marxist theory is the idea of the development of a new type of human being[58]: 'the totally developed individual' who is capable of controlling a rational process of production and distribution within a new form of society – 'an association of free men'. Work – the struggle of man with nature in order to satisfy his needs – is, for Marx, the specifically human activity, which is vital for the self-realisation of man. But in capitalist society man is 'alienated' from his work in two ways: first because the product belongs not to the worker but to the capitalist; second because the bourgeoisie's interest in profit-maximisation leads it to lengthen working hours and to reduce the content of work through division of labour to the point where work became a meaningless drudgery. Work in capitalism does not serve the self-realisation of the worker, but is oppressive, damaging mind and body and causing the overdevelopment of one limited capability at the cost of the complete decay of all other potentialities.

The precondition for human emancipation is therefore the planned control of economic relationships by the workers. Hitherto, economic relationships had functioned like unpredictable natural forces, but once they were understood and controlled by the workers, they could become useful servants for mankind. This would not make work unnecessary, but rational planning would make it possible to reduce working hours and to abolish the rigid division of labour, opening a 'realm of freedom':

> The realm of freedom only begins, in fact, where that labour which is determined by need and external purposes ceases; it is therefore, by its very nature, outside the sphere of material production proper. Just as the savage must wrestle with Nature in order to satisfy his wants, to maintain and reproduce his life, so also must civilised man, and he must do it in all forms of society and under any possible mode of production. With his development the realm

of natural necessity expands, because his wants increase; but at the same time the forces of production, by which these wants are satisfied, also increase. Freedom in this field cannot consist of anything else but the fact that socialised mankind, the associated producers, regulate their interchange with Nature rationally, bring it under their common control, instead of being ruled by it as some blind power, and accomplish their task with the least expenditure of energy and under such conditions as are proper and worthy for human beings. Nevertheless, this always remains a realm of necessity. Beyond it begins the development of human potentiality for its own sake, the true realm of freedom, which however can only flourish upon that realm of necessity as its basis. The shortening of the working day is its fundamental prerequisite.[59]

The 'totally developed individual' in a communist society would still have to work, but the reduction of working hours, the improvement of working conditions and the rational planning of production would make work correspond with human needs, would make it a part of human self-realisation. At this point, the importance of large-scale industry and of the new science of technology for the marxist concept of emancipation becomes evident. Other critics of the misery of early industrial society, including Fourier, some of the Chartists, and even the young Disraeli, longed to return to an idealised pre-industrial world, where agriculture and handicrafts could flourish once more. Nobody saw the evils of early industry more clearly than Marx, but he saw at the same time that the new mode of production bore the seed of human liberation within it. Only large-scale industry could simultaneously satisfy material needs while reducing working hours sufficiently to allow the satisfaction of mental needs. Only modern technology could get rid of an extreme and stultifying division of labour, and make work fulfilling and satisfying. Marx showed that it was not industry and technology in themselves which enslaved the workers, but rather their development under capitalist conditions. Profit and competition – basic principles of the capitalist mode of production – led to inhuman working conditions, unbearable duration of work and extreme division of labour. But these social realities did not blind Marx to the real potential of industry and technology. This becomes evident in an important passage from *Capital*, which we shall quote at length:

Large-scale industry tore aside the veil that concealed from men their own social process of production and turned the various spontaneously divided branches of production into riddles, not only to outsiders but even to the initiated. Its principle, which is to view each process of production in and for itself, and to resolve it into its constituent elements without looking first at the ability of the human hand to perform the new processes, brought into existence the whole of the modern science of technology. The varied, apparently unconnected and petrified forms of the social production process were now dissolved into conscious and planned applications of natural science, divided up systematically in accordance with the particular useful effect aimed at in each case. Similarly, technology discovered the few grand fundamental forms of motion which, despite all the diversity of the instruments used, apply necessarily to every productive action of the human body, just as the science of mechanics is not misled by the immense complication of modern machinery into viewing this as anything other than the constant re-appearance of the same simple mechanical processes.

Modern industry never views or treats the existing form of a production process as the definitive one. Its technical basis is therefore revolutionary, whereas all earlier modes of production were essentially conservative. By means of machinery, chemical processes and other methods, it is continually transforming not only the technical basis of production but also the functions of the worker and the social combinations of the labour process. At the same time, it thereby also revolutionises the division of labour within society, and incessantly throws masses of capital and of workers from one branch of production to another. Thus, large-scale industry, by its very nature, necessitates variation of labour, fluidity of functions, and mobility of the worker in all directions. But on the other hand, in its capitalist form it reproduces the old division of labour with its ossified particularities. We have seen how this absolute contradiction does away with all repose, all fixity and all security as far as the worker's life-situation is concerned; how it constantly threatens, by taking away the instruments of labour, to snatch from his hands the means of subsistence, and, by suppressing his specialised function, to make him superfluous. We have seen, too, how this contradiction bursts forth without restraint in the ceaseless human sacrifices required from the working class, in the reckless squandering of labour-powers, and in the devastating effects of social anarchy. This is the negative side. But if, at present, variation of labour imposes itself after the manner of an overpowering natural law, and with the blindly destructive action of a natural law that meets with obstacles everywhere, large-scale industry, through its very catastrophes, makes the recognition of variation of labour and hence of the fitness of the worker for the maximum number of different kinds of labour into a question of life and death. This possibility of varying labour must become a general law of social production, and the existing relations must be adapted to permit its realisation in practice. That monstrosity, the disposable working population held in reserve, in misery, for the changing requirements of capitalist exploitation, must be replaced by the individual man who is absolutely available for the different kinds of labour required of him; the partially developed individual, who is merely the bearer of one specialised social function, must be replaced by the totally developed individual, for whom the different social functions are different modes of activity he takes up in turn.[60]

This makes it clear, how Marx's goal – the liberation of the working class (and thus finally of all humanity) – and his emphasis on the importance of large-scale industry and technology for the achievement of this goal, necessarily lead him to a new theory of education. On the one hand there is a contradiction between the extreme division of labour in capitalist industry, and the potential of technology to abolish this division of labour by dissolving all special forms of production into conscious and planned applications of natural science. On the other hand, there is a corresponding contradiction between the deskilling of workers to the point where they can carry out only one highly specialised operation, and the need of industry for 'variation of labour, fluidity of functions and mobility of workers'. Capitalist industry had made the worker into a narrow specialist, yet at the same time, it was the principle of the new technology to constantly change the production process, making the specialised worker superfluous. A new machine might at any time cause a worker to join the impoverished masses of the unemployed, replacing him with a new specialist, who had no more security than his predecessor. The solution to these contradictions could only be a versatile worker, whose broad general education and many-sided vocational training qualified him to work at any machine and to understand any production process. The very nature of large-scale industry made polytechnic education a question 'of life and death' for the worker.

And at the same time, large-scale industry offered a potential solution for this question:

As Robert Owen has shown us in detail, the germ of the education of the future is present in the factory system; this education will, in the case of every child over a given age, combine productive labour with instruction and gymnastics, not only as one of the methods of adding to the efficiency of production, but as the only method of producing fully developed human beings.[61]

This was borne out even by the 'paltry education clauses' of the Factory Act of 1833, which, for the first time, had made elementary education a condition for the employment of children in textile mills.[62] 'The success of those clauses proved for the first time the possibility of combining manual labour with education and gymnastics.'[63] Marx quotes reports on the good learning achievements of children who spent half their time at work and half at school. We may be somewhat sceptical about the attentiveness of children who had spent six hours in the factory, and Marx himself was certainly well informed on the deficits of the factory schools.[64] But he saw them above all as the first hesitant steps on the path to combining learning and work in a system of polytechnic education.

At the same time, Marx saw a second tendency in the same direction: the beginnings of technical education, which were a necessary product of the development of industry. Marx wrote *Capital* at the height of the 'first technological revolution'.[65] While Owen had only been concerned with the relatively simple machines of the early textile industry, which required little knowledge from their operatives, then, in the middle of the nineteenth century, a new branch of production had become dominant: the engineering industry. This industry, together with the mining and chemical branches which grew correspondingly, required managers, technicians and new types of skilled workers. Technical colleges and universities were set up for higher level specialists. The first was the *École Polytechnique* in Paris, originally founded shortly after the French Revolution to train officers in new military techniques. It was followed by a whole series of 'polytechnic schools' on the same model: Prague in 1806, Vienna in 1815, Karlsruhe in 1825, etc. These colleges soon started training civilian officials and industrial technicians as well. They were the forerunners of modern technological universities and polytechnics. Lower-level technical schools were also set up for training skilled workers, though they were few in number. Most industrial training took place at work through apprenticeships. The precondition for effective training was a basic general education in reading, writing and arithmetic.

Marx envisaged combining these early tendencies towards vocational training with the simultaneous trend towards introducing general education for working-class children:

> Though the Factory Act, that first and meagre concession wrung from capital, is limited to combining elementary education with work in the factory, there can be no doubt that, with the inevitable

conquest of political power by the working class, technological education, both theoretical and practical, will take its proper place in the schools of the workers. There is also no doubt that those revolutionary ferments whose goal is the abolition of the old division of labour stand in diametrical contradiction with the capitalist form of production, and the economic situation of the workers which corresponds to that form.[66]

The dialectical relationship between education and the mode of production is clearly stated here. Marx does not confine poly-technic education to communist society. Even in capitalist society, the very nature of industry and technology makes it essential to introduce general and technical education for working-class children. But this acts as a 'revolutionary ferment' for the capitalist system, for it is very hard to control and exploit workers who understand the technology of the production process and the structure of society. 'Knowledge is power', as the German pioneer socialist, Wilhelm Liebknecht, remarked. Marx therefore calls upon the labour movement to fight for polytechnic education within capitalism, as an essential part of the general struggle for the emancipation of the working class. This is most clearly expressed in the 1866 'Geneva Resolution' of the General Council of the International Workingmen's Association, which we reprint here in full:

Juvenile and Children's Labour (Both Sexes), 1867

We consider the tendency of modern industry to make children and juvenile persons of both sexes co-operate in the great work of social production, as a progressive, sound and legitimate tendency, although under capital it was distorted into an abomination. In a rational state of society *every child whatever*, from the age of 9 years, ought to become a productive labourer in the same way that no able-bodied adult person ought to be exempted from the general law of nature, viz.: to work in order to be able to eat, and work not only with the brain but with the hands too.

However, for the present, we have only to deal with the children and young persons of both sexes [belonging to the working people. They ought to be divided] into *three classes*, to be treated differently; the first class to range from 9 to 12; the second, from 13 to 15 years; and the third, to comprise the ages of 16 and 17 years. We propose that the employment of the first class in any workshop or house-work be legally restricted to *two*; that of the second, to *four*; and that of the third, to *six* hours. For the third class, there must be a break of at least one hour for meals or relaxation.

It may be desirable to begin elementary school instruction before the age of 9 years; but we deal here only with the most indispensable antidotes against the tendencies of a social system which degrades the working man into a mere instrument for the accumulation of capital, and transforms parents by their necessities into slave-holders, sellers of their own children. The *right* of children and juvenile persons must be vindicated. They are unable to act for themselves. It is, therefore the duty of society to act on their behalf.

If the middle and higher classes neglect their duties toward their off spring, it is their own fault. Sharing the privileges of these classes, the child is condemned to suffer from their prejudices.

The case of the working class stands quite different. The working man is no free agent. In too many cases, he is even too ignorant to understand the true interest of his child, or the normal conditions of human developement. However, the more enlightened part of the working class fully understands that the future of its class, and, therefore, of mankind, altogether depends upon the formation of the rising working generation. They know that, before everything else, the children and juvenile workers must be saved from the crushing effects of the present system. This can only be effected by converting *social reason* into *social force*, and, under given circumstances, there exists no other method of doing so, than through *general laws*, enforced by the power of the state. In enforcing such laws, the working class do not fortify governmental power. On the contrary, they transform that power, now used against them, into their own agency. They effect by a general act what they would vainly attempt by a multitude of isolated individual efforts.

Proceeding from this standing point, we say that no parent and no employer ought to be allowed to use juvenile labour, except when combined with education.

By education we understand three things.

Firstly: *Mental education.*

Secondly: *Bodily education*, such as is given in schools of gymnastics, and by military exercise.

Thirdly: *Technological training*, which imparts the general principles of all processes of production, and, simultaneously initiates the child and young person in the practical use and handling of the elementary instruments of all trades.

A gradual and progressive course of mental, gymnastic, and technological training ought to correspond to the classification of the juvenile labourers. The costs of the technological schools ought to be partly met by the sale of their products.

The combination of paid productive labour, mental education, bodily exercise and polytechnic training, will raise the working class far above the level of the higher and middle classes.

> It is selfunderstood that the employment of all persons from and
> to 17 years (inclusively) in nightwork and all health-injuring trades
> must be strictly prohibited by law.[67]

At a time when the labour movement was struggling against
the evils of child labour, Marx's demand that, in a rational state
of society, every child from the age of nine years should do productive work was highly controversial. As in his view on industry and
technology, we find here that Marx differentiates between a poten-
tially progressive phenomenon and the capitalist perversion of it.
This is made clear by a well-known passage from Marx's 'Critique
of the Gotha Programme' in which he attacks the programme of the
German Social Democratic Party for demanding the abolition of
child labour:

> *Prohibition of child labour!* It was absolutely essential to give an *age-
> limit* here.
>   The *general prohibition* of child labour is incompatible with the
> existence of large-scale industry. It is thus only an empty, pious
> wish.
>   Its implementation – if possible – would be a reactionary step.
> With strict regulation of working hours according to age and with
> other precautionary measures to protect the children, the early
> combination of productive labour with education is one of the most
> powerful means for the transformation of present society.[68]

The Geneva Resolution is a political programme for the
struggle for workers' education within the capitalist system, as well
as an outline for the organisation of education in a society in the
process of transition to socialism. The combination of mental
education, bodily education and technological training[69] are regarded as essential for the further development of the working
class, on its path to emancipation. 'Mental education' refers to the
learning of the basic cultural capabilities (reading, writing, etc.)
as well as a grounding in the natural and social sciences. 'Bodily
education' means the acquiring of gymnastic, sporting and military
abilities from the earliest childhood. 'Technological training' includes not only learning how to use tools, machines and materials,
but also refers specifically to the general scientific and technological
knowledge which is necessary for the control of the production
process. This rough draft for a new form of education was taken up
by Lenin, Krupskaya and other socialist educationalists, when
they started carrying out the theoretical and practical work

necessary for setting up the polytechnic educational system of the first socialist country.

6. Summary

At the time of the industrial revolution, most children of the poorer classes still received no schooling, despite the progressive ideas on education propounded by many eighteenth century philosophers. The social crisis caused by industrialisation, unplanned rural-urban migration, and above all, by the extreme form of capitalist exploitation in the new factories, led to impoverishment of the working class and the breakdown of the family as an instrument for the socialization of the children. The resulting social dangers – epidemics, crime, social unrest – led to attempts by the bourgeoisie to introduce mass education, mainly with the aim of controlling workers more effectively through religious indoctrination and rigid discipline. Education also became a central demand of the new labour movement, and Owenite co-operatives and Chartists set up their own schools.

Towards the middle of the nineteenth century, restrictions on child labour, as well as the growing need for skilled workers with basic education and vocational training, led to the introduction of general elementary education. Robert Owen's schools at New Lanark in the early nineteenth century were a pioneering attempt to give working-class children a non-authoritarian, broadly-based general education, with an emphasis on understanding the society in which they lived. But the paternalism of the experiment, in which there was no room for the ideas and initiatives of the workers themselves, prevented it from having a lasting effect.

The marxist theory of education went a step further in emphasising the role of the working class as the subject of the transformation, both in society in general and in the educational field. Change could not come from wise rulers, but only through the revolutionary practice of the labour movement. The potential for human liberation implicit in large-scale industry and in the modern science of technology play a vital role in the marxist theory of education. Marx examined the factors which were beginning to make mass education necessary within the capitalist system, (in Chapter 6 below, we shall discuss the extent to which Marx's expectations on the development of education in capitalism were in fact met), and showed how the labour movement could develop this to 'a revolutionary ferment', as part of the struggle for a new society. Marx regarded productive work as a vital part of education for all children, and demanded that this should be combined with mental, physical and technological education, to produce the 'totally developed individual' for a communist society.

3.
The First Attempt to Build a Socialist Education System: the Soviet Union 1917–31

The first successful socialist revolution took place in Russia in October 1917. In education, as in other fields, the new Soviet government found itself faced with tasks for which there were no ready-made solutions. From the outset, the bolsheviks understood the vital role to be played by education in shaping the new society, and set out to construct a socialist education system. In this task, their main guide was the marxist theory of polytechnic education. But Marx had only laid down general principles: the need to overcome the distinction between manual and mental work, the importance of linking learning with productive work, the importance of a high level of general education and vocational training for everybody. He had not attempted to make a detailed plan for the aims, form and content of the educational system of a society in transition to socialism. Indeed such a plan could only be utopian in nature, for the new forms of education depended on the prevailing social, economic and political circumstances. Education in the Soviet Union was as much a product of the specific historical conditions of the Russian revolution as of marxist education theory. Before the revolution, Lenin and Nadezhda Konstantinovna Krupskaya, his wife, had begun the task of adapting the principles of polytechnic education to Russian conditions. The educational programme of the bolsheviks was the result of this work.

In this chapter, we shall examine the bolsheviks' educational aims and the difficulties they met in putting them into force. We shall look at the conflict between two basic priorities which ran through the revolutionary years: on the one hand the provision of a high level of general, technological and political education for all workers to allow them to become the real masters of production and society; on the other hand the rapid training of large numbers of economic and technical experts in order to develop rapidly the backward means of production, which threatened the very survival of the revolution. We shall see how the victorious stalinist bureaucracy plumped for the second alternative after 1931, putting a stop to all educational innovation and reintroducing the old 'book-school'. Finally, we shall look at two conflicting models of 'communist personality' and of the methods suitable for creating it – those of Schatzky and Makarenko.[1]

1. Society and Education Before the Revolution

The historical contradiction of the first socialist revolution was that it took place not in the most advanced capitalist country, but in a backward country where the forces of production and the structure of society were still semi-feudal. On the eve of the Russian revolution, less than 15 per cent of the population lived in towns and less than 10 per cent earned their living through industrial work. About two-thirds of the population were peasants – usually owners of very small plots of land, with a low rate of productivity. Most peasants produced for their own bare subsistence, rather than for a market, using the most primitive methods and implements. The main reason for this backwardness was that the peasants had only been emancipated from feudal servitude in 1861. The serfs had had to pay heavily for their emancipation, many became landless labourers and most of the rest were heavily in debt to their former masters, or to moneylenders. The miserable situation of the poor and middle peasants prevented any investment in improved means of production, such as fertiliser, better implements or draught animals. However, a small stratum of peasants were able to produce for sale, and had sufficient animals and resources to improve working methods. These so-called 'kulaks' – about ten per cent of the peasant population – began developing into better-off capitalist farmers, employing wage-labour on a permanent or seasonal basis.

The very late decline of Russian feudalism – four or five centuries later than in England – postponed the beginnings of industrialisation until the late nineteenth century. When it did begin – at first in textiles, then in mining, iron production and railway construction – the Russian bourgeoisie, small and weak, played only a minor part. Most of the new industries were controlled by British, French, German and US capitalists, who hoped for high profits in a country where the general poverty and the prohibition of trade unions kept wages low. Although industrialisation was rapid by the turn of the century, it had still done little more than scratch the surface of an out-of-date, decaying economic and social system. The few industrial areas, around Moscow, Petrograd, in the Donetz basin and on the Neva, were islands in an ocean of backward agriculture and domestic industry. By 1917, there were still only two to three million industrial workers, a million railwaymen, and three-quarters of a million miners in the whole of Russia. Many workers were only semi-proletarians, who still owned village land and returned there at harvest-time.[2]

How was a working-class revolution possible in a backward country with a tiny proletariat? The basic reason was that what little industry did exist was of the most modern type and fully integrated into the world market. Foreign investors introduced modern large-scale production methods, and workers were concentrated in huge factories: for instance, in 1902, 39 per cent of Russian industrial workers were in plants employing more than one thousand persons, compared with only 10 per cent of workers in Germany.[3] This concentration encouraged the setting up of working class organisations and the development of proletarian consciousness. Extremely low wages and bad living conditions, combined with a total absence of social security, strengthened working-class militancy. At the same time, the incompetent ruling aristocracy had no other solution to the social evils but barbaric repression.

The first explosion of the workers' and peasants' discontent came in 1905, but the old regime still had enough forces at its disposal to quell the risings. The events of 1905 led to a programme of reforms, introduced by the Tsar's chief minister, Stolypin, in a desperate attempt to maintain control and to modernise the economy.

A consultative elected assembly called the Duma was introduced. This was not a real parliament: its powers were very restricted, and suffrage was virtually confined to the propertied classes. The most important measure was a change in the laws of land ownership, aimed at breaking down the old village communities, the mir, and encouraging the spread of capitalist farming by the kulaks.

These half-hearted measures came too late. Russian society was an explosive mixture: the vast impoverished peasant masses called for land reform and an end to exploitation by big landlords, kulaks, and merchants. The small but highly concentrated working class was militant and ready to adopt revolutionary ideas. The old ruling aristocracy was incapable of adapting to new conditions, while the bourgeoisie was too small and weak to carry out its historical role of industrialising and constructing a bourgeois-democratic state. The costly defeats of the first world war demonstrated the rottenness of the whole system, leading to the revolution of February 1917. After a brief interregnum, in which the bourgeoisie showed its inability to rule, a rising of workers, soldiers and peasants put an end to the old system in October 1917. The new form of mass rule which came out of the struggle was the soviet – the system of direct democracy through councils of workers, soldiers and peasants. And the leading political force in the new state were the bolsheviks.

Before the revolution, there was no formal schooling for the great majority of workers and peasants. At the beginning of the twentieth century, no less than three-quarters of the Russian population were illiterate. The education system was the most backward in Europe. After emancipation of the serfs in 1861 there had been calls for the introduction of mass education, but very little had been done. Only a few one-class elementary schools, with attendance for only three to four years, were available to the children of workers and peasants. The majority of teachers were totally untrained, and their pay and social standing were very low. Most schools were run by the orthodox church. The chief content of schooling was religious and chauvinist indoctrination, with the aim of training willing and humble servants for the ruling classes. The beginnings of industrialization led to a need for engineers and technicians, so that some secondary, technical and commercial schools were set up. They were few in number and available only to the children of the urban bourgeoisie and of the kulaks. Apart from this, secondary and higher education was reserved for the aristocracy. There were grammar schools and cadet schools for the boys and finishing schools for the young ladies.

After the upheavals of 1905, liberal and democratic groupings called for educational reforms such as the setting up of new schools with the aim of making education compulsory by 1925; secularisation of education; decentralisation of school administration; more autonomy for universities; and the recognition of the rights of national minorities to use their own languages at school. All attempts to use the Duma to introduce real changes were blocked by the aristocracy, who saw mass ignorance as a main pillar of their rule. But there were some gradual improvements – in particular considerable quantitative expansion and a trend towards secularisation. The number of elementary schools rose from 93,000 in 1905 to 124,000 in 1914, and by the latter date two-thirds were controlled by secular authorities and only one-third by the Church.[4]

The fact remains that the majority of children were still condemned to illiteracy and most of the reforms remained on paper. Lenin estimated that in 1913 the number of children of school age was 22 per cent of the total population, while the proportion of persons attending school was only 4·7 per cent of the population. Four-fifths of all children and young people were robbed of any chance of education.[5]

In Russia, as in other countries, the labour movement grasped the importance of popular education in the struggle to change society. Evening schools and workers' education circles were an important field for political training and recruitment. Krupskaya started her revolutionary work in a workers' 'Evening Sunday School' in the industrial suburbs of St Petersburg. Here she first met Lenin.[6] Lenin's articles in *Pravda* are full of information about schooling in Russia. In exile, Lenin encouraged Krupskaya to study the marxist theory of polytechnic education as well as the most advanced theories of bourgeois pedagogy.[7] The form and content of a future education system were important themes of discussion among socialist and democratic revolutionaries of all groupings. A forum for these controversies was the journal *Free Education*, founded in 1907, in which Krupskaya published some important articles on polytechnic education.[8]

In the years preceding the revolution, certain attempts were made to set up new types of schools for the children of workers and peasants. Experiments of various kinds were made not only by socialists, but also by liberals, populists and anarchists. This kind of practical experience was of great value after the revolution, and Krupskaya later did all she could to encourage progressive educationalists to use their abilities to help the bolsheviks in constructing the new school system. All too few bolsheviks had practical teaching experience. Krupskaya herself was one of the exceptions, having spent several years teaching in an elementary school.

2. The Educational Programme of the First Soviet Government

One of the first measures of the Soviet government after the Revolution of October 1917 was to set up a State Commission for Education, led by Krupskaya, with the task of mapping out a new education system. In addition a People's Commissariat for Education was established, with responsibility for the administration of all forms of education. Lunacharsky was appointed as People's Commissar. His first proclamation on 29 October (according to the old Julian calendar), only days after the victorious rising, informed the population what changes were planned:[9]

- Illiteracy and ignorance were to be combatted through the introduction of free, compulsory, general education for all children, and special courses for grown-ups.
- The aim was set of organising an absolutely secular, unitary school with several levels, for all citizens.
- The cultural and education movement of the working masses and of the growing workers' and soldiers' organisations was to receive support.
- The whole school system was to be put under the control of the local organs of self-government (i.e. the soviets).
- Teachers were to co-operate with other social groups. Immediate steps were to be taken to improve their very poor material situation. This applied particularly to 'the most impoverished, but at the same time virtually most important cultural workers, the elementary school teachers'.

In the course of 1918, a whole series of decrees on education were issued by the Council of People's Commissars. They contained the following radical measures:[10]

- all private and church schools taken over by the state;
- the division of state and church, and of church and school; religious instruction at school was forbidden;
- free, compulsory education for all children;
- the provision of food, clothing and school material for all children;
- co-education;
- the abolition of grading and examinations;
- free access to higher education without formal requirements;

- the abolition of uniforms, which had been required in many state and church schools;
- the abolition of compulsory Latin in higher schools;
- the abolition of hierarchical distinctions among teachers. Equal pay for all;
- the prohibition of punishments and compulsory homework;
- the transformation of all schools into unitary work schools.

A Decree of the All-Russian Central Executive Committee of the Soviets,[11] published on 16 October 1918, confirmed most of the above measures, and then went on to lay down the structure of the unitary work schools. They were to have two stages: a five-year course from the age of eight to thirteen, and a four-year course from thirteen to seventeen. Nurseries for children from five to seven were to be linked to the schools. School was to be followed by vocational training or higher education. Compulsory education was thus to last nine years. The new school was to be open seven days a week, so that children could go there not just for classes but also to pursue their other interests.

Productive work was an essential element of the new type of school. Since the aim of combining learning with productive work has been considerably reduced and distorted in later educational programmes in the Soviet Union and East European countries, it is worth looking at this original programme in detail. The 'Principles for School Work' in the Decree of 16 October 1918 are as follows:

> Article 12: Productive work is to be the basis of school life – not as a means of securing the material upkeep of the school and not only as a method of teaching, but as a productive and socially necessary activity. It must be closely and organically linked to teaching and should brighten the whole environment with the light of knowledge. Productive work should become increasingly complicated and go beyond the frontiers of children's immediate environment, introducing them to the various forms of production, including the most advanced ones.
>
> Note 1: The principle of work will become an effective educational method, where work at school is creative and cheerful, where it is carried out without any compulsive effects on child personality, and where it is organised in a planned and social way. In this sense, the school represents a school commune, which is closely and organically linked with the life of the surrounding world through its work processes.

Note 2: The old form of discipline, which restricts school life and hinders the free development of children's personalities, can have no place in the work school. However, the working people themselves will help the children to develop an inner discipline, without which any rational planned collective work is unthinkable. The children take an active part in all work processes of school life. In this, the organisational aspects which develop out of the principle of division of labour have a very important educational role to play. The pupils thus learn a high regard for the methods of the planned use of human labour power, and develop a feeling of responsibility, both for the individual tasks done by the various members of the collective and for the success of the whole undertaking. To put it briefly: collective, productive work and the organisation of all aspects of school life are to educate the future citizens of the socialist republic.[12]

Krupskaya and Lunacharsky emphasised repeatedly that socialist education was not just a question of the content of teaching but also of its methods. They rejected the traditional 'book-school', and demanded that children should learn by taking part in work and social life. They advocated the 'complex method' of teaching (which was to be a frequent subject of controversy in the years to come). According to the 'complex method' teachers were not to teach according to formal curricula for academic subjects. Instead, they were encouraged to take the problems of the children, of local production and of daily life as their starting point, and to examine them in the light of various disciplines simultaneously. Instead of learning geography or history children were, for instance, to study the village they lived in by taking part in work, talking to farmers and workers and the like. The findings of the children's research were to be discussed and systematised at school. Here is an example given by Krupskaya to explain the 'complex method':

Take a village boy. He carries water, looks after the poultry, helps his father in the fields and his mother in the house, takes care of his little brothers, runs errands and so on. He is a necessary person at home. There are lots of little peasants like this in the villages. This work in the village must be the starting point, it must be examined in the light of science, and in this way the pupil must gradually be drawn into the life of the grown-ups.

For instance, a child has to look after the chickens. What must one do in the work school? Buy chickens and get the children to look after them? Certainly not. One must make use of the work of looking after the chickens which the children do at home, and give it a new content.

One must introduce the children to the different breeds of chickens and their habits, using books like Brehm [a well-known popular book on zoology]. This will encourage the children to observe their own chickens. This will lead to various questions: the hatching of the eggs, artificial hatching, the factories which are built for this purpose, the inner structure of an egg, in order to observe the growth of the chick. How much they will have to tell the people at home, how much they will want to write down what they have heard and read! The care of chickens will be dealt with, and the children will try to apply what they have learnt to their own chickens at home. Then the nutritional value of the egg must be discussed. Nutritional value will however lead to a series of further questions. The same applies to the cooking of eggs. And how many exercises and calculations can be linked with the problem of chickens and eggs! The linking of work with teaching thus means making the work done by the children at home meaningful and interesting, and awakening their powers of observation.[13]

The idea is that parents should come to regard school as useful, and that school should have real influence on the economy, for instance by bringing scientific principles into farming.

The Decree of 16 October 1918, also contained provisions to ensure that pupils and parents could help to control and run the schools:

Article 26: The school collective consists of all pupils and all school workers [i.e. teachers and other staff].

Article 27: The organ responsible for the self-administration of the school is the school council. It consists of:
(a) All school workers,
(b) Representatives of the working population of the school district, in number equivalent to one quarter of the school workers,
(c) Pupils from the older groups (from the age of twelve upwards), in the same proportion as b),
(d) A representative of the Department for Popular Education.

Article 28: The inner life of the school collective is to be governed by mass or group meetings of the school collective, within the framework of the Regulations of the central and local organs for popular education . . . [14]

Krupskaya regarded the active participation of the pupils in organising and running the school as an essential first step in educating workers capable of organising and controlling the production process. This meant that pupils' participation should be a serious matter, in which they really had an important part in decision-making, and not just a game with democratic rules, as in capitalist schools.[15]

These radical changes in education met with opposition, even from within the revolutionary camp. The criticisms of the so-called 'Petrograd group' of educationalists was expressed by Blonsky, a well-known educationalist and psychologist. (It is typical for the tolerance and open discussion of this period, that Blonsky, despite the differences between him and Krupskaya, was given an important post in the Commissariat for Education.) He accepted the unitary work school, but called for maintaining the division between subjects, the systematic form of teaching, precise curricula, and differentiation in various special branches in the eighth and ninth grades. The Petrograd group wanted a gradual process of school reform. Blonsky wrote in 1917: 'By reforming the old school, we show our genuine belief in the possibility of creating a new one.' He went on:

> If the old school is destroyed, and a weak state power which lacks authority orders the creation of a new school according to its plans, will we not meet with passive resistence everywhere, and, what is more dangerous for the children, with pedagogical sabotage? Creating a new school now means risking an obvious fiasco . . . Society justly fears the danger of being left without any schools at all, after the old school has been destroyed, and hasty unauthoritative plans for a new one have been made . . .[16]

Krupskaya's answer to this was that, after the radical transformation of society, the whole way in which school functioned no longer corresponded with the economic, political and social conditions of the country. Revolution in society could not be met with evolution in the school. The revolution was creating new people. The country did not need masters and servants, as created by the old schools, but free, strong and intelligent people, whose education was the task of the new school.[19]

At the Eighth Party Congress of the Russian Communist Party (bolsheviks) in March 1919, the educational policy initiated by Lenin, Lunacharsky and Krupskaya was confirmed and made part of the party programme. Special emphasis was put on the role of education in class struggle. It was seen as an important means of carrying out communist propaganda and creating a communist consciousness. The basic principle of education policy was to be the development of mass initiative. 'Soviets for popular education' were to control schools and kindergartens. Workers and peasants were called upon not only to take the lead in controlling bourgeois experts in the factories, but also to join the school councils, which could elect and dismiss all school workers (teachers). The state was given the task of constructing a network of adult education facilities: libraries, schools for adults, courses, lectures, cinemas, etc.[18]

3. The Need for a Cultural Revolution

In a situation of civil war, starvation and scarcity of virtually all vital commodities, the bolsheviks regarded education as one of their first priorities. Why was it so important? The answer is to be found in a large number of Lenin's speeches of this period. The economic and social conditions in Russia were not ripe for the construction of socialism. The Russian revolution only made sense in terms of the European revolution, which the bolsheviks confidently expected to follow the first world war. In the meantime, they had to hang on to power, win the civil war, get the economy going again, and develop the forces of production as rapidly as possible. But the very backwardness of Russian condition forced the bolsheviks into a contradictory policy. On the one hand, securing of soviet power meant mass rule and control, and this required the rapid raising of the cultural level of the workers and peasants.[19] On the other hand, there were just not enough proletarians with sufficient education and training to administer the country, build up the Red Army, and organise industry. The bolsheviks were forced to rely on the old bourgeois experts, who wanted nothing better than to sabotage the new workers' state.

It all boiled down to the following:

> The old utopian socialists imagined that socialism could be built by men of a new type, that first they would train good, pure and splendidly educated people, and these would build socialism . . . We want to build socialism with the aid of those men and women who grew up under capitalism, were depraved and corrupted by capitalism, but steeled for the struggle by capitalism . . . Socialism must triumph, and we socialists and Communists must prove by deeds that we are capable of building socialism with these bricks, with this material, that we are capable of building socialist society with the aid of proletarians who have enjoyed the fruits of culture

> only to an insignificant degree, and with the aid of bourgeois specialists.[20]

Reliance on bourgeois specialists had its dangers:

> Everybody knows that a certain number of experts have systematically betrayed us. Among the experts in the factories, among the agronomists, and in the administration, we have seen and see today at every step a malicious attitude to work, malicious sabotage.[21]

But, said Lenin, it was impossible to maintain soviet power and build socialism without utilising the technical and cultural abilities of the bourgeois specialists. Without them, he told the workers, there would not even be a Red Army:

> And you know that when two years ago we tried to create a Red Army without them, it ended in guerilla methods and chaos; the result was that our ten to twelve million soldiers did not make up a single division. There was not a single division to fight, and with our millions of soldiers we were unable to cope with the tiny regular army of the Whites. We learned this lesson at the cost of much bloodshed, and it must now be applied to industry.[22]

The specialists could not be made to work by force alone. Lenin insisted on the necessity of offering them material rewards in the form of high pay. In addition, it was necessary to control them by putting a workers' commissar alongside each specialist and by surrounding them with communists.[23]

The low educational level led also to the danger of bureaucratic rule. The old czarist bureaucracy had been defeated and removed, but the lack of educated workers and peasants had made it necessary to recall many former officials. Even where officials had been recruited from the masses, there was the risk of bureaucratic deformation and lack of control:

> The result of this low cultural level is that the Soviets, which by virtue of their programme are organs of government *by the working people*, are in fact organs of government *for the working people* by the advanced section of the proletariat, but not by the working people as a whole.[42]

Of course, the problem of bourgeois specialists applied as much in the schools as in the factory or the army. According to Victor Serge, 'The greater part of the old teaching staff resisted, sabotaged, misunderstood and only awaited the end of Bolshevism.'[25] The old 'All Russian Teachers' Association' took a counter-revolutionary stance and had to be disbanded and replaced with a new 'Internationalist Teachers Association'.

So the bolsheviks were in a cleft stick: they could not do without the bourgeois specialists, and yet reliance on them led to bureaucratism and the erosion of the revolution from within. There was only one way out: the rapid raising of the cultural level of the workers and peasants, so that they would soon be capable of effectively controlling the specialists, and, in the long run, of replacing them. The victory of the political and social revolutions could only be maintained, said Lenin, if they were followed by a cultural revolution.[26] This meant that workers and peasants had to take over all that was good and useful in bourgeois culture and technology, and adapt it for use in building socialism. Lenin described this task in detail in his speech to the youth organisations in 1920:

> Proletarian culture must be the logical development of the store of knowledge mankind has accumulated under the yoke of capitalist, landowner and bureaucratic society. All these roads have been leading, and will continue to lead up to proletarian culture, in the same way as political economy, as reshaped by Marx, has shown us what human society must arrive at, shown us the passage to the class struggle, to the beginning of the proletarian revolution.[27]

Lenin criticised the idea that one could 'learn communism' without systematic study. Abandoning the abstract learning by rote of the old school did not mean doing away with school itself: 'You can become a communist only when you enrich your mind with a knowledge of all the treasures created by mankind.'[28] The correct application of this knowledge depended on the training of youth in communist morality and ethics. These were based on the requirements of the collective struggle of the workers and peasants to destroy the old society and build a new one: 'We say: morality is what serves to destroy the old exploiting society and to unite all the working people around the proletariat, which is building up a new, communist society.'[29] Communist education meant linking every aspect of learning with the struggle of the proletariat and the working people against the old society. Education must not be restricted to school, but must be involved in the real struggles, the 'storms of life'.

Lenin explained what he meant by this in a concrete way: the introduction of electric power in the Soviet Union was vital for the further development of the forces of production and for the construction of socialism. Being a communist hence meant learning about electricity and taking an active and creative part in the struggle for electrification.[30]

In short, Lenin regarded the rapid building of a socialist education system as an essential condition for maintaining Soviet power. The priority of the task is illustrated by the fact that Lenin made no less than 270 speeches and statements on the subject and signed 192 decrees on education in the five years following the October revolution.[31] He was always aware of the tragic dialectic which made the job so difficult:

> This cultural revolution would now suffice to make our country a completely socialist country; but it presents immense difficulties of a purely cultural (for we are illiterate) and material character (for to be cultural we must achieve a certain development of the material means of production, must have a certain material base).[32]

4. Society and Education 1917–31

The Period of War Communism

It was one thing to call for a new culture and to pass decrees for radical changes in education. It was another matter to realise these measures in the difficult situation of the years following the revolution. Victor Serge has described the situation of the schools in 1918:

> Everything had to be improvised. The old textbooks were good only for fuel . . . The schools themselves were tragic ruins. They lacked paper, pencils, notebooks, and pens. In winter, the ragged children met around little stoves installed in the middle of the classrooms, where they often burned the remaining furniture to keep out the cold. There was one pencil for each four children; the teachers were starving.[33]

Krupskaya remarked that most of the teachers had never even heard of polytechnic education before 1918. Neither their training nor the equipment of the school were suitable for combining learning with productive work. And on top of all this, most teachers opposed the revolution and were just waiting for its collapse.

Yet in 1918 there was enormous revolutionary elan, willingness to try experiments, to take over the best of western progressive ideas, and to revive populist traditions in education associated with Tolstoy and the Narodniks. Revolutionary workers, full of thirst for knowledge, threw themselves into the struggle to transform education, setting up new schools, adult courses, workers colleges and nurseries. There was free and open discussion inside and outside the party.

The outbreak of the civil war in the summer of 1918 brought great setbacks. The white armies, armed and supported by the Western powers, occupied vast areas, cutting off a large proportion of the bolsheviks' supplies of food and raw materials. Class struggles within the areas held by the bolsheviks sharpened. Most industry was still in private hands, and the owners refused to support the war effort. To survive the bolsheviks had to nationalise all industry virtually overnight, introduce strict rationing, centralise economic control, and send many of the most militant workers to the front. The years of 'war communism' were a period of starvation and hardship, and a period of increasing bureaucratisation, as a vast system of ministeries, offices and permits was set up to administer the scarcity.

The introduction of nine years' compulsory education in this situation was an illusion. The most pressing problem was to care for the tens of thousands of orphaned, homeless and hungry children who wandered through town and country, forming gangs and stealing to stay alive. At the height of the civil war, the Soviet government introduced free school meals for children and young people, and set up children's homes and colonies, Makarenko's famous Gorky Colony was one of many. The number of children in homes rose from 30,000 in 1917, to 75,000 in 1918, 125,000 in 1919, 400,000 in 1920 and 540,000 in 1921/22.[34] In this period it was generally not possible to introduce even the five-year first stage of the unitary work school. The second stage, for children from thirteen to seventeen, was available for only nine per cent of children in this age group in 1919.[35] Young people in socialist Russia were still growing up illiterate.

But even in these hard years, progress was made. All schools were taken over by the state and formally changed into unitary work schools. Co-education was introduced. Workers', peasants' and youth organisations took initiatives to fight illiteracy and to improve vocational training. A whole series of new types of educational institutions began to develop: schools for illiterate or semiliterate young people and adults, schools for the political education of party members, 'schools of factory youth', which combined elementary general education with vocational training for young people employed in factories, 'schools of peasant youth', which linked general education with the theory and practice of agriculture, 'workers' faculties' which were to give class-conscious workers the basic education necessary for going on to university, where they would become 'red specialists'. Of course, this meant that the new education system was anything but 'unitary'. Competing school types and methods, important as they were in this early phase, were later to become a problem.

The First Party Conference on Popular Education (December 1920–January 1921) was the beginning of a move away from the ambitious aims of the early decrees, of adaptation to the grim reality. The duration of the unitary work school was reduced from nine to seven years – as a 'temporary measure'. For the next ten years Krupskaya and Lunacharsky found themselves fighting – and gradually losing – a battle against the watering down of their aims of a high level of general education and of linking learning with productive work.

The New Economic Policy

The bolsheviks paid a heavy price for victory in the civil war: thousands of revolutionaries were killed and large areas devastated. Industry virtually collapsed: production fell to fifteen per cent of the 1914 level, and many workers left the towns to find food. Relations between the Soviet government and the peasants were severely strained, for during the civil war it had been impossible to provide industrial goods to pay the peasants for food supplies. Armed workers' detachments had been sent into the country to requisition grain, and the peasants hit back by producing less. The New Economic Policy (NEP) which replaced war communism in March 1921 was an attempt to get the shattered economy going again. It was a return to a mixed economy: large-scale industry, railways, banks, and foreign trade remained in the hands of the state, but small and medium industry was opened to private capital. Grain requisitions were stopped, and peasants were permitted to sell their surplus products on free markets. Foreign capital was re-admitted and trade agreements made with capitalist countries.[36] The idea was to use private initiative to restore economic stability, while at the same time improving and gradually extending the socialist state sector.

The NEP was an economic success, but it had dangerous political consequences: it sharpened the trend towards the establishment of privileged strata, which had already started with the bureaucracy of war communism: first, the state and party officials, who could no longer be adequately controlled by the depleted and demoralised working class; second, the bourgeois specialists in industry, commerce and administration, who were paid very high salaries to encourage loyal and efficient work; third, the reborn class of industrial and commercial capitalists in non-state enterprises; and fourth, the kulaks, who were the main beneficiaries of the free agricultural markets. Together, these groups were known as the 'Nepmen', and they began to form a wealthy, powerful class, which appeared to many revolutionaries as a portent of the restoration of capitalism.[37] By the time Lenin died in 1924, embittered debates on the correct future policy for building socialism were shattering the unity of the party leadership.

Obviously the change in policy and the discussions on the future course had important consequences for education. The rehabilitation of the economy required the rapid training of large numbers of skilled workers, engineers and technicians. Vocational training, which had been neglected in the civil war years, became a foremost priority. In 1920 a Committee for Vocational and Technical training was set up in the Russian Soviet Socialist Republic. It was responsible not only for all forms of vocational training, but also for higher education, which was seen principally in its role of providing highly trained cadres for state and the economy. This meant that important powers were taken out of the hands of Lunacharsky and Krupskaya. In the following years there was considerable disagreement between the Commissariat for Education and the Committee for Vocational and Technical Training on the priorities in educational policy and the best means of achieving them.

In July 1920, the Council of People's Commissars issued a decree which required all workers to undergo vocational training, and which mapped out the future training system. On the lower level were various types of technical and trade schools intended for young people who had had four years of general education. They led to qualification as a skilled worker. In 1921, a new type of Factory School for Apprentices' (FZU) was set up, in which vocational training took place entirely within a factory. This became the main type of basic vocational training. Apprentices worked in the factory during training, receiving practical and theoretical instruction on the side. Training was to the level of skilled worker or foreman.

Political education played a certain part in the course, but it was not in any sense polytechnic education, for rapid specialisation in a specific trade was the express aim. The advocates of this type of training actually spoke of 'monotechnic education', to differentiate it from what they regarded as high-flying illusions. The FZU grew rapidly: from 45 schools with 2,000 apprentices in 1921 to nearly a thousand schools with 90,000 apprentices by the end of the 1920s.[38] 'Schools for peasant youth' played a similar part in rural areas. By 1928, there were about 1,100 with 90,000 pupils, who were later to play an important part in setting up the new collective farms.

A level higher was the 'technikum'. This was a college for training various types of technicians, managers, agronomists, teachers, etc. The completion of the seven-year school was the condition for admission. The structure and methods of the 'technikum' were based to a large extent on the pre-revolutionary middle schools. Again, polytechnic education had little influences on the courses, which were closely related to the needs of industry and other sectors for middle-level cadres. Despite rapid expansion – by 1927 there were over a thousand of these schools, with 190,000 students – they could not keep up with the growing economic need for trained people.[39]

In 1918, the universities and higher technical colleges had been opened to the workers – access was to be without examination. But this measure remained a dead letter, for higher education facilities were quite inadequate, and few workers or peasants had enough basic education to follow the courses. The 'workers' faculties', which we have already mentioned, were an attempt to solve the latter problem. But by 1923 free entry was abolished, strict quotas proclaimed, and higher education, too, was closely geared to the need for experts and engineers. All in all, vocational and higher education returned to old hierarchical structures, and to a system of narrow specialisation. The rapid meeting of economic needs was given priority over the political aim of reducing the dominant position of experts, and securing workers' control over production.

In general education Lunacharsky and Krupskaya were able to maintain their influential positions until the end of the twenties. Their basic aim remained the replacement of the old 'book-school', which had been cut off from working life, by the work school based on polytechnic principles. However, the material development of the school system left much to be desired. By 1923 Krupskaya had to admit that only 50 per cent of Russian children were receiving any schooling at all, and that it would be a considerable step forward to achieve a four year first stage of the unitary work school for all children.[40] Seven years compulsory schooling was still a distant dream. As late as 1929, Krupskaya was complaining that half the children aged between eight and twelve (with the exception of those from the Moscow and Leningrad areas) could not read or write.[41]

The realisation of the second stage of the unitary work school (the seven-year school) lagged far behind economic needs. The seven-year school was training far too few middle-level personnel, and it was using old-fashioned methods and not relating its work to local needs.

> The number of seven-year schools and of their graduates is minute (according to figures for 1927–28, only 7.4 per cent of pupils who enter the first class reach the seventh class – that includes schools for peasant youth and seven-year factory schools). The social composition of the seven-year school is also bad, for it is a well-known fact that the children of the worst paid workers and the children of the poor peasants leave school early (workers' and agricultural labourers' children are only 23.6 per cent of the total in the seventh class).[42]

It appears that by the mid-1920s, class privilege was once again creeping into the education and vocational training system.

At every debate or conference where education policy came up, we find Krupskaya fighting a rearguard action against the abolition of polytechnic education and project teaching methods. For instance, at the Third All-Russian Trade Union Congress of 1920, the trade unionist Koselyov attacked the work school and called for narrowly specialised training, to bring Russian industry up to world levels. Krupskaya replied that a socialist state could not simply take over capitalist methods of raising efficiency.

> From our point of view, vocational training must not mentally cripple a person, by forcing him into narrow specialisation from an early age, it must not restrict his horizon, its only purpose must be

C

to serve his all-sided total development. Vocational training must not educate a worker who only carries out instructions, who works mechanically. It must train the worker to be the master of production.[43]

A few years later, proposals were made to abolish the second stage of the work school, and replace it with more factory youth and peasant youth schools, directly linked to special forms of work. The philosophy behind the proposals was that workers and peasants did not need general education: 'One does not need geometry to bake cakes.' Krupskaya replied that workers and peasants wanted to be the conscious creators of the communist order, and not just the people who carried out instructions from above:

Polytechnic education has the aim of studying modern technology in general, its main achievements and its foundations, the inter-relationships between the various branches of production and development tendencies of modern technology. It aims to show where this development is leading us.[44]

Krupskaya went on to attack the Soviet trade unions for taking up a 'conservative, handicraft point of view' in this question, and for not recognising the necessity of a broadly based training to allow workers to master technology and adapt to changes in production methods.[45]

But Krupskaya and her associates at the People's Commissariat for Popular Education were fighting a losing battle. Bureaucratic rule was getting more and more firmly established in party, state and industry. By 1927, Stalin was strong enough to expel Trotsky, Zinoviev and Kamenev from the Politbureau, the Central Committee and, finally, the party. A purge of party members suspected of sympathies with the left got under way. Strict discipline and obedience became the chief virtues demanded of a communist. The bureaucratic leaders had no use for workers educated to run and control production. They wanted large numbers of specialists, trained to absolute conformity. The move away from polytechnic education gained new momentum.

The result was new teaching plans for all subjects, emphasising systematic formalised learning and rejecting the 'complex method'. Krupskaya attacked the draft for the new curriculum for work study in the second stage of the work school as being 'unpolitical, it is no way connected with the task of constructing socialism'. The curriculum reduced polytechnic education to unrelated specialised techniques, and replaced productive work with lectures and excursions.[46] Krupskaya had to retreat more and more from her position. She took to quoting Lenin's views on the importance of polytechnic education, hoping that his authority still carried weight. But increasingly, the views of experts like Gastev, the founder of the Central Institute for Labour, came to prevail. Gastev, for example, emphasised the priority of rapidly training skilled workers like carpenters and mechanics, and demanded the reduction of polytechnic education in the schools to basic vocational training. In vain did Krupskaya repeat the question:

> Do we want to reproduce the old division of labour, do we want to make the workers narrow specialists who only know their own special job and are therefore permanently bound to it, or do we want to train specialists in the sense meant by Marx and Lenin?[47]

In vain did she point out how Gastev's ideas contradicted the political aims of the revolution:

> The worker is not just somebody who carries out orders here. Today he carries out orders, tomorrow he can be an inventor, and the day after tomorrow an important organiser in a factory. Gastev does not want to see this.[48]

By the time Krupskaya wrote this, in 1928, the stage was set for a counter-revolution in education.

The First Five-Year Plan and the 'Cultural Revolution' from Above

Once Stalin had got rid of the Left Opposition and consolidated his dominant position in the party, he set about carrying out his programme of building 'socialism in one country'. The first five-year plan of 1928–33 proclaimed forced collectivisation and an industrialisation of unprecedented scope and speed. The poor peasants (about five to eight million of the 25 million peasant household) were called upon to form collective farms. The state was to give technical assistance, while land and animals were to be confiscated from the kulaks, who made up one and a half to two million households. Stalin called for a general attack on the kulaks, and their extermination as a class. The result was a period of violent class struggles and upheavals, which did as much to change Russia as had the revolution of 1917.

Stalin's programme did not go as planned, because a large

proportion of the biggest peasant stratum, the middle peasants (15–18 million households), sided with the kulaks. They were attached to their private property and were not convinced that collective work would bring them any benefits. Stalin sent young communists, troops and GPU (political police) units to the countryside. The peasants were forced into the collective farms by machine guns, armed searches and requisitions. Millions of kulaks and middle peasants were turned out of their homes and sent to Arctic regions. The desperate resistance of the peasants took on destructive forms: grain was burnt, implements smashed and cattle slaughtered. Peasant individualism was so ingrained that many preferred to eat meat just for once rather than give their animals to the state. The number of horses fell from 34 million in 1929 to 17 million in 1933. Thirty million cattle and 100 million sheeps and goats were butchered.[49] This was a catastrophe for an agricultural system which was still based on horses as the main source of energy and animal manure as the main fertiliser. The result was a new famine, not only in the towns but also in the countryside.

Industrialisation now became a question of life or death. Only the introduction of tractors and of chemical fertiliser could make it possible to feed the population. This meant building new factories, oil refineries and chemical plants, raising coal and iron production, and rapidly extending electrification. The original extremely ambitious, targets of the five-year plan had to be increased even further, and the fulfilment of the plan in four years was proclaimed. Labour power was provided by the peasants who had been driven from the land.

The first five-year plan was an agricultural and industrial revolution on an unprecedented scale, but it was not a socialist revolution. Collectivisation and industrialisation took place under the iron dictatorship of the party bureaucracy. The workers and peasants had no voice in decision-making; anybody who dissented was branded a class-enemy and dealt with accordingly. There was no more talk of workers and peasants controlling specialists and managers through the soviets. One-man management was the rule. Creativity and initiative were not sought after. Participation in building socialism meant hard work and unquestioning obedience. A system of draconian disciplinary measures, combined with material incentives was devised. There were very large wage differentials and most workers were on piece-rates. 'Socialist emulation' and Stakhanovism were further measures designed to press as much work as possible out of the workers.[50] People who did not work hard enough or who were suspected of political dissent were sent to labour camps. Many large projects, such as the White Sea canal, were actually carried out with the slave labour of hundreds of thousands of political prisoners. In the second half of the 1930s Stalin turned against the old bolsheviks of the revolutionary period. Thousands were executed or imprisoned after show trials. All those who had been members of the Politbureau up to the death of Lenin were executed – except Stalin himself, of course, Tomski, who committed suicide and Trotsky who was exiled and, finally, murdered.

In circumstances like these, education aimed at making workers and peasants fit to control production and run society is quite unthinkable. Stalinism meant three things in education: first, training in unquestioning conformity; second, the production of vast numbers of engineers, technicians, managers and other 'cadres'; third, a drive for mass literacy to allow the introduction of modern methods in agriculture and industry. Stalin echoed Lenin's call for a 'cultural revolution'. However, he did not mean a movement based on the interests and initiatives of the masses, but a revolution from above, strictly controlled by party directives. A five-year cultural plan was proclaimed in 1928, as a vital precondition for the fulfilment of the economic plan.

One of the first measures was the dismissal of Lunacharsky as Commissar for Education, and attacks on leading educationalists as 'right-opportunists'. The new commissar, Bubnov, had previously been in charge of the political administration of the Red Army. He introduced military command structures and discipline in the commissariat, forbade free discussion on aims and methods, and called for an educational campaign in order to move 'the education system from the rear of the column to the first rank in socialist construction'. Bubnov demanded mass mobilisation in the 'cultural campaign': led by the 'general staff' (i.e. the commissariat), a 'cultural army' of workers, young communists, and pioneers was to carry out shock attacks against illiteracy, lack of schools, etc.

However, stalinism did not mean an immediate break with polytechnic methods. On the contrary, at first they were regarded as essential instruments for the rapid introduction of new technologies and the corresponding training of the labour force. From

1929 to 1931 the Research Institute for Marxist-Leninist Education, directed by V. N. Schulgin, had considerable influence on education policy. Schulgin argued that school was a product of class society and that it, like the state, would wither away during the transition to a communist society. He wanted pupils and teachers to spend an increasing proportion of their time working in factories and on farms, visiting cinemas, libraries and laboratories. The school was only to have the function of organising the children's work, the teacher that of advising children which work processes would help them to learn. Children were no longer to learn at school but through work itself. Curricula and text-books could only hinder learning processes.[51] The consequence was a partial return to the 'complex-method'. But in 1931 Bubnov attached Schulgin's theory:

> The present period is a period of sharpening class struggle. We must use every means to strengthen the proletarian state. From this point of view all discussions on the 'withering away of the state' at the present time are totally unnecessary and harmful for us. All prattle of this sort must be attacked without quarter ... No less harmful are the discussions on the 'withering away of the school'. These disorganise the teachers who are now fighting the battle for the school, who are supposed to stabilise and transform it; for the school is one of the strongest levers for strengthening the proletarian state in the present period.[52]

A few months later the Central Committee of the CPSU issued an important decision on primary and middle schools. Polytechnic education was henceforth to mean the 'solid and systematic learning of the sciences, especially physics, chemistry and mathematics'. The project teaching of the 'complex method' was strictly forbidden. Measures were to be taken to strengthen discipline and to make sure that the teacher took the leading role in the learning process. Collective management of schools was replaced by strict control by a headmaster.[53] In 1932, a further decision of the central committee introduced unitary curricula for all subjects. Teaching was to take place in fixed class-groups, with a predetermined plan of work. The main instrument of systematic teaching was to be the formal lesson, using a prescribed text book. Regular marks and annual examinations were introduced.[54] It was a resurrection of the old 'book-school' which Krupskaya had always fought against. At first there were still claims that the school was based on polytechnic education, but in fact 'productive work' was now mere handicraft work, quite unrelated to modern technology, let alone to the economic and social structures of society. Finally, in 1937, even this pretence was dropped: a decree of the Commissariat for Education ordered the abolition of work in the schools. The workshops were 'liquidated', teachers with suitable training were put to teaching physics and mathematics, the others dismissed with one week's notice. Courses for handicraft teachers in training colleges were abolished.[55] Krupskaya wrote a series of letters to party leaders condemning the measures, but her voice went unheard.[56] It was probably only her name that saved her from becoming a victim of the show trials.

Stalinist methods did achieve a quite remarkable quantitative expansion of the education system. By the outbreak of the second world war illiteracy had been almost stamped out and at least four years of schooling was available to almost every child. Middle level vocational training and higher education grew by about 500 per cent between 1928 and 1940. But it was not socialist education, but formalised teaching with strict discipline aimed at training obedient workers who did not think for themselves. Vocational training was geared to the rapid production of narrowly specialised cadres, foremen and skilled workers. Education had the same function as in capitalism: social selection and the maintaining of class privileges. By the end of the 1930s, school uniforms, special schools for the children of officers and school fees for secondary and higher education were being introduced.

5. Education for the New Society: Two Conflicting Models

We now want to look in more detail at the aims and methods of socialist education as exemplified by two projects which played an important part in the development of Soviet educational strategies: the 'First Experimental Station of the People's Commissariat for Education'; and the Dzerzhinsky Commune, a youth labour commune set up by the GPU (Stalin's political police) in 1927. These two projects are closely associated with the ideas of two famous Soviet educationalists: the first with S. T. Schatzky and the second with A. S. Makarenko. But the great difference between the two models is not so much a result of varying educational ideas, as of the different political and economic context in which they took place.

As we have already pointed out, the bolsheviks were faced with the task of inventing and constructing a new educational system, to fit people for the task of building a socialist society. There was a theoretical basis for this task: the marxist theory of polytechnic education as interpreted and adapted by Lenin and Krupskaya. But there was no blueprint for the concrete realisation of this enormous undertaking. In the immediate post-revolutionary years, the bolsheviks encouraged a period of experimentation in which progressive teachers, educationalists and workers tried out a great variety of models, such as the open labour colony 'Bolschewo', described by Otto Fenichel, Vera Schmidt's psycho-analytic 'children's laboratory', Makarenko's Gorky Colony, voluntary youth communes, etc. There were thousands of projects and a great blaze of new ideas. We cannot attempt to look at them all in detail, so we will describe just one – Schatzky's experimental station – as an example for the creativity of this early period.

Makarenko's Dzerzhinsky Commune belongs to a different epoch of Soviet history: it is a product of the educational policy of the victorious stalinist bureaucracy. The teaching aims and methods developed by Makarenko in his earlier Gorky Colony now take on the character of conscious and systematic preparation of young people to serve as 'new cadres' in the realisation of Stalin's plans for rapid industrialisation.

A comparison of these two projects gives a vivid impression of the requirements made of education in two succeeding stages of the development of Soviet society. They are based on varying views of what socialism means, and of the characteristics necessary for its construction. Although both Schatzky and Makarenko speak of education for a new society, of collective education, and of linking learning with work, they mean quite different things by all these concepts.

The First Experimental Station of the People's Commissariat for Education

Schatzky had been a leading progressive educationalist before the revolution.[57] In 1905, together with his friends Zelenko and Sieger, he set up a summer colony in the country for working-class children from Moscow. The colony was co-ordinated with nurseries and clubs for children in Moscow itself. The project soon provided facilities for 450 children, and a 'settlement association' was set up to run it. The aim was to set up children's communities and to study them. The experience gained in this way was to form the basis for changes and innovations in education. This 'education in movement' became a main principle for all Schatzky's ideas and projects. An early innovation in the settlement was the setting up of textile, wood and metal workshops for the children.

In 1907, the 'settlement' was forbidden on the charge of 'trying to introduce socialism among little children'. It started up again two years later under a new name, and in 1911 Schatzky set up a new colony in the Kaluga district. Here, according to his own description, he got to know the social and economic conditions, the customs and beliefs, of the poorest strata of society. He also learnt to place trust in children and came to realise that they were quite capable of collectively organising their own lives according to their own interests, if they got the right sort of support from grown-ups.

In 1916, Schatzky obtained the backing of the Moscow City Duma for a new project: an Experimental Station for Education, embracing all age groups and the most important forms of work. It was to start with nursery school and go on to elementary and secondary school. Children's clubs, workshops, a library, and a children's colony were to form part of the project.[58] After the revolution the experimental station was taken over by the People's Commissariat and its scope extended. Schatzky did not believe in confining education to the school; children were to learn by studying and taking part in the life and work of the community around them. In this way the school was to change not only the consciousness of the children, but also to influence production and social life in town and country. For Schatzky education meant community work. In accordance with this concept, the real field of work of the experimental station was not just the educational facilities it contained, but also a whole working-class district of Moscow, and a rural area in the Kaluga district containing three big estates, five main villages and about 60 small villages.

The following passages from a paper setting out the aims and structure of the experimental station give a good idea of how Schatzky tried to carry out his educational plans:

> As the main task of the Experimental Station is investigation and experimentation, the various types of activity must be continually developed out of the work process itself. It is therefore not possible to lay them down comprehensively and in detail beforehand. How-

ever, the most important activities are as follows:

1. Popular education in every form. This includes:

(a) Pre-school education in town and country;

(b) First and second stage schools of various types, according to local conditions. The Experimental Station is to provide material to answer the following questions: what forms are to be taken by the work school in town and country; what types of productive work are to be made the basis of school life, taking local conditions into account; which types of school can be set up under rural conditions, taking account of the peculiar and complex system of settlement (of the country); e.g. complete schools with the necessary number of departments in larger settlements and smaller schools in the familiar environment of the village;

(c) Facilities outside school for children and young people in the form of children's clubs, playgrounds, work colonies for children, etc. . . .

(d) Facilities outside school amongst the adult population aimed at supporting their intellectual and aesthetic development. These include: schools for adults starting with ABC-schools and going on to peasants' high schools and similar universities and technical colleges, libraries, clubs for grown-ups, popular theatre, musical education for the people as well as the task of organising people's houses as centres of education outside school, and the methods of work in these.

2. Agricultural experiments (the carrying out of experiments with improved methods of cultivation, vegetable growing, garden work, livestock-raising) and getting the local population to take part in them.

3. Handicraft and industrial methods taking account of local conditions (experiments with regard to the introduction of new working methods and the participation of the population in questions of technical progress).

4. Socio-cultural work for the development of communal instincts and habits of collective work . . .

5. Hygienic and medical tasks . . .

6. Statistics . . .

7. Publishing . . .

8. The task of training personnel for various types of cultural work. Here we are not thinking of training narrow specialists, but rather a particular type of cultural worker with the following characteristics:

(a) The ability to become orientated in various types of cultural work and to discover their interrelationships;

(b) Linking cultural and social work (experience in productive work) in a single person;

(c) A creative attitude towards work and the disposition to seek new ways of doing things.

9. Setting up educational exhibitions, both fixed and mobile.

10. Establishing active links to organisations active in popular education, particularly those of an experimental nature.[59]

The children's colony had originally functioned in the summer only. The working-class children from Schatzky's Moscow children's club had come out for a few months, often returning year after year. But from 1918 onwards the colony became a permanent year-round dwelling place for the children. In 1923 it was combined with a nine-year boarding school. Schatzky's aim was a community of children of various ages, together with grown-ups. The children were to run the community themselves and to find their own patterns of living and organisation, without being dictated to by adults. A vital role in the colony was played by work, of which there were two types: the daily tasks necessary for running the colony, such as cooking, cleaning, administration; and productive work like growing vegetables, building roads and water pipelines, etc. The guiding principle was that the children were to decide in democratic assemblies what work needed doing, and how it was to be carried out. The right of the children to decide was taken seriously: at one stage they decided that they did not want to work, and restricted their activities to the minimum necessary for providing meals, etc. The adults were annoyed, but did not intervene. After a while, the children decided that productive work would be more interesting than just playing, and started organising it again.

The children got into the habit of holding regular assemblies which discussed all important matters, took decisions on all aspects of work and life, and made general rules for the colony. If anybody broke a rule, he or she was warned by the assembly. After three warnings, a child was expelled from the colony. Work and lessons did not take up all the time of the children: free play, sports and theatre also played an important part. Schatzky regarded such activities as essential for maintaining children's natural curiosity.

In the schools of the experimental station, formal subject teaching was replaced by the 'complex method'. Schatzky was a leading exponent of this form of teaching, and helped to work out the People's Commissariat of Education's new teaching plans for the unitary work school issued in 1923, embodying the complex method. The essence of these new plans was that children should no

longer learn abstract school subjects, but should learn by studying
and participating in the life of the community around them. Instead of learning reading, writing, geography, etc., children were
to investigate all aspects of a topic such as 'health' or 'the village'.
Children and teachers were to organise their own studies, going
outside the school and looking at the real problems associated with
such themes. Children were to work in fields connected with their
studies, and help to bring in new working methods. The school
was to cease to be a mere institution of learning and to become the
centre of children's life and work, caring for their material well-
being by providing food and clothes. But Schatzky did not want to
undermine the role of the family in education. His aim was to
influence family education methods and family life in general by
making school a living part of the community.

Schatzky's critics attacked him for not educating children for
the class struggle which was going on around them. Indeed
Schatzky was strongly opposed to forms of education which prepare children for a predetermined future and for involvement in a
particular political party.[60] He argued that adults had undergone
a very one-sided education and did not really understand the
world of the children. By allowing children to develop freely and
to organise their own life and work, Schatzky thought they would
develop in an all-sided and creative way. Play was the children's
form of work, through which they took possession of the material
and social world and came to understand their own needs and
interests. Schatzky regarded the free and autonomous development of the children's community as the best preparation for
future class struggle. People brought up in this way would be able
to recognise their own interests and fight for them collectively.

As the struggle on educational policy intensified in the late
1920s Schatzky's position became increasingly precarious. He had
not joined the party until 1928; a year later he was attacked for
'right deviationism' because his model of the work school was
based on agricultural rather than industrial work, and because he
rejected Schulgin's notion of the 'withering away of the school'.
Krupskaya publicly defended Schatzky, which saved him for the
time being. He began adapting his views to conform with stalinist
policies: he spoke in favour of forced collectivisation (for which the
peasants of the Kaluga district burnt down his house), and engaged in a self-criticism, rescinding his views on the complex
method after it had been forbidden by the party in 1931. Neverthe-

less, he was dismissed from his job as director of the experimental station in 1932. The station was then reorganised on stalinist lines. For over twenty years Schatzky's ideas on education were completely suppressed in the Soviet Union. It was not until after the Twentieth Party Congress in 1956 that a selection of his works was once again published.

The Dzerzhinsky Commune

In looking at the work of A. S. Makarenko (1888–1939) it is difficult to distinguish between myth and reality. After his death, Makarenko was canonized by official propaganda as the greatest of communist educators. His work is known mainly through his fascinating educational novels, which do not necessarily give an accurate picture. It was not until after 1956 that any discussion of the real problems of Makarenko's methods became possible, by which time it was difficult to get objective information on what actually happened in his educational projects.[61]

After fifteen years as a school teacher, Makarenko was appointed director of the Gorky Colony in 1920. This was one of the homes set up in the civil war period to deal with the thousands of orphaned and destitute children. In 1923 the Gorky Colony was recognised by the People's Commissariat for Education as an experimental and model institution, but in the succeeding years there was increasing criticism of Makarenko's educational methods. Krupskaya publicly criticised the forms of discipline and punishment used in the Gorky Colony. It is not certain whether Makarenko left the Gorky Colony voluntarily or whether he was dismissed. In any case, he departed in 1927 and soon afterwards attacked the educational concepts of the People's Commissariat for Education.

At the end of 1927, Makarenko was appointed by the GPU to run a new home for children and young people in the Ukraine. The GPU was a political police force, one of Stalin's main instruments for suppressing and terrorising his opponents. Its responsibility for public order included the prevention of hooliganism by young people, and to this purpose it ran various labour camps and prisons. In setting up the new colony, it was also concerned to find ways of re-educating children and youths to play an active role in industrialisation and class struggle. The GPU named its new colony after the founder of the political police, Felix Dzerzhinsky, and financed it through deductions from the pay of Ukrainian GPU members.

Makarenko brought sixty boys and girls from the Gorky Colony with him. By 1932, the Dzerzhinsky Commune had over three hundred members. The basis of life in the commune was productive work. The whole collective was organised in groups with seven to fifteen members, each responsible for a specific form of work: metalwork, turning, carpentry, tailoring, foundry work, nickel-plating. In 1932 a factory for making electric hand drills was also set up. The children had to work four hours per day, more when it was necessary to fulfil the plan or to carry out urgent jobs. Makarenko remarked that labour discipline was poor at first, though he attributed this to inability on the part of the personnel in charge of the various departments. After a year, it was decided that the Dzerzhinsky Commune should pay its own way and all work was to be based on the principle of profitability. Mechanisation and division of labour was introduced and, starting in 1930, all communards were paid according to the same piece-work scales as grown-up workers. Methods like 'socialist emulation' and 'shock-working' were used to raise productivity. Production commissions were set up in all departments. They organised regular discussions on increasing production. Strict labour discipline was maintained by the Komsomol (Young Communist League) as well as by specially appointed 'commanders'. All communards were trained as skilled workers in several trades, and received a general education equivalent to middle-school levels. In 1930 the Dzerzhinsky Commune set up its own 'workers' faculty' to prepare young people for entry to university. Skilled work, general education and collective training – these were Makarenko's principles for training the 'new cadres' urgently needed by the Soviet state.

Makarenko's ideas on collective training are crucial for his concept of communist personality: all members of the commune were assigned to work-groups. Each work-group had a commander – a child or youth appointed or elected for three to six months. The commander sometimes had one or two deputies.

> Commanders are always to be appointed when there is no firmly established collective, and when the Komsomol organisation is not yet capable of adequately guiding opinions in the collective . . .
>
> In well organised collectives with a strong Komsomol organisation, the commanders should be elected . . . A pupil should be

elected as commander, who is loyal to the interests of the home, a good pupil, a shock worker in production, who is superior to the others in qualification, and who is marked by characteristics like tact, energy, talent for organisation, consideration towards younger persons and honesty.[62]

The commanders had considerable power: they could give orders to other communards at work and school, in the dormitories and outside. They were responsible for all everyday decisions, for maintaining discipline, for making sure that the dormitories and classrooms and the clothes and faces of the communards were clean. Orders from commanders had to be obeyed at once, and all communards had to salute them. The commanders made daily reports to the director of the commune on the work and discipline of their departments.

The chief organ of self-government in the Dzerzhinsky Commune was the Commanders' Council. Its members were all the commanders, the director of the commune, the deputy director, the manager of the household, the manager of the production sector, the doctor, the secretary of the Komsomol and the members of the commune administration. The director of the commune had the task of making sure that commune assemblies did not make any wrong or harmful decisions. All discussions had to be carefully prepared in advance. In this the director was aided by the Pioneers and the Komsomol. These organisations were present in all departments and were meant to take the lead in activist work and 'socialist emulation'. In 1930 Makarenko proudly declared that the Komsomol has become the 'real director' of the commune, and that there was no need for teachers any more. Instead there was now a 'teachers' collective' consisting of the school-teachers, engineers, foremen, work instructors, GPU members, administrators and 'above all and principally the Party and Komsomol group'.[63]

Military organisation and drill played a big part in Makarenko's collective training. The pupils wore uniforms and did military training. The commune was guarded by armed sentries. Flags and military music were prominent at festivities. The new 'Soviet Patriotism' called for by Stalin was a main feature of the Dzerzhinsky Commune.

Makarenko believed that giving children and young people responsibility was vital for their education as active Soviet workers. There were three stages in setting up an educational commune: to start with, the educators had to make clear and firm regulations. Once a core of pupils who accepted the principles of the director had become established, they were to be given a leading part. In the final stage the aim was that all communards should voluntarily accept the rules and discipline of the Commanders' Council. All members of the commune possessed the full rights of a Soviet citizen. They had the right and the duty of taking part in productive work, which brought benefit to themselves and the collective. Each communard was responsible for his or her own work and behaviour and had to be prepared to accept collective criticism and practise self-criticism. Makarenko summed his method up:

> We give the children's and youth collective a school, a workers' faculty, a factory, engineers, a production and finance plan, wages, duties and the right to responsibility. And that means – we give it discipline.[64]

A Comparison of Educational Principles

Both Schatzky and Makarenko wanted to educate people capable of building a new society; both regarded collective education, based on the self-government of the pupils, as the best way of achieving this aim; both regarded productive work as an important part of the learning process. But there the similarities end: Schatzky and Makarenko meant quite different things by these principles, and had quite different methods of achieving their basic aims.

Schatzky wanted the children to develop freely, rather than being pressed into a pre-determined mould by well intentioned grown-ups. He wanted to preserve children's natural curiosity by allowing them to decide on their own collective play and work-processes. This meant that children's assemblies in schools and homes should be real decision-making bodies, without any form of manipulation by teachers. School was to help children to understand the work and problems of the surrounding communities; its teaching was to be based on local conditions, rather than on general curricula. Children and teachers were to go outside the school and learn from work and daily life. Productive work was important in education not for its own sake, but as an instrument to help children understand society. High productivity and strict work-discipline had no place in Schatzky's educational concepts. Individual interests and abilities were to develop in the collective process of the self-organisation of the children's community. Schatzky demanded that children should not be educated for the future, but allowed to run their own lives in the present. This, he argued, was the best way of bringing up creative, totally developed people, who would take a conscious and active part in building a new society.

Makarenko had a clear idea of the sort of 'communist personality' he wanted to achieve: the well-trained, disciplined, skilled worker, accustomed to accepting and exercising authority, loyal to the party and state. Collective education did not mean that children could do as they liked, but rather that they learnt to accept the authority of the collective and to take a voluntary part in strengthening this authority. The system of elected and appointed commanders was particularly important for getting young people used to discipline and self-discipline. Productive work was the other main instrument of education. It was disciplined industrial work, controlled by foremen and commanders, and motivated by piece rates. There was not the least attempt to reduce the gulf between manual and mental work, or to eliminate rigid forms of the division of labour. Military structures, drill and uniforms were further mechanisms to secure the submission of the individual to the all-powerful collective.

Schatzky's aims and methods corresponded with the marxist aim of the totally developed individual, and he came close to achieving the sort of school planned for all Soviet children by Krupskaya and Lunacharsky. But Stalin had no use for autonomous, creative people. Makarenko's method of collective education met his requirements far better: unconditional acceptance of the authority of the hierarchical collective provided a suitable preparation for unconditional obedience to the orders of the stalinist party and state.

4

Education in Eastern Europe Since Stalin: the German Democratic Republic

Education in the Soviet Union during Stalin's rule was marked by a complete departure from the principles of polytechnic education. Practical work was abolished. Soviet schools adopted the same rigid methods, hierarchical structures and abstract content as capitalist schools of the period. However, Soviet education was not static: there was considerable quantitative growth at all levels. Illiteracy was stamped out and basic education up to the age of fourteen made generally available. The second world war led to widespread destruction of educational facilities, causing the postponement of plans for ten-year compulsory education, but most of the lost ground was made up by the 1950s.

The creation of the Soviet bloc in Eastern Europe after 1945 meant the export of Soviet educational methods to the countries concerned. At first, of course, this led to the copying of the Stalinist school system. But after Stalin's death in 1953 important changes were made in Soviet education, and these were closely followed in Eastern Europe: a return to the principles of polytechnic education was proclaimed and new ways of linking school with work introduced.

These changes and their causes are the subject of the present chapter. Our account concentrates on the German Democratic Republic (GDR), partly because it is interesting to see how polytechnic principles are applied in the most industrially developed Soviet-type society, and partly because information was most readily available to us on that country. However, we argue that the GDR experience is representative of the general pattern of educational developments in the Soviet Union and in other Eastern European countries. As we will show, the leaders of the GDR have followed closely the twists and turns of Soviet education policy. It is also interesting to compare developments in the GDR with those in the German Federal Republic (see chapter 6) – two countries with very similar cultures and historical backgrounds, but with opposing political systems. The degree to which educational change follows a similar pattern is often striking.

1. Education Policy Since 1945

Stalinist Education Prior to 1958

In the first few years of occupation after 1945 no attempt was made to build up an independent state in the Soviet zone of Germany. The four powers had agreed to administer their zones in such a way as to permit their reunification as a demilitarised, democratic state as soon as circumstances permitted. Between 1945 and 1949 the main concern of the Soviet Military Administration was to restore the war-shattered economy and to eliminate Nazi influence. The 'anti-fascist, democratic school reform' of these years was concerned with the restoration of damaged schools, the improvement and democratisation of education and – above all – with denazification. When they came to power in 1933, the Nazis had dismissed not only all communist and socialist teachers, but also those with democratic leanings,* and had used the schools as an instrument of ideological indoctrination. So the Soviet Military Administration dismissed no less than two-thirds of all teachers and replaced them with 40,000 workers, farmers and other persons who had little or no training as teachers.[1] Other measures were the establishment of a unitary school, based on an eight-year elementary school, and open to all; the prohibition of private schools; a strict division between state and church in education; and a programme to raise the level of schooling in rural areas. Access to higher education was via a four-year high school similar in structure to the traditional German *Gymnasium*. Selectivity remained: the proportion of high-school pupils from the families of workers or farmers was still only 34 per cent in 1950.

* The *Berufsverbot* (political blacklisting) which was introduced in West Germany in 1972, has a long tradition – German rulers have always regarded school as an instrument of political control. After the 1848 Revolution, thousands of democratic teachers were dismissed. The same thing happened in 1933. In modern West Germany, half a million civil servants have been investigated and some thousands dismissed. In East Germany, political control of teachers is even more drastic.

The introduction of Soviet educational methods started with the founding of the German Democratic Republic in 1949. The intensification of the cold war in the late 1940s finalised the division of Germany. Each side started building up its German state as a 'buffer zone' and, at the same time, a 'show-case' for its own social system. In East Germany, the ruling Socialist Unity Party (SED)[2] started to construct a society on the Soviet model. The main priority was the rapid reinforcement of the industrial basis, in particular the build-up of heavy industry. All major industries were nationalised, a highly centralised state-planning system set up, and a five-year plan on the stalinist model adopted.

This meant new tasks for the schools. The SED defined them as follows:

> The German democratic school has the task of educating patriots who are loyal to their homeland, their people, the working class and the government, and who will achieve the unity of a peaceful, in-dependent, democratic Germany by fighting the imperialist occupiers and the Adenauer clique,
>
> who will preserve eternal friendship with the Soviet Union, the People's Democracies and with all people who are fighting for peace and progress,
>
> who regard creative work as a matter of honour and fame,
>
> who increase and protect socialist property,
>
> who contribute with all their strength to the enhancement of the people's democratic basis of state power, and who are full of love and trust for our People's Army.[3]

Considerable changes in the structure of education and in the content of methods of teaching were necessary. Teachers were called upon to study and adopt the methods of 'marxist education' (which meant, in reality, Soviet education). The guiding principles were the leading role of the teacher and systematic learning in formal lessons.[4] Great emphasis was put on mathematics and science, while arts subjects were regarded as secondary. A start was made with introducing Soviet forms of school organisation – in particular the ten-year high school. One-class schools in rural areas were closed and replaced by central schools with the same curricula as urban schools. A new educational institution was introduced with the aim of breaking the power of the old upper and middle-class intelligentsia – 'workers' and farmers' faculties': special courses designed to raise the educational level of members of these social classes, so that they could study at university. The aim was the creation of a new 'socialist intelligentsia' which would support the aims of the SED.

Productive work was not part of the school curriculum at this stage, but some attempts were made to reduce the gulf between school and factory – partly because it was becoming apparent that many young people had a contemptuous attitude towards manual work and were unwilling to take factory jobs. One system was 'sponsorship' (*Patenschaft*) of a particular school by a factory or collective farm. The pupils visited the factory or farm, had talks from workers, and often spent some period working there. The success of such schemes encouraged discussion on the general introduction of polytechnic education.

The Introduction of Polytechnic Education

In 1958 there was a far-reaching structural reform of education in the GDR. One cause was the need to raise the skill-level of workers to meet the ambitious targets of the seven-year economic plan which began in 1959. But the main factor was no doubt the changes in Soviet educational policy following Stalin's death. Starting in 1954, work in school workshops and gardens was reintroduced in Soviet schools. In 1956 a new subject called 'the foundations of production' was tried out in selected schools. In the autumn of 1958, party leader Nikita Khrushchev and the Central Committee of the Soviet Communist Party attacked the school system for being cut off from life, and for not providing adequate preparation for factory and farm work. New educational laws were passed in 1958 and 1959. The whole school system was to be reorganised to link general education, vocational training, and productive work. Polytechnic education was declared to be the guiding principle of the new Soviet schools. Productive work and vocational training was to take up no less than a third of school time in the ninth, tenth and eleventh grades. School-leavers were to be fully qualified, skilled workers. This new policy was referred to as the 'professionalisation' of education.[5]

Changes in the GDR followed a similar pattern: late in 1958, a 'school day in production' was introduced, which meant that all pupils were to spend one day a week working in a 'socialist enterprise' in industry or agriculture. In 1959 a new 'Law on the Socialist Development of the School System' was enacted. It made the 'ten-year general polytechnic high school' the basic school form for all children from the age of six to sixteen. The new high school was to be generally available by 1964, though this target was not in fact met until the mid-1970s. The new law redefined the aim of education:

> Education in the socialist school is to be closely linked with productive work and the practice of socialist construction. School is to prepare young people for life and work in socialism, to educate them as all-sided polytechnically educated people, and to secure a high level of education. School trains children and young people in solidarity and collective behaviour, in love for work and for the working people, and develops all their mental and physical capabilities for the well-being of the people and the nation.

This aim was to be met through polytechnic education in the form of handicraft classes for the lower grades and work in socialist enterprises from the seventh grade onwards. Access to higher education was via an 'extended high school' from the ninth to the twelfth grades. Pupils were to be prepared for the *Abitur* (equivalent of A-levels), while at the same time receiving vocational training in a skilled manual occupation. After passing the Abitur, young people had to do at least one year of manual work before being eligible to apply for higher education. Various types of evening and external courses were to be set up to encourage working people to qualify for higher education.[6]

The new policy proved difficult to implement. The 'school day in production' had been introduced suddenly by the SED leadership, without preparing teachers, parents, pupils or factories for it. There was considerable opposition. Teachers felt incompetent to supervise polytechnic learning and feared that they might have to do manual work themselves. Many parents and pupils suspected (rightly as it often turned out) that doing certain jobs while still at school might decide their future occupation.[7] Above all: where were 450,000 workplaces for the pupils of the seventh to twelfth grades to be found? Many factories and farms regarded the young people as a nuisance, who would interfere with the fulfilment of the production plan. There was a great lack of suitable instructors. Another problem was the type of work done, which was not always a help in achieving the SED's aim of getting children to 'love work': 'Now I know for the first time how stupid and strenuous such jobs are', said one pupil – 'Now I will study hard, so that I don't have to do a job like that later on.'[8]

The Departure from 'Professionalisation' Since 1965

The mid-1960s saw a new about-face in education policy both in the Soviet Union and the GDR. The difficulties in implementing the policy of 'professionalisation' of education were one reason for this. More important were economic and technological demands on the education system. The centralized planning system left over from the Stalin era was running into difficulties. The rigid form of plan targets led factory directors to concentrate purely on fulfilment or over-fulfilment in terms of quantity. Questions of quality and effective use of resources were neglected, leading to growing inefficiency. There was a contradiction between what was rational for the individual enterprise and what was rational for the whole economy. By the beginning of the 1960s, production growth was falling back.

The result was a radical change in economic policy, known as the 'Liberman reform' in the Soviet Union and in the GDR as the 'NÖSPL' (*Neue Ökonomische System der Planung und Leitung* – new economic system of planning and management). The function of central planning was reduced to setting out general perspectives and targets. Each factory or combine was given much greater autonomy in deciding how to meet its target and in its relationships with the plants which supplied its raw materials and purchased its products. Allocation of resources was to be through price mechanisms rather than central administrative decisions. By achieving their production targets, factories were to make profits which were to be used partly to finance investments and partly to reward the directors and the workers with premiums. This system of 'economic levers' (i.e. profit motives) was to ensure that the interests of workers, directors and the plant as a whole coincided with the interests of society: higher production, more efficient use of resources, rationalisation. As we shall see below, the new system of 'economic levers' was to have important consequences for the official concept of 'socialist personality' and hence for the education system.

At the same time there was considerable discussion on the educational consequences of the so-called 'scientific technological revolution'. This refers to the introduction of new methods of production and work organisation, such as electronic data processing and control, which led to higher productivity and intensification of work. Such techniques were vital to the Soviet bloc in its economic competition with the West, especially in the case of the GDR, where population losses in the war and the departure of skilled workers since had led to a serious labour shortage. The 'scientific-technological revolution' made new demands on workers: some needed a much higher level of scientific and technical training, while others were required to develop qualities of flexibility and mobility. The problems involved are very similar to those experienced in capitalist countries in the 'third technological revolution' and appear to have more or less the same consequences for the education system, as the analysis of educational change in West Germany in Chapter 6 will show (see also Appendix).

These changes made the 'professionalisation' of education an actual barrier to further economic progress. It meant that children had to decide far too early (sometimes in the eighth grade) on their future occupation. Their training was far too specialised, and related to short-term labour needs of local factories, rather than to the long-term needs of the economy as a whole. The aim of reaching a high skill level through linking factory training with school education proved to be illusory. At the same time, the universities were reporting that 'professionalisation' had caused the general education level of new entrants to sink dangerously.[9]

By the mid-1960s the Soviet education authorities were abandoning vocational training in schools and cutting back the hours spent on practical work. There was even talk of abolishing polytechnic education altogether. This did not take place, however. Instead new curricula were introduced, redefining polytechnic education: it was no longer to be regarded as preparation for specific occupations, but rather as a general principle of education. The task of polytechnic education was to give pupils a basic understanding of the scientific and technological foundations of all production processes.[10]

Developments in the GDR followed the same pattern. The new 'Law on the Unitary Socialist Education System' of 1965, and further regulations passed in succeeding years gave polytechnic education at high school a new orientation. It was to serve as the basis for general education and all forms of further education and vocational training.[11] School was to be related to future work in the sense of general preparation and orientation, but not in the sense of specific vocational training. The linking of Abitur (A-levels) with training as a skilled worker was abandoned (it had in fact only been partially carried out). The principle of polytechnic education was to guide the choice of teaching topics and material in all subjects. In addition, the subject 'introduction to socialist production' was given special prominence, with the aim of helping young people understand the relationship between economics and technology. The 'school day in production' remained part of the curriculum, but was now intended to teach pupils about production methods in general rather than to get used to a likely future job. Polytechnic education was to contribute to the 'total development of personality', to help fit pupils to 'master the scientific-technological revolution'. Its basic theme was to be technology, understood in a very broad sense as something which mediates between nature and society. By studying technology young people were to learn how planned social activity combined with knowledge of scientific laws led to changes in production processes.[12]

2. The Education System of the German Democratic Republic

General Structure

The essential features of the present education system of the GDR are typical of education in Soviet-type societies. There is a unitary education system in which all educational processes from nursery school to university are centrally planned, coordinated, and directed towards a common goal. This goal is declared to be: 'a high level of education for the whole people, the education of all-sided and harmoniously developed socialist personalities, who consciously shape social life, transform nature, and lead a fulfilled, happy life worthy of human beings.'[13] The main way of reaching this goal is a 'socialist education, centred round education to work.'[14] Equality of opportunity for members of both sexes and of all social classes is said to be an essential part of this system. This does not mean that all children receive the same education: selectivity is according to ability and talent, and there are special schools to encourage children who are especially gifted.

Education is run according to the principles of democratic centralism. Basic decisions are made by the SED as 'the party of the working class' and carried out by the appropriate ministries and administrative bodies. Headmasters are appointed by the state and are personally responsible for 'the political, educational and organisational management of the school'.[15] In this they are helped and controlled by the local party organisations: the SED group, the FDJ (*Freie Deutsche Jugend* – Free German Youth, which organises young people aged 14 to 25) and the Pioneers (for children up to 14). There are parents' committees, with purely consultative functions, but no elected pupils' representatives – their interests are said to be taken care of by the FDJ or the Pioneers (about 90 per cent of pupils are in one or the other).

The development of education is linked with general economic and labour-market planning. The five-year and the annual plans each contain targets for the growth of education and the number of school-leavers and graduates with specific qualifications. The aim of planning is to make sure that the education system meets current and expected future labour requirements of the economy. Regional plans are made to co-ordinate schools and vocational training establishments with local industry and agriculture. Pupils are given advice and guidance from a relatively early age to make sure that their individual occupational wishes do not diverge too widely from actual opportunities. Higher education graduates are directed into specific jobs.[16] The system sounds very efficient in meeting labour needs, but the question remains as to how much room it leaves for individual self-development and choice.

To get a clear picture of the GDR's educational system it is not sufficient to examine merely the polytechnic high school (although it does make the main contribution to developing 'socialist personality'). This institution can only be understood in its relationship with pre-school, occupational and higher education; all these institutions work in a co-ordinated way to achieve the desired educational aims, and we shall therefore look at each of them.

Pre-school Education

A great deal of emphasis has been put on developing pre-school education. One reason is the severe labour shortage which makes it essential to release women from household duties for productive work. Another is the belief that early planned education is essential for combatting social inequality and for the achievement of the declared educational aims. Nursery school is not compulsory, but no less than 80 per cent of three- to six-year-old children do attend – a figure which is far higher than in most other countries, possibly the highest anywhere. A lot of effort has been put into training nursery staff – the ratio is one for every fourteen children.[17]

The tasks and methods of nursery school are laid down in a state plan.[18] There is a certain amount of formal teaching, aimed at laying the foundations for learning to read, write and count, although this seems to have been reduced lately. The main emphasis is on creating specific character traits which are the first steps towards a later 'socialist personality': self-reliance, working towards a goal, initiative, and a feeling of community.[19] The main way of developing these traits is through intervention by the teachers in the children's games. Play is guided so that certain desired moral and behaviour patterns result from it. Rewards and punishments are used, but only in the sense of praise or criticism. Particularly important are role-games, often started by the teacher, in which the children take on social roles (e.g. a worker, a shop assistant, a frontier soldier) and thus learn the forms of behaviour expected of citizens of the GDR. Social behaviour and love of work is also encouraged by getting the children to take on regular tasks like setting the table or tidying up. Sometimes children work in the garden of the kindergarten. Another method used is excursions to factories, farms, police stations, etc., after which role-games are encouraged, to reinforce the impressions made by the visits. One way of teaching the required attitude towards work is by encouraging children to make things with handicraft methods, working persistently and constantly. Children are trained to keep at a job until they have finished it. Group work and production of things for other people (e.g. presents for parents, old people, groups of workers) are also useful in encouraging a collective, socialist attitude towards work.

Schools

The central institution of the GDR education system is the ten-year polytechnic high school. Compulsory education starts at the age of six and continues until sixteen. In principle, all children attend the same schools, except for children with physical or mental disabilities, for whom there are special ESN schools.[20] But there are certain forms of differentiation. In 1974, about ten per cent of children left after the eighth class (aged fourteen) to start an apprenticeship. They, however, spend two or three days a week in a vocational school, which is supposed to ensure that they reach the general educational level of the tenth class. Other children enter preparation classes for the 'extended high school' after the eighth grade (these take place within the normal high school). After the tenth grade all children take an exam to decide on who is to enter the extended high school (which is comparable to a British sixth-form college). Obviously those who have been in the preparation classes have the best chance. In 1973, 11·6 per cent of pupils leaving the tenth grade went on to the extended high school. Marks are not the only criterion: political and ideological attitudes also play a part, and so does 'social origin'. It is hard to say quite what the latter means, since it is claimed that the educational disadvantages of the children of workers and peasants have long since been overcome. One pointer is the demand for special treatment for the children of parents 'who have made special achievements in the construction of socialism', which could refer to state and party bureaucrats. The extended high school prepares pupils for the *Abitur* (A levels) and for entry to higher education. In 1974, 9·6 per cent of the appropriate age-group passed these exams at the extended high school, and it may be assumed that most went on to university.[21] Obviously there is a high degree of selectivity here, but it is hard to say whether it is based on achievement, as claimed, or on class criteria.

Another way of gaining access to higher education is through special occupational training courses which last three years and which combine a vocational qualification with *Abitur*. However, it seems that this *Abitur* is recognised only for entry to specific engineering, technological or officers colleges. About ten thousand students per year enter higher education in this way.

A further form of selectivity is the 'special schools' and 'special classes' set up to encourage children with special talents. These sometimes start as early as the third grade. There are special schools for sport, music, languages, technology, science and mathematics. Their task is to provide experts and leading cadres for economy and science. In 1970 there were 26 such schools. The present figure is unavailable. It may be suspected that these schools are designed to secure the privileges and the self-regeneration of the state and party leadership, but it is impossible to prove this.

The East German form of 'polytechnic education' takes three

forms in the ten-year high school: first, it is brought into all general education subjects; second, there are special subjects devoted to polytechnic education; third, there is the 'school day in production'. We shall look at these three aspects in turn.

Bringing polytechnic education into general education means relating the choice of teaching topics to the problems of production and social organisation. This is easiest in subjects like mathematics and the natural sciences. Here it is a matter of not teaching just abstract scientific laws, but of always showing their practical application in the production process. But working life can be brought into arts subjects too: a language book can describe factory work, pupils can learn to paint by depicting what they have seen on a visit to a collective farm. Indeed, artistic subjects are officially regarded as particularly important in achieving the educational aim of getting children to 'love work and working people'.[22] Subjects like history and geography can be used to show the development of the forces of production, and the way in which society is organised in different areas. To make sure that teachers do bring polytechnic education into general teaching in the desired way, the school authorities have issued binding teaching instructions and textbooks for all subjects.[23] GDR educationalists totally reject the 'complex method' advocated by Krupskaya. No attempt is made to relate teaching to the actual situation, problems and interests of the children. Pupils have no scope for deciding what they want to learn. All teaching is according to highly systematic compulsory curricula. This applies even to the voluntary technical and scientific working groups, which have been set up for older pupils outside normal teaching hours.

The special subjects devoted to polytechnic education are handicraft classes for grades one to six and the subject 'introduction to socialist production' (which is usually combined with technical draughtsmanship) for grades seven to ten. Handicraft classes are not just traditional woodwork and the like, but are meant to teach basic technical principles through working with various materials, using technical kits and building electrical models. The 'introduction to socialist production' is the most important polytechnic subject, and is worth looking at more closely. Its aim is to teach pupils the technical, technological, economic and social foundations of the production process. By learning about methods of production, children are to begin to think about problems of economic organisation and political structures. These relationships make the subject an extremely important instrument for teaching children to 'love work' and to accept the SED's ideology on the part to be played by workers in building up the economy of the GDR.

The best way to understand this function is to read the official school books for the subject. Here are a few passages from the book used in the ninth grade for teaching children about the technology and economics of socialist agriculture:

> The people in the GDR are the social owners of the means of production. This means that they have an interest in the development of the socialist state, for the more that is produced, the better it is for the living standards of the population. A socialist attitude of people towards the socialist state does not develop of its own accord. Consciousness and a socialist attitude towards work develops through collective work in fulfilling the works' plan and through the mutual personal relationships of the workers and collective farmers. This expresses itself in excellent production achievements, in maintaining labour discipline, in co-operation in making and fulfilling the production plan . . .
>
> The plan is the working programme of the working people, which they have made themselves . . .
>
> In socialism, work is a moral duty and a matter of honour and respect. More and more working people are becoming conscious of their responsibility . . .[24]

To prove the last point, the children are shown a table which shows the growing number of workers and peasants who have been awarded the title of 'meritorious activist' (*Verdienter Aktivist*) or 'meritorious foreman' (*Verdienter Meister*). But, they are told, idealism is not sufficient to maintain high production. That is why most workers are paid piece-rates, or receive premiums for fulfilment or over-fulfilment of the plan. Piecework – regarded in capitalist countries as an especially severe form of exploitation – is described as a basic principle of socialism. Another important lesson in this school book concerns the leading role of the SED:

> The most class-conscious and progressive workers, collective farmers and members of the intelligentsia are organised in the SED. They have created the programme for the planned construction of socialism. The strength of the SED lies in its unity and its rigid discipline . . . Its strength also lies in its marxist-leninist theory.[25]

The book shows in diagram the vital role played by the SED and its sub-organisations in running the economy, and then sets pupils a task: 'Show in the case of your place of work [i.e. where the pupil has his 'school day in production'] the leading role of the SED in the political and economic work with working people.'

The third aspect of polytechnic education at high school is the 'school day in production'. As already mentioned, the emphasis has moved away from the original aim of vocational training and of recruiting apprentices for specific jobs. The aim now is not only to teach pupils about production technologies but also to show them the social and organisational structure of a 'socialist' factory. Pupils are instructed by specially trained polytechnic teachers as well as by foremen and workers, who are released from normal work, and who receive instruction in teaching methods. The 1965 law required factories to provide the necessary organisational and material facilities for the 'school day in production'. There is usually a special teaching room in the factory, known as a 'poly-technic cabinet', which contains drawings, tables, machines, in-struments and other teaching aids. These allow the instructors to demonstrate technological methods to pupils without interrupting production. However, it is regarded as essential that pupils should spend a considerable part of their 'school day in production' doing real productive work, in order to form a correct attitude towards manual work.

A guiding principle for all education is 'political-ideological, moral and social training'.[26] We have already shown this for the 'introduction to socialist production'. It is meant to apply in the same way to all aspects of school life. An East German educational-ist states the principle as follows:

> The unity of the teaching and learning of scientific knowledge in the various fields with the learning of the ideology of the working class, that means the scientific view of the world and of society of marxism-leninism.

Young people are to be convinced of the superiority of socialism, not in an abstract way, but by convincingly explaining to them the structure of 'socialism as it really exists in the GDR'.[27] Very im-portant instruments for achieving this are the youth organisations – the FDJ and the Pioneers – which organise social activities and excursions, make contacts with factories, farms, and army units, and generally take care of the ideological training of young people. Within the school classes they appoint 'learning officials', who have the task of helping weaker pupils. Sometimes, a pupil who is disorderly and unwilling to work may be excluded from the FDJ. This is regarded as a 'very severe punishment'.[28] It is easy to see why: since selection for higher education depends not only on learning achievements but also on behaviour and ideological attitude, exclusion from the FDJ is probably tantamount to exclusion from higher education.

Vocational Training

Article 25 of the Constitution of the GDR declares that all young people have the right and the duty to learn an occupation. Accordingly, 99 per cent of those who do not go on to higher education enter an apprenticeship. This lasts two to three years. A 'State Office for Vocational Training' co-ordinates all vocational training, and makes sure that the number of people trained for the various jobs meets the needs of the economy. School-leavers make contracts with factories or collective farms. During the first year of training, the apprentice spends two days per week doing practical work in the factory or farm, and three days in a vocational school; in the second and third year, this becomes three days practical work per week and two days theoretical.

By international standards the proportion of theoretical training is very high. This is connected with the aim of making all workers capable of 'mastering the scientific-technological revolution'. Training is organised so as to give all workers a broad general understanding of the foundations of the production process before going on to specialisation. In this way workers remain flexible and mobile, and capable of learning new working methods, as technology develops. One measure to ensure this has been the reduction in the number of recognised skilled occupations from 972 in 1958 to 306 in 1972. Highly specialised occupations have been linked together to allow more general training. Another measure has been the introduction of 28 so-called 'basic occupations'. This means that young people start their training with a fairly general course in the 'basic occupation' and then specialise in the last year.

Take as an example the training of a building worker. After leaving the tenth grade of high school the building apprentice spends two days per week on the building site and three days in the vocational school. (Big enterprises run their own schools; otherwise, the local authority is responsible.) In the first eighteen months the apprentice has general courses in 'state citizens' studies' (*Staatsbürgerkunde*), sport, methods of mental work and (voluntarily) Russian. Theoretical training includes the following courses: basic electronics, basic automatic control technology, basic data processing, plant management, properties of materials, building machinery, building methods, technology, construction of foundations, draughtsmanship, planning and management of the building process. Practical training (on the building site) consists of surveying, brick-laying, plastering, interior work, concrete and reinforced concrete work, pipe-laying, steel construction, machine work. After eighteen months, the apprentice decides to spend the last six months learning one of the following specialised occupations: road and drain work, bricklaying, reinforced concrete work, plastering, steel construction.[29]

Training for all other occupations is organised in a similar way. Clearly, a significant part of the course is concerned with knowledge and skills which are relevant for all modern production processes. This broadly-based training realises important polytechnic principles, and is a step towards overcoming narrow overspecialisation. One wonders how educational authorities will react to the tendencies towards deskilling of labour inherent in some of the most modern forms of automated production.[30] One sign that this problem is arising is the official criticism of the 'overemphasis on theory' and the demand for more practical work during training, following the Eighth Party Congress of the SED in 1971.[31]

Higher Education

Selection for higher education in universities, technical universities, teachers training colleges, etc., is on the basis of school achievement, and of political and ideological criteria. In 1970, 12·2 per cent of the appropriate age group were admitted to higher education. This proportion was found to be too high for actual economic needs, and was reduced to 10·2 per cent in 1974.[32] The usual channel for access to higher education is the extended high school, but entry may also be made through various forms of vocational training, as well as through adult education in the form of full-time or evening courses.

University education generally lasts four years. The number of students for various courses, as well as the form and content of

D

the courses, are centrally planned to meet expected economic needs. The first two years are devoted to a broadly-based general course with special emphasis on intensive study of marxism-leninism. This is regarded as the 'absolutely essential basis for forming students' socialist personality'.[33] Productive manual work is not part of university courses. The last two years of higher education are devoted to specialised training for particular occupations. Upon graduation, most young people are assigned to particular jobs – they seem to have very little choice in the matter. A very small proportion stay on for post-graduate research. As one would expect, the main emphasis is on scientific and technological subjects. Only about ten per cent of students take arts and social science courses.[34]

There is no doubt that university graduates have a privileged position in society, both in terms of income[35] and power. The question is are they a real 'meritocracy' selected only according to ability and political reliability, or does class privilege play a part. Until 1966 figures were published on the social origins of students in higher education. In that year the figures were as follows: children of manual workers – 31 per cent; non-manual workers – 25 per cent; farmers – 6 per cent; intelligentsia (i.e. people with higher education themselves) – 30 per cent; self-employed persons – 5 per cent; others – 3 per cent.[36] Although the share of workers is certainly higher than in capitalist countries, these figures show clearly the overrepresentation of the intelligentsia.

It is said that this problem became even more marked during the early 1970s,[37] but it is impossible to say for sure, as figures are no longer issued. An East German sociological study found that the children of workers and peasants more frequently fail to meet required class standards than children of the intelligentsia, and therefore have to repeat a class. The intelligentsia are more inclined than members of other social classes to encourage their children to stay on for the extended high school.[38] These discrepancies make it all the more surprising that special measures to favour workers' and farmers' children are no longer regarded as necessary (the 'workers' and farmers' faculties' appear to have been abolished).

3. Does the GDR Have a Socialist Education System?

All in all, there can be no doubt that the GDR has developed a modern and efficient education system since 1945. Education has had a very high priority, and a big share of scarce financial and manpower resources have been put into this sector. Every child in the GDR today can attain a high level of general education and vocational training, and can be virtually certain of getting a job which matches his qualifications. Does this mean that the GDR has a socialist education system, based on the marxist principles of polytechnic education, and devoted to producing 'totally-developed individuals'? To answer this question, it is necessary to look more closely at economic and social structures in the GDR, and then to re-examine the official concept of 'socialist personality', which is supposed to be the final aim of education.

Class and Power in the GDR

In marxist theory, socialism is regarded as a phase of transition from capitalist to communist society. Its essential feature is workers' rule, aimed at creating the conditions necessary for communism.[39] In 1963, the leadership of the SED declared that the socialist revolution had come to a victorious conclusion and that the GDR was now a socialist society, controlled by a socialist state. At the same time, the 'new economic system' (NÖSPL), which we described above, was introduced.[40] 'Economic levers' in the form of piece rates and premiums were to ensure the rapid and rational development of the forces of production. In 1967 minor changes were made in the NÖSPL and it was renamed the 'economic system of socialism' (*Ökonomische System des Sozialismus*). Walter Ulbricht, leader of the SED until 1971, declared that socialism in the GDR was an 'independent social formation'; in other words, no longer a transitional form but a particular type of society with specific social and economic structures. Ulbricht regarded the structure of socialism as essentially similar to communism – transition from one to the other was mainly a question of raising the level of the forces of production.[41] The main interest of the party and the working class was therefore in raising the level of the productive apparatus to world standards. As Kurt Hager, a leading SED theorist, put it:

> The victory of socialism requires above all higher labour productivity than in capitalism. This is to be obtained through the systematic and planned introduction of the most modern achievements of science and technology and of socialist production, and through the development of socialist consciousness and the socialist collective work of working people.[42]

This implied taking over the most advanced capitalist forms of technology and labour organisation. This, in turn, meant abandoning the aim of abolishing the division between mental and manual work and of creating a classless society.

According to official theory, there are two classes in the GDR: the workers and the collective farmers. They differ according to their relationship to the means of production: the workers own these indirectly through the socialist state; the collective farmers directly, as owners of the collective farms. Official theory does speak of a 'special stratum', the intelligentsia, within the working class. It is not a class, because it has the same relationship to the means of production as other workers, but it has a special status because of higher levels of education, responsibility, and income. The two classes and the stratum of the intelligentsia are said to be 'non-antagonistic', because they share the same interest in raising production. Is this really the case?

The intelligentsia are mental workers. There is no alternation between mental and manual work in the GDR, in the sense that manual workers might in turn take over supervisory or administrative tasks. Members of the intelligentsia receive much higher incomes than manual workers.[43] This applies not only to basic rates, but also to premiums. These are paid not only to actual production workers but also to managers, supervisors, and engineers. Since premiums are related to basic rates, they do nothing to reduce income inequality. Leading state and party officials are especially privileged: in addition to high salaries, they get perks like official cars and residences, and the right to make purchases in special shops for luxury goods.

Mental and manual workers differ not only in income but also in power: factories, like schools, are run according to the 'democratic centralist' principle of one-man management. Basic economic decisions are still made at the central planning level. The local execution of the plan is decided upon not by the workers, but by the directors of factories and state farms. In theory plans are submitted to the critique of the workers before being finalised.

In practice, this means that local party and trade union organisations make suggestions on the most efficient way to carry out the plan.[44] Both party and trade unions are centrally controlled, and leave no room for democratic decision-making by the workers. The official line of the SED is that since the working class rules anyway – through the dictatorship of the proletariat as exercised by the SED – any real form of democratic workers' control is superfluous. This, of course, is the real reason why piece rates and other material incentives are so important: since workers have no real say in running production and society, they have to be cajoled into working hard through material incentives.

All this indicates that the intelligentsia is in reality a privileged ruling class. It rules not through formal ownership of the means of production, but through factual control over them by virtue of holding the leading positions in state and party. The official class theory is unmarxist: it reduces the definition of class to a single criterion – ownership of the means of production – and declares that the intelligentsia cannot be a class because its members do not formally possess the factories. This class theory excludes the questions of real control of production, of common class consciousness and of common material interests and social privileges. On all these criteria, the intelligentsia is a specific class – a new state bourgeoisie. This class reacts violently to any threat to its power, using its monopoly of the means of repression (police, courts, army) to silence all critics.

Socialist Personality and the Development of the Forces of Production

So what is this 'socialist personality' which East German leaders ceaselessly declare to be their aim? We have seen that the SED reduces the question of building socialism to that of the rapid development of the forces of production. But socialism is not just a quantitative question. It means that workers must control their own living and working conditions, and be able to change them so as to satisfy their own needs and interests. Socialism means a process of *qualitative transformation* in the forces of production, so that they not only produce the things needed by the working people, but also produce them in such a way as to make work itself a way of fulfilling human needs. 'Economic levers' like piece work and premiums, combined with rigid labour discipline and the domination of manual workers by mental workers, are quite in-compatible with socialism and the aim of working towards the classless society of communism.

The 'socialist personality' of the SED is not what Marx meant by the 'totally developed individual'. The aim of the SED is to make everybody into highly motivated, disciplined workers, with a high level of technological education and a broadly based vocational training, able to adapt to the changing demands of the modern production process. 'Mastering the scientific-technological revolution' does not mean that workers decide what technologies to introduce and how to use them to meet their own ends; it means that workers must be flexible and mobile, and capable of learning new tasks to meet the requirements of economic and technological changes decided upon from above. Upon close examination, the characteristics ascribed to the 'socialist personality' turn out to be surprisingly similar to the technocratic demands for 'non-process-specific abilities' made in advanced capitalist countries.[45]

Of course, the concept of the 'totally developed individual' advanced by Marx (and taken up by Lenin and Krupskaya) in-cluded the ability to work hard and to master modern technology, but it went a lot further. Marx envisaged a worker who not only understood technology, but also its economic and political basis and the consequences of its use. Knowledge was to make the working class capable of controlling and transforming the forces of production to meet its own needs and interests. This is the real historical task of the transitional stage of socialism, which can only be accomplished when the workers themselves really determine what is to be produced and how. The 'totally developed indi-viduals' in a socialist society would not need piece rates and 'economic levers' or the dictates of an all-knowing party to make them follow their own interests. They would understand their own interests and decide upon them collectively with their mates. The concept of the 'totally developed individual' means that the rapid abolition of the distinction between manual and mental work, and above all of the domination of manual workers by mental workers, is the first priority of the socialist revolution. By abandoning this aim, the ruling bureaucracy of the Soviet bloc has made it quite clear that it does not want socialism.

This general analysis of political and educational aims is confirmed by an examination of the content of education in nurseries, schools, vocational training and universities. In nurseries the process of training hard-working, conformist people starts through the constant planned intervention of teachers in children's games. Instead of learning spontaneously through play, based on their own situation, experience and problems, children learn pre-determined moral and behavioural norms. In high school, children are pumped full of knowledge according to fixed, centrally planned curricula. Hard work and pressure for moral and political conformity pervade school life. Political education does not permit children to recognise their own interests and to work out methods of fighting for them – it is merely compulsory indoctrination with the ideology of the SED. The process of selection for higher education and desirable jobs helps to ensure conformity: a young person who has not shown his 'love for work' during the 'school day in production' and in school itself, or who has not shown his 'socialist personality' by active membership in the FDJ, is not likely to get far. Vocational training is designed to produce competent, motivated workers, able to adapt to changing conditions, but it in no way creates the conditions for a reduction of the gulf between manual and mental work. University education leads to a privileged position in society. It is cut off from manual work, and is designed to ensure loyalty to the aims and leadership of the SED.

The SED has taken the marxist concept of polytechnic education and robbed it of its real content. Instead of 'totally developed individuals' capable of creatively transforming society, the aim is the well-trained, hard-working, conformist wage workers. This leads to a double contradiction. First, by stifling originality and creativity from the earliest age the SED may well defeat its own aim of the rapid development of the forces of production. Scientific creativity is the result of the free development of children's curiosity and thirst for knowledge. The systematic inculcation of prescribed formal knowledge leaves little room for this. By taking measures to prevent children and young people from coming to political conclusions which it does not want the SED may also prevent them from making the scientific discoveries it does want.

Second, even in the emasculated form in which it is practised in the GDR, polytechnic education does raise questions about the political and social implications of the production process. The SED does all it can to keep the population of the GDR ignorant of the real problems of society, and treats them as if they were politically infantile. But in the long run highly educated people will not be willing to restrict their horizon to applauding the distorted reports of success set before them by the official media. They will become aware of the real deficiencies and problems of the society in which they work and live. The contradiction between constantly telling working people that they are the rulers of society, and in reality excluding them from any form of control will not remain latent for ever.

5.
Education and Cultural Revolution in China

In 1949, after two decades of warfare, the Communist Red Army finally defeated the US-backed troops of the Kuomintang,* and the Peoples Republic of China was proclaimed. The conditions for building socialism were even less favourable than in Russia in 1917. China was an enormous, backward agricultural country, hardly touched by modern industrial technology. Ninety per cent of the population were peasants – nearly all of them illiterate. The traditional rural economy was in a state of collapse; continuous political chaos since the overthrow of the Emperor in 1911, the Japanese invasion, and the long drawn out civil war had led to indescribable misery for the masses. Starvation, epidemics, child prostitution were the order of the day. To an even greater extent than Russia, China confronts us with the paradox of an attempted socialist revolution in a country with extremely underdeveloped forces of production and a tiny proletariat.

Education has played a vital role in the Chinese Communist Party's strategy for building socialism. It has been one of the main objects of dispute in inter-party conflicts as well as in the Cultural Revolution. This is not surprising: the very backwardness of material conditions in China has given a special importance to the subjective factors of consciousness and knowledge. The great efforts put into building and transforming the educational system have led to results which have astounded most western educationalists. The basic principles have been taken from the marxist theory of polytechnic education. In this chapter we will describe

* The Kuomintang (KMT – Nationalist Party) originated in the democratic revolution of 1911. Under the leadership of Sun Yat-sen, it tried to reunite China and to introduce Western political forms. After 1927, the KMT became dominated by rich landowners and merchants. Led by Chiang Kai-shek, the KMT was the party of reaction, backed by the USA in the fight against communism.

the development of education in China, try to show how the various institutions are organised and how they function, and try to assess to what extent polytechnic education is in fact practised in China.

Anyone who tries to examine education in China encounters very serious difficulties. First, information on events in China is difficult to obtain, often inexact, incomplete and out of date. For instance, it took years for reliable reports on the Cultural Revolution or on the disappearance of Lin Piao to get through. The student of China has to piece together apparently unrelated facts, like a mosaic, and knows that the final picture will never be complete. Second, statistical data and official material (regulations, school plans, curricula) is hard to obtain. Third, nearly all information that does come to us tends to be ideologically filtered and influenced – in one direction or another.[1] This makes it very difficult to assess the accuracy of data. In particular, it is extremely hard to know what the conditions and consciousness of ordinary people are like, and to what extent they can participate in political decision-making. Fourth, the great size and diversity of the People's Republic – the enormous range of geographical and economic conditions, the cultural differences between the various peoples of China, and the differences between town and country – all prohibit easy generalisations. Fifth, the development of the education system has been strongly influenced by economic and political events, in particular by the 'struggle between two lines' which has had a decisive effect on all aspects of life in China since the mid-1950s. The periodic dominance of the one or the other line has meant not only changes of political orientation and economic policy, but has also led to far-reaching changes in the aims and structure of education. It is impossible to understand education in China without understanding the political and economic causes and effects of the 'struggle between two lines'.

1. Education in China Before 1949

Changes in education are always a reaction to changes in economic and social structures. The process which led to the development of mass education in the People's Republic began with the undermining of the ancient Chinese social order by western imperialism from the middle of the nineteenth century.[2] Before this there had been a highly developed educational system reserved for children of the ruling class. It was based on the Confucian social philosophy, the main principle of which was the innate inequality of human beings. This was used to justify hierarchical and patriarchal class and family structures. On the highest pinnacle stood the emperor – the bearer of the 'Mandate of Heaven'. He ruled his enormous empire with the help of the mandarins: state officials appointed on the basis of success in competitive exams. In return for loyal and competent service as administrators, the mandarins received a monopoly with regard to education and political influence, as well as considerable material rewards. Only sons from well-off families could become mandarins, for success in the exams was dependent on many years attendance at an expensive private school, where the teachings of Confucius and other scholars were learnt in a highly mechanical manner. This meant that state officials came from the class of the wealthy landowners. Having a mandarin in the family raised its status, power and material well-being. The family clan was the most important safeguard for the stability of the traditional order. The principle of inequality operated within the family too: the son was subordinate to his father, the wife to her husband, a younger brother to an older brother. Women were, in general, totally devoid of rights. The relationship between emperor and people was meant to be similar in character to that between father and children.

Formal education was available only to the elder sons of mandarins and big landowners. Girls were trained at home for their future role of serving in the family of their husbands. There were no schools for the children of the great peasant masses, who made up ninety per cent of the population. From an early age they had to help in the fields, or to serve the landlords. Children were regarded as the property of the parents – they could be sold, made to marry against their will or even killed. Girls were seen as a useless burden. If a father was asked how many children he had, he would only count the boys.

Traditional China was a self-sufficient, inward-looking society. An efficient irrigation system for rice farming had been developed at the beginning of the Imperial period, but after that the means of production stagnated. The Chinese had little contact with other nations. There was not much incentive for international trade, of the sort which had played such a part in transforming feudal society in Europe. When change did come it was due to outside influences: the military power of western imperialism forced China to open her frontiers to opium and other products of christian civilisation, made her cede harbour territories for European merchants, and allowed the entry of missionaries, diplomats, soldiers and other bearers of western culture. Military defeat and the accompanying economic upheavals compelled the Chinese ruling class to take notice of the superiority of western technology and industrial production methods. Demands for a modernisation of education followed.

In 1911 a nationalist revolution overthrew the ancient Imperial order. Many of its leaders had received a western education, either in mission schools within China or abroad. One of the first acts of the republican government was to proclaim new educational plans. It set out to replace the Confucian system with one based upon modern American and Japanese cultural concepts, and bourgeois ideals of economic, technical and scientific efficiency, and 'political freedom'. The intention of these plans was to train a new economic and technical elite, capable of dragging China into the modern capitalist world: there were no plans for mass education. But the intentions of republican government remained a dead letter. Sun Yat-sen and his followers were unable to hold power, and China sunk into the chaos and dissolution of the warlord period.

In the early 1920s, there was a new upsurge of democratic, anti-imperialist struggle, strongly influenced by the success of the Russian Revolution. The Kuomintang (KMT) was reorganised with the aid of Comintern instructors and formed a revolutionary alliance with the Communist Party of China, which had been founded in 1921. A military academy was set up at Whampoa to train officers for the struggle to reunite China – its military director was Chiang Kai-shek and its political leader Chou En-lai. Cadre-training courses for workers' and peasants' organisations were also introduced, but mass education programmes were still not the order of the day. The rightward turn of the KMT in 1927, in which Chiang's troops massacred untold thousands of their erstwhile communist allies, certainly put a stop to any ideas of educating the people.[3] In 1937, only 15 per cent of all Chinese children attended primary schools and only 10 per cent attended middle schools. The vast majority of the population remained illiterate – 'blind', as the Chinese say.

The first real attempts at mass education took place in the rural soviets set up by the CCP under the leadership of Mao

Tse-tung in Kiangsi. Chiang's coup had forced most surviving communists to flee the cities (although the Politburo remained in hiding in Shanghai), thus cutting them off from the small but militant proletariat. The strategy adopted by Mao and the Red Army led by Chu Teh was to organise peasant risings and to set up soviet governments in liberated areas. The towns were to be abandoned for the time being, while the communist party rebuilt its strength through long drawn-out rural guerrilla warfare. The mobilisation of the poor and middle peasants was to be achieved by making land reform a major part of the political programme. The Red Army soon became a peasant army, whose leadership consisted mainly of intellectuals.

Mao's new strategy, maintained through more than twenty years of civil war, led to the victory of the CCP in 1949, and helped in several ways to determine the special characteristics of the Chinese revolution. First, the strategy of rural guerrilla warfare went against marxist theory and the experience of the Russian revolution. It was rejected by the existing leadership of the CCP, the Comintern, and other communist parties. At one stage, Mao was even excluded from the Politburo and the Central Committee. The Chinese revolution therefore developed in isolation from world communism. Even after the second world war the Soviet Union still recognised the KMT government and handed over the cities of Manchuria to it. Second, the relationship between workers and peasants was quite different from that in Russia, where the risings of the urban proletariat in 1917 had led to a rapid capture of state power. During and after the civil war relations between town and country became increasingly conflict-ridden; collectivization in 1928 meant appalling repression for the rural population. The Chinese revolution, however, was based primarily on the peasant masses. The experience of the Long March (1934–35) and of the guerrilla struggles from 1927 to 1949 led to a mass mobilisation of the peasants, who became the real subject of the revolution. This had important consequences for development strategies after the liberation. Third, in Russia the bolsheviks seized state power and then had to defend it against white armies and foreign intervention. At the same time they had to feed the population and try to build up a new economic and social order under the worst possible conditions. In China, the long drawn-out war of liberation gave the communists time to gain experience in production and administration. They were able to try out new models on a small scale before having to run the whole society. (This applied to the educational system, whose embryonic forms were developed in the liberated areas before 1949.)

The first Soviet Government was proclaimed in a mountain area of Kiangsi Province in 1931. Article twelve of its constitution laid down the following educational aims:

- the Chinese Soviet Government recognised the right of all workers, peasants and other working people to gain an education;
- the introduction of free schools for all children was to be embarked upon immediately;
- educational establishments were to be run by the people, with support from the party.

Great efforts were made to set up schools and adult education courses during the Yenan period (1935–45) and the Third Revolutionary Civil War (1946–49). Mass education was an important part of the CCP's strategy for mobilising the masses and gaining their active participation in the revolutionary struggle. Only by making the peasants the subject of the revolution could the initially small and isolated Communist Party hope to win. Peasant support was not enough – active initiative and leadership were essential, and these could only be achieved by making peasant interests a primary concern, and through effective mass education.

Wherever the Red Army went, it gained the support of poor and middle peasants by driving away the landlords, redividing land, cutting taxes, and abolishing traditional symbols of subservience like bound feet and long plaits. The rule of gentry and corrupt officials was replaced by self-government in elected soviets on the village, district and provincial levels. Police and militia duties were taken over by the peasant organisations in order to allow the Red Army to concentrate its forces at the front. Mass mobilisation for increasing rural production, through more efficient methods and bringing waste land into cultivation, drew in all sections of the population. Special organisations were set up to involve and politicize women, children and old people. These changes were most dramatic for women, for they had been completely subservient in the old society. Now they had an important social role in the new Young Communist League, the Anti-

Japanese Societies, in nursing, schools and agricultural brigades. For the first time they could work with men on an equal footing.

General literacy was the aim of the CCP. However, the complicated Chinese written language was a major obstacle to mass literacy. (The degree of education in China can be measured by the number of characters a person knows; since each character represents an object or idea, the choice of what characters to learn can determine the political content of education.) Soldiers and party members started learning characters, and passed their knowledge on to the peasants wherever they went. Basic education belonged to the programme of all mass organisations, and was always combined with political education: the texts used told of the red flag and the Red Army, and explained that the Red Army was the army of the poor people.[4] By the time a peasant had learnt to read he also knew the basic doctrine of the CCP.

Despite military and economic difficulties, schools were set up in the areas liberated by the Red Army. When Edgar Snow visited Yenan, capital of the liberated area in northwest China, in 1936 (only a year after the Long March) he was informed that more than 200 elementary schools had been set up already in the area, as well as a training college for elementary teachers, an agricultural school, a textile school, a trade union school and a party school with four hundred students. There were also military and medical academies. The standard of these schools was certainly not high – in northwest China 95 per cent of the population were illiterate and the cultural level was very low, so that teachers were scarce. There were enormous problems: virtually no books and no presses to print them, no school buildings, no teaching material. But education was always related to the needs of production and the military struggle. Political instruction played a major part.[5] The very backwardness of conditions compelled the use of polytechnic principles: pupils had to make their own writing brushes, teachers their own equipment. Self-reliance and self-organisation were essential, and the political aims of education were quite clear to all participants. The Yenan experience helped to shape China's new educational system after the liberation, particularly in the phases of the Great Leap Forward (1958–60) and the cultural revolution (1966).

2. Society and Education 1949-76

Learning from the Russians (1949-57)

The first few years after the liberation were devoted to restoring order, getting the devastated economy going again, and building the foundations for a transition to socialism. The problems were enormous. Traditional agriculture had reached the limits of its capacity. Climatic and geographical factors restrict arable land to only 12-15 per cent of China's total area – for each Chinese only one sixth as much land is available on average as for each inhabitant of the USA or Russia. Immediately after 1949 the return of peace combined with better nutrition, hygiene and health care to produce a population explosion: China's population rose from 550 million in 1950 to 825 million in 1975.[6] The country's small industrial base had been largely destroyed (and had been designed to serve the interests of foreign capital and not the Chinese people anyway). There was a lack of all the factors necessary for economic and social development: food for the masses, fertiliser and machinery to improve agricultural productivity, capital and experts to build up industry.

The situation in education was similar. Only about 15 per cent of children had access to primary schools; these schools were concentrated in the towns of the eastern seaboard, their quality was very poor and the teachers hardly trained. Secondary schools were even scarcer. Their curriculum was scholastic and unrelated to ordinary life; the pupils came from the landowning and bourgeois classes. Many secondary schools had been founded by foreign missionaries and were shaped by imperialist culture and ideology. What little higher education existed was quite unrelated to the development of the technical and scientific skills required for building socialist industry. The construction of a socialist education system was thus from the outset not just a problem of quantity and quality, but also of combatting the bourgeois and elitist mentality of existing intellectuals. And yet the CCP could not do without these intellectuals: there was nobody else to serve as teachers and experts.

At first China tried to emulate the development model of the Soviet Union. With the aid of Soviet experts, a first five-year plan on the stalinist pattern was introduced. Agriculture was to serve as the main source of capital accumulation for industry; investment was concentrated in heavy industry. The core of the programme was 150 big, specialised heavy industrial plants employing the most modern technology. The machines were to be provided by the Soviet Union and installed by Russian experts. The economy was controlled by centralised ministries in Peking. A hierarchical chain of command delegated immediate authority over production to powerful factory directors. Material incentives (premiums, piece-rates) were to encourage workers to raise productivity.

The educational system had two principal tasks in this development model: one was to quickly train the experts needed for the new industries; the other was to bring about mass literacy and raise the level of basic education, regarded as the preconditions for involving peasants and workers in the struggle for building a socialist society. Conflicts about education in subsequent years concerned the relative priority of these two tasks. What was more important, highly qualified scientists and technicians, or a population with a socialist consciousness – experts or reds?

The 1949 Common Programme of the Chinese Government (this served as the 'temporary constitution' of the People's Republic; its provisions were confirmed in the Constitution of 1954)[7] was strongly influenced by the Yenan experience. It called for general mass education, the linking of theory and practice as a basic educational principle, and the relating of education to the interests of the people and the requirements of socialist construction. A rapid quantitative expansion followed: the number of children attending primary school rose from 24 million in 1949 to 64 million in 1956; secondary school attendance rose from 1 to 6 million; the number of students in higher education quadrupled to 441,000.[8] Campaigns for the political re-education of the bourgeois intelligentsia were carried out, and special courses were set up to train party and military cadres for administrative tasks.

But rapid expansion made it difficult to realize the political aims of educational change. Reliance on the old intelligentsia and on Soviet aid was unavoidable. Nearly all the new textbooks were translated from Russian. More than 600 Russians taught in Chinese colleges and universities, training Chinese lecturers and teachers. Many Chinese students were sent to the Soviet Union – 36,000 by 1959.[9] It must be remembered that this was a period in which polytechnic education had been completely abolished in the Soviet Union – narrow specialisation, mechanical learning, and political conformity were the essence of stalinist education. Chinese students had to copy out the lecture notes of the Russian lecturers and learn them off by heart. There was no question of making learning relevant to everyday life, or of allowing students to take creative initiatives. Obviously, teachers trained in this way used similarly repressive methods in their own teaching. Although the contents of the Soviet-influenced learning were new to the Chinese, the methods were not: they were like the learning-by-rote of the Confucian schools. The old teachers of landlord or bourgeois origin felt quite at home with these methods, while students of worker or peasant origin found themselves under great stress, and were often unable to pass the exams. So despite the intentions of the Common Programme, higher and secondary education remained instruments of class privilege.

The mass literacy campaigns in factories and on the land, which were closely related to the introduction of agricultural co-operatives, did much more to introduce principles of polytechnic education. Local people were helped to produce their own text books, based on their own names and the characters for tools, crops and animals. School children labelled objects in the village with the appropriate character, as a learning aid. Literacy classes, often combined with political education, were carried out during work-breaks in factories and on construction projects. Evening classes were introduced for peasants. By 1958, illiteracy had been reduced to below ten per cent in many areas.

By the mid-1950s, it was becoming clear that the Soviet model was not suitable for Chinese conditions. Industrial production had risen sharply, but at the expense of agriculture. The neglect of this sector began to cause shortages, which threatened further industrial growth. The transport system was not adequate to serve a highly centralised industrial apparatus. In addition, centralisation was creating an inflated and inefficient bureaucracy. Altogether, the Soviet model emphasised the wrong priorities, for China had very little capital but a great reserve of human labour power.

The contradictions in education were similar to those in society in general: primary education in rural areas began to stagnate, examinations were tightened up, old hierarchical structures were revived, pupils of bourgeois origin had much better chances in education than did those of worker or peasant origin. The rapid development of secondary and higher education was taking place at the expense of general mass education. Scientists, technicians, trained cadres and administrators began to achieve privileged positions in party, state and economy. Bureaucratic deformation of the party and factional struggles were the inevitable results. Within the party leadership, the group around Liu Shao-chi successfully opposed attempts to introduce productive work into the schools. Liu summed up their educational position: 'Universal education is still not too urgent now: the question now is still higher education and the need for specialists.'[10]

In 1956, to deal with growing unrest among intellectuals, Mao proclaimed the 'Hundred Flowers Campaign' encouraging criticism in the cultural and political spheres: 'Let a hundred flowers bloom, a hundred schools of thought contend', was the slogan. But the campaign was rapidly stopped when it became clear that most of the criticisms expressed by intellectuals showed that they wanted to regain their old elite power-positions, and to run education without party interference. A new 'rectification campaign' was then started to combat 'commandism', 'bureacratism' and 'mandarinism' in party organisations. In an important speech 'On the correct handling of contradictions among the people'[11] in February 1957, Mao analysed the economic, political and social tensions which had not been solved by attempts to copy the Soviet model. This speech heralded the transition to a new policy for the construction of socialism which involved a radical change in educational priorities.

The Great Leap Forward (1958–60)

The main principles of the new policy were: rural and local industries instead of centralised heavy industry; small and medium-sized enterprises using traditional or intermediate technology instead of large factories using imported modern technology; decentralised decision-making; greater influence of production teams and local party committees instead of one-man management; the 'mass-line' – active involvement of the people in planning and initiating development projects; maximum utilisation of labour to 'create capital' in big irrigation projects and the like.[12] A new form of social organisation became necessary – the peoples commune, embracing 10–30,000 persons. About 74,000 communes were set up throughout China. They had the tasks of organising agricultural and industrial production, carrying out all administrative work, and setting up local militias. They were responsible for social welfare and education. Villages and small towns were integrated into the commune as subordinate production teams or production brigades. Village co-operatives and individual farmers brought all their land and tools and animals into the commune; only small gardens with perhaps a few fruit trees and chickens were allowed to remain private property. Commune members were paid according to the amount of work done, payment being partly in the form of produce and partly in money. The communes organised decentralised rural industries, with the aim of using seasonal labour reserves. The 'backyard steel-furnaces' were a well-known aspect of this policy, but typically rural industries also played a big part, with the production of fertilisers, building materials, food processing, agricultural implements. The communes also co-ordinated the mass mobilisation of labour for flood control and irrigation projects.

The Great Leap Forward was an attempt to reduce the differences between town and country, industry and agriculture, mental and manual work. Political understanding and will-power became more important than technical expertise in the fight against economic backwardness. Small-scale technology and decentralised decision-making gave mass education priority over the training of highly qualified specialists. It was more important to be 'red' than 'expert'. It became necessary to extend and improve mass education and to re-educate the intelligentsia to serve the people, instead of to seek elitist privileges for themselves. Both these aims were to be achieved through a re-orientation of the educational system, based on combining learning with productive work. In addition, this new policy aimed to mobilise additional reserves of labour for the vast projects being undertaken.

New educational principles were laid down in 1958 by the Central Committee of the CCP in the document 'Education must be combined with Productive Work', which declared:

> We insist on the educational principle of all-round development. We consider that the only method to train human beings in all-round development is to educate them to serve working-class politics and combine education with productive labour . . .[13]

Responsibility for education was to be decentralised: local authorities, factories and communes were encouraged to set up their own schools. Part-time and spare-time schools were to be introduced, based on the principle 'that every capable person can teach'. In time these could improve their curricula, equipment and teaching staff with government aid. Open political discussion by teachers, students and pupils was to be encouraged with special emphasis on the making and exhibiting of 'dazibao' (big character posters).[14]

The new policy led to a great upsurge of effort in mass education. The communes set up vast numbers of primary and secondary schools: in 1960 there were 91 million primary school pupils, and in 1958 over two million secondary school pupils in 22,600 schools run by people's communes. Entry requirements for higher education were changed to admit workers' and peasants' children more readily – by 1959 half of the new students came from these classes. Students and professors, pupils and teachers spent periods doing agricultural work, labouring on irrigation projects, and set up workshops, blast furnaces and repair shops. Literacy campaigns and spare-time schools were organised by factories and communes. By 1959, 30 million people were enrolled in various types of courses. Polytechnic education seemed destined to become the basic principle of Chinese society.

The Three Hard Years (1960–62) and the Return to the Soviet Path (1961–65)

The early enthusiasm of the Great Leap Forward was soon dashed to the ground. Three consecutive years of severe floods led to a food crisis, aggravated by the diversion of labour to large-scale projects. Rural industry often turned out to be inefficient and wasteful. There was considerable peasant opposition to rapid collectivisation – especially where attempts had been made to break down family structures in the communes. The break with the Soviet Union in 1960 exacerbated the economic difficulties: suddenly all Soviet experts were called home, often taking vital plans with them. Necessary parts for industrial plants were not delivered. These set-backs led to a crisis in the party leadership: Mao was replaced by Liu as President of the People's Republic, although he remained party chairman. A partial return to the policies of the first five-year plan took place: economic planning was centralised once more, the power of management strengthened, material incentives for workers reintroduced. The communes were not dissolved, but some of their tasks were devolved to the production brigades. Peasants were allowed to cultivate private plots and sell the products on free markets. Capital accumulation for investment in heavy industry became once more the main economic priority. Correspondingly, tendencies towards bureaucracy and elitism reappeared.[15]

The consequences for the educational system were obvious: the training of specialists again took precedence over mass education. The percentage of school-age children actually attending school sunk from 87 to 56. The number of secondary schools run by communes declined to 3,715 with 266,000 pupils in 1962.[16] This was partly due to closure of schools and partly to the re-centralisation of control. Teachers were called upon to concentrate on especially gifted pupils. A system of elite schools was set up, including boarding schools for the children of cadres.[17] Technical knowledge became more important than political education and productive work in schools was reduced. Exams were once again tightened up: 'The method of examination is to treat candidates as enemies and ambush them', said Mao.[18] The old Chinese method of learning-by-rote and reciting books was resurrected; grammar and the correct writing of characters were re-emphasised. All in all, there was a return to an elitist, class-biased educational system.

The Cultural Revolution and After (1966–76)

These developments caused considerable discussion and dispute inside and outside the party. As early as 1962, Mao and his supporters started a 'Socialist Education Movement' aimed at raising political consciousness, particularly in rural areas. The Movement was ineffective, for it received little support from leading party officials, but it did have considerable influence on sections of the People's Liberation Army, led by Defence Minister Lin Piao. Lin began to use his very considerable power to support left elements in the party bureaucracy. Matters came to a head in the Spring of 1966 with a dispute about the ideological content of a play written by Wu Han, a leading member of the right-controlled Peking City Council. Mao and Lin threw their weight behind the critics of the play and called for a 'Great Proletarian Cultural Revolution'. Although Mao was still party chairman, very large sections of the leadership supported the technocratic line of Liu Shao-chi. Mao's strategy was to mobilise masses of ordinary people to support his policies. So we have the strange paradox of the party chairman writing a big-character poster calling on revolutionaries to 'Bombard the Headquarters'. We cannot describe the cultural revolution in any adequate way here and will give only a very schematic account of what seems to have happened, as a precondition for discussing educational changes. The reader who wants more information is referred to the appropriate literature, some of which is named in our footnotes.

It should be noted that the cultural revolution was in fact concerned not only with culture, but with all aspects of political, economic and social life. The name 'cultural revolution' indicates the new priority accorded to social consciousness as an instrument for transforming society. Enlarging and remoulding the education system became tasks of the utmost urgency. This is made evident by the so-called 'Sixteen Points' drawn up by the Central Committee of the CCP on 8 August 1966. This document is widely regarded as the manifesto of the Cultural Revolution. The aims of the movement are defined as the struggle against those people in power 'who have taken the capitalist road', criticism and rejection of reactionary bourgeois academic 'authorities' and the ideology of the bourgeoisie and all other exploiting classes, as well as the transformation of education, literature, art and all other parts of the superstructure which do not correspond with the socialist economic bases. The method of the movement is to be the mobilisation of the masses. 'Don't be afraid of disorder', exhorts the document. One of the 'Sixteen Points' deals with education:

> In the Great Proletarian Cultural Revolution a most important task is to transform the old educational system and the old principles and methods of teaching. In this great Cultural Revolution, the phenomenon of our schools being dominated by bourgeois intellectuals must be completely changed. In every kind of school we must apply thoroughly the policy advanced by Comrade Mao Tse-tung of education serving proletarian politics and education being combined with productive labour, so as to enable those receiving an education to develop morally, intellectually and physically and to become labourers with socialist consciousness and culture.[19]

The 'Sixteen Points' also called for mass criticism of party and state officials, and for the establishment of Cultural Revolution Committees in all areas, to control and combat existing institutions. These were to be elected on the basis of direct democracy, following the example of the Paris Commune of 1871.

Mao called on the masses to expose and criticise the 'capitalist roaders'. In response a new movement of students and young people mushroomed into being: the red guards. They travelled to Peking in millions, attacked party officials, dragged them through the streets in dunce's caps and forced them to carry out self-criticisms. From Peking and the other cities they poured into the countryside by train (they were allowed free travel), in commandeered lorries, or on foot in 'long marches'. The only problem was that the capitalist roaders soon got the idea, too, and formed their own red guard groups. Before long there were three main red guard movements – rightist, moderate and leftist – which fought each other tooth and nail.[20]

Mao's main rivals – Liu Schao-chi, Teng Hsiao-ping and Peng Chen – were soon disgraced and dismissed, as were thousands of lesser cadres. But the removal of administrators, the mass travel, and the permanent discussions led to disorganisation of the educational system and the closure of most schools and universities, as well as to serious disturbances in production and transport. This became particularly serious when groups of workers started taking the call for class struggle seriously, and carried out strikes to improve their material situation. These struggles came to a climax in January 1967 with the 'Commune of Shanghai' – an attempt by workers to realise the direct democracy on the 'Paris Commune' model promised by the 'Sixteen Points'.[21]

This all got a bit too much for the Maoist leadership, who started taking measures to tame the cultural revolution. The red guards were ordered to stop travelling around the country and, in particular, to stop interfering in factories and people's communes. In November 1966 they were forbidden to arrest, judge and torture people and – a little later – forbidden to search dwellings, seize property, and to make people kneel and wear dunce's caps. The party leadership ordered students and middle-school pupils to return to university and school by March 1967. It seems that all these instructions were more or less ignored by the young revolutionaries. There were increasing reports of armed battles between rival red guard groups, between red guards from Peking and peasants and workers in the provinces, and between red guards and the army. These were no trivial matters – heavy weapons and even warships were used, and there were many dead and wounded.[22] Schools and universities remained closed. By now the party had more or less ceased to exist as a political institution. Mao resorted to the last power factor remaining more or less intact to restore order: the People's Liberation Army (PLA) was called in. Revolutionary committees were set up in each province based on the 'triple alliance' of revolutionary mass organisations (i.e. red guards, 'revolutionary rebels', etc.), revolutionary cadres (i.e. rehabilitated party and state officials), and the local PLA garrisons.[23] For a while, these revolutionary committees became the effective government. Similar committees were formed at lower levels – in communes, factories, work brigades and the like. This was not the end of the cultural revolution, but it led to a slowing down and a change in character. The influence of the PLA was strengthened, and with it that of Lin Piao, who was publicly designated as Mao's closest comrade-in-arms and successor.

The PLA was also sent into the schools to supervise their reopening, help in setting up the 'triple alliance', and assist in carrying out the task of 'struggle-criticism-transformation'. At a school in Shanghai, for instance, three hundred soldiers were sent in to control 1,800 pupils – a ratio of one soldier to six pupils. The pupils were organised in platoons and companies, did military drill and studied the works of Mao Tse-tung with the soldiers.[24] It took quite a while for the educational system to start working normally. Groups of pupils were still travelling around in 1968, and some university faculties were not re-opened until 1970 (teachers' training departments), or even 1973 (psychology).

In economic policy, the cultural revolution led to a partial readoption of the methods of the Great Leap Forward: mass initiatives again became more important than the plans of experts; material incentives were superseded by political consciousness; import of modern technology was rejected in favour of national independence using traditional methods; decentralisation and mass control replaced the centralised control of production from Peking ministries. The simultaneous development of agriculture and industry was called for with the slogan: 'agriculture is the basis, industry the leading factor'. The cultural revolution aimed at the abolition of hierarchies, the questioning of the value of narrow specialisation and expertise. The primacy of politics in every area of social and cultural life was the goal.

The cultural revolution was an attempt by Mao and his followers to return to the 'mass line' of the Yenan period and of the people's communes during the Great Leap Forward.[25] It was a partial success for Mao: the leading 'capitalist-roaders' were removed from positions of power, widespread criticism of bureaucratism in state and party took place, leading to important changes, and elitist methods in education came under attack. But just as in the Hundred Flowers Campaign ten years earlier, Mao found that the movement developed its own dangerous dynamic and threatened to get out of control. The promises of direct democracy were rapidly rescinded and the PLA became the new stabilising factor. Only a few years after the cultural revolution the in-fighting within the party leadership broke out with new ferocity.

In September 1971 Lin Piao suddenly disappeared. The cultural revolution had catapulted Lin to the position of second most important person in China, but in the subsequent years conflicts within the reorganised party and the PLA had reduced his influence. The events of 1971 have not yet been completely cleared up, but it appears that Lin and his supporters attempted to carry out a coup d'état. There were rumours of an air-raid on Mao's Shanghai residence. After the failure of the coup, Lin tried to flee to the Soviet Union, but his plane crashed in the People's Republic of Outer Mongolia.[26] The months following Lin's disappearance saw great disorder in state and party leadership. His most prominent supporters were arrested, and thousands of officers and functionaries were criticised and dismissed. It was said to be the greatest purge in the history of the CCP, except for the cultural revolution itself.[27] The victims included many of the exponents of the left 'mass-line' in the cultural revolution, so that the events following Lin's disappearance certainly meant a strengthening of the right. The affair also showed how seriously China's rulers really took the masses: it was over a year before the people were even informed that the second most important leader was a traitor and that he had been removed.

Two years after Lin's demise, in 1973, a campaign for the criticism of Confucius and Lin Piao was proclaimed. These two names were meant to symbolise all proponents of elitist, undemocratic practices in various sectors of society. Discrimination against women and contempt for manual work were special targets for criticism. The movement was a very restricted re-run of the cultural revolution. Many of the abuses attacked in this campaign were things that were supposed to have been abolished during the cultural revolution, such as entry examinations for higher education which discriminated against workers and peasants, and educational privileges for the children of cadres ('slipping in through the back door'). The campaign appears to have been an attempt of the weakened party left, led by Mao, Chiang Ching and the Shanghai group (later to be known as the 'gang of four'), to regain control and fight the rightward trend.

In the long run they failed. After the death of Chou En-lai (January 1976) and Mao Tse-tung (September 1976), the struggle broke out more violently than ever. In the summer of 1976 Chiang Ching and the Shanghai group seemed to have the reins of power in their hands. Teng Hsiao-ping, who had seemed destined to succeed Chou as prime minister, was purged for the second time together with many of his supporters. But in October a military action instigated by Hua Guo-feng led to the arrest of Chiang Ching and her followers. A virulent campaign against the 'gang of four' at all levels of party and state then followed. Thousands of cadres were removed from their positions. The Eleventh Party Congress of the CCP in August 1977 confirmed the victory of Hua and the again reinstated Teng. Western observers have been full of delight at the new 'pragmatic' development policy based upon the import of advanced technology, material incentives for workers, improved training for experts, and a modernisation of the economy.

3. The Education System after the Cultural Revolution

We shall now look more systematically at the changes in Chinese education following the Cultural Revolution. Our description is based on published reports as well as on discussions with colleagues who have visited the People's Republic. The picture is full of contradictions, so that we can often only give varying information, which leads us not to answers but to further questions. The analysis applies to the first half of the 1970s; what has happened since the take-over by Hua and Teng is anybody's guess. Ours is that the path of economic development is once more on the model of stalinist Russia, and that education will take a corresponding turn – but most predictions about China tend to be mistaken!

Principles and Structures

The 'Sixteen Points' of 1966 called for a transformation of education, literature, art and all other parts of the superstructure which did not conform with the socialist economic base. This implies that Mao and his supporters regarded the economic structures (factory management, people's communes) as already socialist and, at least partially, controlled by the workers and peasants; they can hardly have meant that the still very backward technical level constituted a 'socialist economic base'. Culture and education, on the other hand, were parts of the superstructure still controlled by bourgeois intellectuals. As we saw earlier, trained personnel were so scarce in 1949 that the new communist government was forced to give important tasks to intellectuals of landlord and bourgeois origin, particularly in the education system. Various attempts at 're-education' had not succeeded in making these intellectuals 'serve the people'. They continued to seek power and privileges for themselves, and had considerable influence even within the party. Mao and his supporters regarded this as an obstacle to further socialist development of both base and superstructure. Perhaps in 1949 it had been thought that it would be possible to dispense with the pre-revolutionary intellectuals once a new generation of socialist intellectuals had been trained. But by 1966 it was evident that the new intellectuals were not much different from the old ones, for they had been trained in the same tradition. The cultural revolution thus appears as an attempt to re-educate intellectuals by making them learn from the workers and peasants and through the experience of productive work.

But the cultural revolution was more than this: it was an attempt to compensate for material backwardness through political consciousness. Rapid economic development was vital if socialism was to be built in a very poor country with an exploding population. In the Soviet Union Stalin's strategy for solving a similar problem had been extreme compulsion and exploitation of labour, combined with material incentives, through the system of Stakhanovism. This system had been tried in China in the first five-year plan without much success. The cultural revolution was meant to create a new socialist morality with the aim of getting people to work very hard without much material reward.

Culture and education were to become the main levers for transforming backward means of production. Behind this strategy one may see a shimmer of Robert Owen's theory of changing society through formation of character, which Marx criticised in the Third Thesis on Feuerbach.[28] Be that as it may, it meant that education became a chief priority, and that a new type of education was necessary. Education was to take place everywhere and at all times: in fields and factory, on the street and in the theatre, as

well as in schools and universities. Education must include everybody and continue throughout life. The new educational principles
were roughly as follows:

1. Education was to serve proletarian politics.

2. In all areas it was to be combined with productive labour.

3. The length of studies at school and university were to be
reduced.

4. There were to be fewer, but better, courses; all teaching
material was to be thoroughly revised.

5. Pupils were not only to study, but also to learn how to do
industrial and agricultural work, and about military matters, in
order to be capable of taking part in the struggles of the cultural
revolution.

6. School teaching was to embrace the problems of everyday
social and economic life. Theory and practice were to be linked.

7. Girls and boys were to receive the same education and
vocational training.

8. The proportion of students from workers' and peasants'
families was to be systematically raised.

9. Control of education was to be decentralised to allow
work brigades, communes and factories to set up their own schools
and run them according to local conditions and needs.[29]

To what extent were these principles put into force? We will look
first at a few general aspects and then examine the various parts of
the education system, with special attention to the extent to which
learning is combined with productive work.

The red guard movement was intended by the leaders of the
cultural revolution to involve young people at schools and universities in proletarian politics. Mass travel and 'long marches'
were planned to allow youth to learn from workers and peasants,
and to get them to take part in productive work. This was intended
as a temporary phase pending the transformation of the schools.
We have seen how this movement got out of hand and was stopped
fairly rapidly. It is hard to say to what extent the educational aims
were achieved.

The reorganisation and decentralisation of education started
with the abolition of the Ministry of Education in 1966. Large
numbers of schools, nurseries and other educational facilities
were taken over by local productive units. The usual form of
control was the 'triple alliance' in which local workers and

peasants, PLA soldiers, and the 'revolutionary teachers and pupils' were jointly responsible for running schools. Again an assessment is difficult. In the early stages the purpose of the 'triple alliance' was to cool things down, restore order and get schools working again after the turbulence of the early months of the cultural revolution.[30] Later the 'triple alliance' seems to have been an important instrument of the 'open-door policy' of bringing workers, peasants and soldiers into the schools as educators. It is difficult to say whether decentralisation has been maintained. The Ministry of Education was re-established in 1975. The new Minister of Education Chou Yung-hsin made scathing remarks about the results of the cultural revolution: 'A wall full of big character posters does not make a university'. He attacked the peasant-students for their lack of secondary education: 'They can tell us the difference between leeks and wheat, but if you put a piece of litmus-paper in their hands it is too much for them'.[31]

Reduction in the length of school and university studies was carried out. There seem to have been regional variations, but on the whole primary school was reduced from six to four or five years, lower middle remained at three years, and upper middle was reduced from three to two years. All middle school leavers were to spend at least two years 'serving the people' in a commune, a factory, or the PLA before being eligible to go on to higher education, which was reduced from four or five to three years.

Of course not many places were available in higher education. Selection was to be made by the masses in the work or military units, not through exams to test academic ability. The criteria for selection were a high level of political consciousness and involvement, successful participation in practical work, and good health. Students had to be unmarried and their selection was to be confirmed by the appropriate cadres.

It is reported that when the universities were reopened about 1970 a large proportion of new entrants were 'worker, peasant and soldier students'. For instance, of the 6,900 entrants to Tsinghua University in Peking in 1973, 50 per cent came from factories, 35 per cent from communes and 15 per cent from the army.[32] (This does not mean that these were not children of intellectuals or cadres, for they too are supposed to do two years productive work after leaving school.) However it is apparent that entry through examination was re-introduced in at least some cases around this time, for one of the main targets for attack in the campaign to criticise Confucius and Lin Piao were university entrance exams which favoured persons of bourgeois origin.

To sum up: it is clear that some important principles of the cultural revolution with regard to the structure of education were realised at least in part. But there was a definite tendency away from these principles in the early 1970s, well before the big move to the right connected with the takeover of Hua and Teng in late 1976.

Nursery Schools

Most Chinese children are still educated in the family until the age of seven, when they enter primary school. Since most mothers work in agriculture or industry, this often means that children are looked after by grandparents or other older people. For a complete picture of how Chinese children are socialised it would be necessary to examine family child-rearing practices, but we have neither the space nor the information to do this here.[33] It is hard even to say how many children go to nurseries. Estimates for the cities range between 30 and 60 per cent of children aged two-and-a-half to seven. The proportion in the countryside is certainly much smaller. However, nursery provision is remarkably high for an underdeveloped country, and even compares very favourably with developed countries like Britain.

Nurseries are often run by agricultural work brigades or communes, by factories and offices, and by local revolutionary committees. Their opening hours correspond with the long working days of the parents. Many remain open all night to care for the children of shift-workers or of workers who have to stay away from home for a period. Western observers report that nursery activities are organised according to a fairly rigid timetable, and that the teachers decide what is to be done rather than the children.[34] Typical timetables show a strong emphasis on physical development through organised gymnastics and pre-military exercises, but also through free play and going for walks. Formal teaching takes up about 40 minutes to two hours per day, depending on the age of the children. The types of games and toys described by visitors to nurseries do not seem very conducive to developing creativity and initiative: role games are usually directed by the teacher with the aim of showing a particular moral lesson. There are very few toys (which is, of course, in part a reflection of underdevelopment) and those that do exist lead to receptive mechanical play (e.g. with clockwork tractors) rather than to creative games which develop problem-solving and research abilities.

The children are instructed in gymnastics, singing, dancing, drawing and painting (in particular copying, which is a preliminary exercise for learning to write Chinese characters), reading (about fifty basic characters), counting up to ten, Chinese language and politics. The theme which runs through and links all subjects is moral training. Stories, dances, songs, pictures, reading lessons, counting – all are related to working hard, serving the people and behaving according to socialist ethics. For instance children are told the story of the revolutionary hero Lei Feng, and then asked to think of ways of emulating Lei Feng in their daily activities. The 'big apple' game ends with the moral that only an egotistic child would keep the big apple for himself; a child who has thought about the teachings of Mao and the example of Lei Feng or Norman Bethune will give away the big apple and keep the small one for himself. Lessons are well planned and prepared and take place in a disciplined atmosphere. Teachers join in games and activities. Spontaneous ideas and projects have no place. Public control of moral and intellectual development takes place through regular criticism and self-criticism sessions.

An important factor in the development of socialist morality and political consciousness is participation in productive work. One aspect of this is that children are expected to do the daily chores of the nursery, like making beds and tidying up. In addition they care for the garden, doing regular tasks like weeding, planting vegetables and flowers, and harvesting the products. Every week there is a period of 'industrial work' usually lasting about 20 minutes. This is contract work for local factories: folding cartons, testing and packing torch bulbs, sorting out beans to get rid of bad ones, sorting out parts for a sewing-machine factory (to give just a few examples mentioned by various visitors). The basic principle is that this is real, necessary, productive work, which helps make useful products. The children are not just being occupied or learning about work through simulation – they are really taking part in social production. To make this quite clear, children are often taken to visit the factory for which they work, where they proudly see how their own products are utilised. In rural nurseries children are sometimes sent out for short periods to help with weeding the fields and similar tasks.

Before the cultural revolution, nurseries merely had the function of looking after children while the parents were at work. They had no clear educational aims. Since the cultural revolution nurseries have received the task of laying the groundwork of a 'socialist personality' by teaching children the 'five loves':

- love for Mao Tse-tung;
- love for the CCP;
- love for the socialist motherland;
- love for productive work;
- love for the workers, peasants and soldiers.

Further aims of education are: love of the collective of fellow pupils, respect for discipline, acceptance of group criticism, readiness for self-criticism, and willingness to make sacrifices in the name of internationalism.

Primary School

Virtually all Chinese children of the appropriate age-group attend primary school. Estimates as to their number vary from 127 million (1972)[35] to 145 million (1974).[36] The only areas where primary schools are not yet available for all children are thinly populated border areas inhabited by semi-nomadic minority groups. Children generally spend five years at primary school (compared with six before the cultural revolution), starting either at six and a half or seven and leaving at twelve to thirteen. Classes appear to be very big: over fifty on average, even in the urban schools visited by Kessen's group. They are probably often even bigger in rural areas. Each class has a class-teacher, but also receives a considerable number of lessons from subject-teachers. Teachers have a long working week (from 7 a.m. to 5 p.m., 6 days a week) but spend sometimes as little as 15 hours actually teaching. The rest of the time is spent preparing classes, correcting work, taking part in teachers' conferences and political education classes, meeting pupils' representatives, supervising workshops and visiting parents in their homes. Teachers are expected to visit all their pupils' parents from time to time, and to discuss learning problems with them. This too is part of the 'open-door' policy. It is said that parents can come to the school at any time and sit in on classes, as well as speaking to the teacher.

Elementary school lasts all day, usually from 8 a.m. to 4 p.m., with a fairly long dinner break during which most children go

E

home. In rural areas school dinners are often provided. Physical exercises are an important part of the daily timetable. Other subjects taught are Chinese language, politics, mathematics, music, painting, general knowledge (including basic science, geography and history) and productive work.[37] Learning Chinese script takes up anything from a third to a half of elementary school lessons. Children are expected to learn the 2,500 characters necessary for basic literacy by the time they leave elementary school.

Teaching methods are, in the eyes of visiting western teachers, often formal and old-fashioned. The teacher sits on a dais facing the class and lessons are often recited by heart. (It is reported that Chinese teachers are trying to reduce the use of these traditional methods and to increase pupil participation and initiative; this is no doubt very difficult in classes with fifty children.) Priority seems to be given to thorough preparation of lessons by the teachers – otherwise it would be possible to increase their classroom teaching hours and reduce the size of classes. All reports emphasise the high level of discipline and concentration in school classes. This is not, however, based on repressive teaching methods, for all forms of punishment are forbidden. Praise, encouragement, moral pressure, criticism and self-criticism are the techniques used. Teachers frequently contact parents in cases of lateness, indiscipline, or learning difficulties.

As in the nurseries, moral and political education is the all-pervading principle. The examples and tasks in all subjects contain political lessons, and emphasise that the purpose of learning is to qualify oneself to serve the people. Love for the workers, peasants and soldiers, and respect for physical labour are constant themes. The Kessen group reports that the first English lesson in an elementary school started with the quotation from Chairman Mao: 'You should concern yourselves with affairs of state and carry through the Great Proletarian Cultural Revolution to the end'.[38]

The communist children's organisation, the 'Little Red Soldiers', plays an important part in moral and political education. This organisation was set up during the cultural revolution to replace the disbanded 'Young Pioneers'. Children can become members from the second or third grade onwards. Fifty to ninety per cent of elementary school children are members. Criteria for acceptance as a member are: concern for political issues, serving

the people, working hard at school, participation in physical training, readiness to take part in criticism and self-criticism. Little
Red Soldiers help teachers by keeping the class tidy, cleaning the
blackboard, etc. They supervise other children in lining up for
physical training, and sometimes in the workshops as well. In some
classes Little Red Soldiers go around first thing in the morning to
make sure that each child is washed, tidily dressed and has a clean
handkerchief. Little Red Soldiers are supposed to be shining
examples, working hard at school, and carrying out social tasks
(like helping old people) in their spare time. The stories concerning moral behaviour discussed in political education classes
often give Little Red Soldiers as examples. All the Little Red
Soldiers of a class form a platoon. All the platoons of a school form
a company, with appointed commanders, responsible for various
tasks, such as supervising productive work or leading the propaganda group. The Little Red Soldier organisation is important in
getting children used to discipline and responsibility. It is also a
powerful instrument to ensure moral conformity and early political
orthodoxy. Refusal of admission, or expulsion, is a very serious
matter, since selection for further education is based on political
criteria.

Productive work plays a big part in elementary school.
Pupils produce components for local factories in the school workshops. They often spend a week of each term working in the
factory itself and another week in an agricultural commune. The
exact forms of organisation seem to vary considerably from school
to school, taking local circumstances into account. Examples of
work done in school workshops are producing parts for a lorry
repair plant, assembling and packing shuttlecocks, painting toys
and making chess figures.[39] In factories and farms the children
seem to take part in all tasks as far as their strength and knowledge permits it. It is common for a factory to send a worker to a
school for a period of a year or more to supervise the workshops.
Sometimes retired workers take on this task. Again, this is part of
the 'open-door' policy, and helps children to get to know workers
and to learn from them.

Secondary School

For many Chinese children full-time education ends at thirteen.
Exact figures on attendance at junior and senior middle schools

are not available, but it is certain that not all children receive a secondary education. In 1974, there were said to be 36·5 million middle school pupils.[40] Facilities appear to be better in town than in the countryside: it is said that 90 per cent of urban primary school leavers go on to junior middle school, and half to three-quarters of them stay on for senior middle school. In the country, about three-quarters of primary school leavers go to junior middle school. About half the junior middle school pupils go on to senior middle school.[41] (All these figures must be regarded as unreliable estimates.) The criteria for selection are unclear. Primary school children do take regular exams and get marks, which presumably play some part. But political criteria are also important. These include class origin – children of workers and poor peasants being favoured – and moral and political behaviour. Membership in the Little Red Soldiers is probably a help.

Since the cultural revolution the length of middle school has been reduced to five years – three years junior and two years senior. The basic aims of education and the structure of the middle schools are similar to those of primary schools. The red guards play a part similar to that of the Little Red Soldiers in primary schools. The subjects generally taught at middle school are Chinese, politics, mathematics, physics, chemistry (the last two often being combined as 'general knowledge of industry and agriculture'), history, geography, foreign languages (usually English first and Russian or another western language later), physical training and culture. Apart from the usual political and moral aspects, the main principle is that all knowledge should be related to the needs of production and everyday life. For instance, the Kessen group reported that in the schools they visited mathematics was not divided up into algebra, geometry and trigonometry, but was integrated and related to practical problems.[42]

Productive work plays an even bigger part in middle than in primary schools, and is closely related to preparing pupils for their future occupational roles. Pupils do regular contract work for factories in school workshops. As is to be expected, the physical and mental demands made are higher than in primary school: pupils are expected to repair and maintain their own machines, and to build workshops where necessary. Examples are often given of improvements and inventions being made in school workshops. Workers from local factories act as advisers and supervisors. This type of work is regarded as an essential complement to actually working in factories, for it is possible to experiment, to strip down and explain machines, which could not be done in factories where production must be maintained.

Middle school pupils also spend up to a month each year working in factories and up to another month in agriculture. Productive work is aimed not only to improve technical understanding, but also to further the political education of pupils by raising their respect for manual labour. In addition, older workers and peasants, with whom pupils often stay, tell them about the misery of the pre-revolutionary 'bitter years' and about the class struggles since 1949. Pupils sometimes make 'long marches' of several hundred kilometres to their places of work. In principle, middle school pupils are supposed to spend about 30 per cent of their time doing productive work. However, the organisational form for productive work varies from region to region. The Kirin Programme called on pupils to:

> Follow Chairman Mao's teaching 'rural students should make use of their vacations, weekends and holidays and spare time to return to their own villages to take part in production'. The primary way is for the students to participate in production in the people's commune, the production brigade and the production team, while their participation in labour arranged by the schools is secondary.[43]

After completing middle school, the young people are 'sent down' to the villages or into the factories. Workers, peasants and revolutionary heroes come to the schools to explain the necessity of sending educated people where the state needs them. Pupils may express wishes as to where they are to go, but these are often not granted. An only child is generally permitted to stay near his parents. Since schooling is still more highly developed in the cities of the eastern seaboard, many young people are sent from there to underdeveloped western regions, like Tibet and Sinkiang. They are often expected to spend the rest of their lives there. After two years farm or factory work, young people with middle school education may apply for university places. Only a very few young people are allowed to go straight from school to university. This occurs when there are shortages of trained people with special abilities. Interestingly, the case usually mentioned is that of people with language proficiency for training as interpreters, which indicates that the use of foreign books and technologies still has a high priority.

Higher Education

Universities are probably the most difficult section of Chinese education to generalise about. Before the cultural revolution they were, by virtue of their position in society, centres of bourgeois thinking, traditionalism and class privilege. They were shattered by the cultural revolution, and remained closed for years. Most, but apparently not all, institutes and faculties were re-opened between 1970 and 1973. Length of studies was cut from five to three years. 'Mao Tse-tung-thought propaganda teams' of workers, peasants and PLA soldiers came into the universities to stop the fighting between rival red guard groups and to supervise the reform of curriculum. The new principles were a great emphasis on politics, teaching future intellectuals to serve the people, and combining study with productive work. Students are supposed to spend about a quarter of their time working in factories or communes.

It is impossible to say how many university students there are in China. The figure had risen from 116,500 in 1949, to 441,000 in 1957, and 775,000 in 1962;[44] it seems likely that the number fell immediately after the cultural revolution. It is obvious that only a very small proportion of middle-school leavers can go on to higher education, and nearly all those work at least two years in factories or communes before being eligible. Their applications must be supported by the members of their work teams and by local political cadres. Candidates must be in good health and unmarried. On the basis of these criteria, the various communes and factories send lists of qualified applicants to the Revolutionary Committee of the university, which then interviews candidates to make sure that they have an adequate educational level to follow the courses. Written examinations are sometimes used for this purpose. It is impossible to say what the relative importance of political criteria, interviews and exams is in selecting students. By 1973 there were numerous reports of complaints about the reintroduction of rigid exams which favoured students of bourgeois origin. Another target of the 'campaign to criticise Confucius and Lin Piao' was the practice of 'slipping in through the back door' – which refers to cadres using their influence to obtain university places for their own children.[45]

There is no doubt that the content of university courses has changed very considerably since the cultural revolution. Study is closely related to the needs of students' future work, whether in production or in tertiary sectors like health services, education or culture. Since nearly all students have worked before studying, it is not difficult for them to relate their studies to social practice. As far as possible, productive work done while at university is connected with theoretical studies. For instance, during a one-year course in computing at the faculty for industrial automation students helped to assemble relatively simple computers. While doing theoretical work on transistor circuits they were set the task of assembling a complicated computer from scratch. After they had gained such practical experience, and theoretical knowledge of the technology, they were instructed to design a new computer.[46] Another example is that of students studying high polymer techniques in the chemistry department, who do laboratory work after going into the theory, and then go to work in a plastics, chemical fibre or rubber plant.[47] Such direct linking of study and application is, of course, easier in scientific or technological subjects than in the arts, but here too students work in factories and communes, and use this experience to shape their future cultural work.

Another form for relating production and education are the '21 July Workers' Colleges', so named after an instruction from Chairman Mao of 21 July 1968. Here, instead of bringing productive work into the university, the principle is to set up colleges within the factory. The first workers' college was set up by the Shanghai machine-tool factory. Workers are selected for higher education and receive theoretical instruction, usually from the scientific and engineering personnel of the factory. Both students and teachers continue to work in the factory so that their studies are closely orientated on the practical problems which arise. After completing training the workers return to their old jobs, where they are able to make innovations, or they receive new tasks within the plant. Where necessary some lecturers are brought in from existing universities. It appears that a large number of '21 July Workers' Colleges' have been set up in the last few years. It is not possible to compare the level of qualification of these worker-students, with that of graduates of conventional universities, for no data is available. One risk is that their training might be too closely related to the situation of a particular factory.

Finally, mention should be made of another new institution, although strictly speaking it belongs to the field of adult education rather than higher education: the '7 May Cadre Schools'. Again the name comes from an instruction from Chairman Mao – that of 7 May 1966, which was of great importance for education policy.[48] These schools were set up in large numbers during the cultural revolution to 're-educate' cadres who had become alienated from the people. The first cadres sent to them had an uncomfortable time, for they had to build the schools themselves, using primitive tools and without outside help. Again, it was an attempt to return to the 'Yenan Spirit' – through hard manual work and privation, the cadres should regain an understanding of the life and work of the people. In the meantime, the '7 May Schools' are firmly established. Cadres go there on a voluntary basis (although there appears to be considerable moral pressure to do so). They spend six months to a year in out-of-the-way areas, doing hard physical labour and studying marxism-leninism and Mao Tse-tung thought.[49] It is said that a period at a '7 May School' does help to break down bureaucratic and elitist attitudes. However, one cannot help wondering why this 're-education' takes place in a group consisting only of fellow cadres, rather than through living and working among the workers and peasants, as was often the case during the cultural revolution.

4. A Tentative Assessment

Achievements

It is very difficult to come to any definite conclusions about the Chinese education system. One reason for this is the glaring contradictions in the available data, which are due not only to the different points of view of the observers (one has the feeling that most visitors to China have seen only what they wanted to), but also to the real contradictions of a huge, complex society caught up in a process of transformation and class struggle. Let us start with an indisputable fact: the three decades since the establishment of the People's Republic have witnessed an enormous and rapid expansion of mass education. Before 1949, most children received no formal schooling whatsoever. Today all children attend elementary school until the age of thirteen. A large proportion continue in secondary education. Higher education is still relatively restricted, but has none the less expanded considerably. The number of persons in full-time education in China is three to four times the size of the whole British population! In purely quantitative terms,

China may justly be regarded as an example for all developing countries.

Chinese education is, however, not just important for quantitative reasons. Attempts have been made to develop a qualitatively new type of education, based on the combination of learning and productive labour, and emphasising political and moral training. The stated aim is that: 'Our educational policy must enable everyone who receives an education to develop morally, intellectually and physically and become a worker with both socialist consciousness and culture.'[50] To achieve this aim, it has been necessary to break down ancient and deeply ingrained traditions. Before 1949 education was an automatic entitlement to privilege. The educated man had a complete contempt for manual work, to the point that he would not even carry a parcel through the streets. Destroying this mentality was one of the main aims of the radical changes in education associated with the cultural revolution. In its qualitative innovations Chinese education is of interest not only for underdeveloped countries – it must be taken seriously by teachers in advanced industrial countries as well.

When one compares education in China today with education in capitalist countries during the period of industrialisation, it becomes clear how different the role of workers and peasants in the process of social transformation is intended to be. But this leads to questions: first what type of knowledge and skills does the Chinese pupil actually receive in the educational system; second, who decides on educational aims and on the use to which knowledge is put; third, is the final result anything approaching the marxist concept of polytechnic education?

The Content of Education

The main conflict concerning the aims of education has hinged on the question: is it more important to be 'red' than 'expert' to build a socialist society? Answers to this question have varied according to the prevailing political line and the corresponding changes in development strategy. It would be mistaken to think that the conflict has been finally resolved. However, a few generalisations are possible. Every child learns the basic cultural techniques of reading, writing and mathematics. He also receives instruction in history, geography, basic natural science and politics. Every child learns about the culture of his country and learns to express himself

through painting, dance and song. Physical training is strongly emphasised and contributes to a high level of health. Every child
learns how goods to satisfy the material needs of society are produced, and takes part in this production him or herself, through
work in both agriculture and industry. Political and moral training
plays a very big part in all aspects of education. A child learns to
accept social control and criticism, to practise self-criticism, to
subordinate his own needs to those of the collective. Discipline and
self-discipline are important educational aims. Individual initiative, creativity, and problem-solving abilities seem to be of
secondary importance (although there are conflicting reports on
this subject).

It may be assumed that the product of this educational
system is a person with a relatively high level of literacy and
general knowledge; a person who has the mental disposition
necessary to adapt to different types of work in a changing
economy; a person motivated to work hard and serve the community, even in unpleasant tasks; a person who is politically loyal
and who accepts the authority of work collectives and political
leadership. This type of person seems well suited to build up a
modern economy in a backward, impoverished country. But is he
capable of controlling and criticising authority, of making sure
that the new form of society serves his own interests as a producer,
and not those of a privileged ruling class? Is he going to be able to
make himself the subject of social transformation, and not just its
tool? That is the question.

Masses and Morality

The answer cannot be found by looking at the educational system
in isolation from the rest of society. Polytechnic education not only
involves combining general and technical education with productive work, it also means equipping the producer to run and
control production and society. And that is only possible if he is
actually going to have the right to share in the exercise of political
power. It all boils down to the question – who rules?

> Who decides whether to set up a school? Who finances it? Who
> selects the staff? Who selects the best educated workers, so that
> they can go to university to perfect themselves? Who is always
> right, according to the thought of Mao Tse-tung? The only answer
> is: the masses.[51]

For subscribers to this type of mindless Maoism there is no problem: the masses run everything. But who are these masses? Are they the masses who demonstrated against the 'Black Line' of Liu Shao-chi, and for Mao Tse-tung and his close comrade in arms Lin Piao in 1966? Or are they the militant oil-workers of Dagang who condemned the anti-party Lin Piao clique in 1973? Are they the hundreds of thousands of people who demonstrated against the dismissal of Teng Hsiao-ping on Peking's central Tiananmen Square on 5 April 1976, or the workers' militia who came and beat them up on the orders of the 'gang of four'? Or are they the crowds who demonstrated in support of the arrest of the 'gang of four' and the reinstatement of Teng six months later? If you look through back numbers of Chinese periodicals, like *China Reconstructs*, you cannot help getting the impression that the masses are always full of enthusiasm for the party clique which happens to be on top at the time. If the dominant clique changes, the masses are always there to criticise the old leaders as counter-revolutionary traitors. Or can it be that there are alternative sets of masses, which can be mobilised by the opposing factions in the 'struggle of two lines'? Or that there are various masses which, upon closer examination, turn out to be members of different classes, with contradictory interests? We cannot give adequate answers to all these questions. But the 'mass line' is an empty slogan as long as the various cliques in the party leadership treat the population with contempt, not even informing them of momentous events until years afterwards.

Who does rule? The 'dictatorship of the proletariat' has two aspects in China: one is the leading role of the party. This temporarily broke down during the cultural revolution, when strife within the CCP leadership made the party completely ineffective, but has since been re-established. The other aspect is the control of every work-brigade, commune, school, university, factory, etc., through a revolutionary committee, based on the 'triple alliance' of party cadres, PLA soldiers and revolutionary masses. But these committees are not elected by the masses – they are appointed by the local party leadership, after 'consultation with the masses' (whatever that means).[52] In other words: the party rules at every level. Now, that is hardly surprising in a socialist country. The party is supposed to embrace the most advanced and class-conscious workers – it is the vanguard of the revolution. The problem is that structures within the party are hierarchical, with a clear chain of command from top to bottom. There are no effective mechanisms to allow party members to control the leadership. Struggles within the party leadership may lead to splits and conflicts throughout the party, but the question as to which line is to prevail is decided at the top. It percolates down to the normal party member in the form of purges and self-criticism.

The party leadership controls the base, and through the appointment of revolutionary committees it also runs things in every sector of society. The revolutionary committees are not an instrument of mass control over production and politics. Their functions are to pass party instructions on to the masses, to pass information on problems of production and everyday life from the masses to the party, and to exercise moral and political control over each individual. This third function is often highly repressive. For instance, people are not allowed to travel anywhere without a permit from the revolutionary committee of their work-unit. Even visits to friends in another part of the same town require the appropriate permit, which is checked by patrols of the workers' militia. Revolutionary committees exercise considerable control over personal life. For instance, hospitals and doctors have to inform the appropriate revolutionary committee if an unmarried women becomes pregnant. This is anti-social behaviour, which leads to interrogation of the woman, and to a black mark in the record of both the mother and the father of the child.[53]

The power of revolutionary and party committees is very great: for instance, an applicant for university must present a certificate from the appropriate committee confirming that he has correct political and moral attitudes. Any form of nonconformity is enough to jeopardise his future. Serious deviation from required attitudes and behaviour may lead to a person being sent to a commune or labour camp in a remote area for 're-education', through hard work and privation. Of course, 're-education' is preceded by mass discussion, and self-criticism by the culprit, but this does not alter the fact that such measures have a clearly punitive character.

It is at this point that the problematic nature of moral education and the emphasis on productive work becomes clear. Since the criteria for correct attitudes and behaviour are not set by the masses themselves, but by the party leadership, the education system functions not as a method of developing workers' ability to exercise political power, but rather as a system of social control over the workers. Moral behaviour is inculcated from earliest

childhood. Children who do not conform (for example by not becoming 'Little Red Soldiers') have no chance of further education
or of entering the party hierarchy.

The very concept of 're-education' through productive work
implies that the difference between manual and mental work has
not been abolished, that manual workers are still dominated by
mental workers, and that manual work is still widely regarded as
inferior. 'Re-education' through productive work takes on a punitive nature. Who is re-educated? Cadres who have the wrong
attitude and support the wrong lines, and young people who do
not work hard enough. But why are there cadres who get so
alienated from the masses that they need re-education? Why can
they not be controlled by the workers and peasants of their own
workplaces, instead of being sent off to special '7 May Cadre
Schools'? The whole concept shows that it is not possible for
workers and peasants to control party cadres, let alone depose
them. Re-education for normal workers has a much more severe
character and is completely separate from re-education for cadres.
A worker may be sent for re-education in a remote region for
several years, and even when this time is up he or she may not be
granted a permit to return to the east. Re-education for cadres is
usually voluntary and lasts six months to a year.

Briefly, our view is that behind the ideology of the mass-line
and the moralism of serving the people lie the economic and
political interests of a new ruling class: the party bureaucracy,
which holds all the reins of power in its hands. Evidence for this
theory is presented by a remarkable big character poster put up in
Canton in November 1974.[54] Its authors, under the name of Li Yi
Zhe, describe the concentration of power in the hands of a small
privileged class of leading cadres: a new bourgeoisie, which ex-
propriates surplus product by controlling and utilising collective
property for their own benefit. This class has developed a concealed method of passing on power and property to its children, by
securing educational privileges through the method of 'slipping
through the back door'. The much publicised 'struggle between
two lines' is interpreted by Li Yi Zhe as a power struggle between
two fractions of the ruling bourgeoisie. The real underlying class
struggle is between the new bourgeoisie and the masses of the
people. The poster reports the drastic measures taken by the
bureaucracy to suppress anyone who tries to criticise them:
'arrests, murders, fabricated accusations even barbaric tor-

tures . . .'[55] It mentions that the authorities of many cities have set up 'work-troupes for maintaining the cleanliness of the political appearance of the city'. These have the task of tearing down big character posters which do not conform to the official line, thus destroying the main form of popular political expression.

The Contradiction in Education

Mao Tse-tung's 'worker with both socialist consciousness and culture' is not Marx's 'totally developed individual'. There are similarities and differences between these two concepts. The main similarity is that both require a broadly-based general and technical education and involvement in productive work. The main difference is that Marx saw polytechnic education as part of the process whereby workers would be able to take control of production and society, and shape them in their own interests. The Chinese education system inculcates its pupils with moral values designed to make them willing and competent workers, eager to use all their abilities to achieve economic and political aims set not by themselves, but by an all-powerful party bureaucracy.

The contradiction in Chinese education is between the high level of technological and economic knowledge it imparts to future workers, and the political and moral education designed to make them serve the interests of a new form of bourgeois dictatorship. Mao Tse-tung once wrote:

> Where do correct ideas come from? Do they drop from the skies? No. Are they innate in the mind? No. They come from social practice, and from it alone; they come from three kinds of social practice, the struggle for production, the class struggle and scientific experiment.[56]

If Chinese workers learn to master technology and production, no amount of moral stories about big and little apples or about the exploits of Lei Feng are going to pull the wool over their eyes for ever. Complete realisation of the marxist concept of polytechnic education is not possible under the present economic and political circumstances, but the Chinese educational system does embody enough progressive aspects to make it a 'revolutionary ferment' for Chinese society.

6.
Polytechnic Education and the Transition from School to Work in Modern Capitalism

'The truth is that most young people leave school politically and economically illiterate', declared the British Trades Union Congress in its contribution to the 'great debate' on the 1977 government Green Paper.[1] This suits the interests of employers and the state in a capitalist society – the less workers understand about the economy and society they live in, the more easily can they be ruled. Yet in the last few years tendencies have become apparent in major capitalist countries towards attempting to reduce the gulf between schooling and the reality of work and everyday life. One such attempt has been the introduction of a new subject in West German schools known either as *Arbeitslehre* (literally 'learning about work') or as *Polytechnik*. In this chapter we shall examine this new subject as a case study of the current changes in the aims and methods of capitalist schooling. But first we will look briefly at the historical development of the relationship between school and work, and try to relate the current educational debate taking place in Britain to the type of changes which are occurring elsewhere.

1. Trends in the Relationship Between Production and Education

As Marx wrote *Capital* he was able to observe the effects of the 'first technological revolution':[2] the development of the engineering industry and corresponding changes in mining and chemicals were leading to a reversal of the historical trend towards de-skilling of labour which had started with capitalist manufacture. Skilled workers, technicians and managers were becoming necessary, and special training institutions were being set up. The tendencies towards general elementary education for the whole working class and technical training for a part of it made up one pillar of the marxist education theory. The other was the goal of the 'totally developed individual' necessary for the transition to a new form of society.

Over a century later, it is clear that the technological development of the forces of production under capitalism has not led to a 'totally developed' worker. Because such workers would be a powerful 'revolutionary ferment', the employers and the state have sought – and found – ways of creating the skills necessary for the production process without raising economic and technological understanding to a level which would endanger bourgeois domination. They have followed two main strategies. First, a sharp divide is imposed between school and production, so that the necessary cultural capabilities may be learnt while practical knowledge of the economy and society is kept to a minimum. Second, a hierarchy is created within the working class, in order that certain sections may gain technical skills without raising the cultural level and social consciousness of the whole class.

The Division Between School and Production

The compulsory elementary school set up for working-class children in the second half of the nineteenth century in most capitalist countries was completely cut off from the sphere of production. (It should be remembered that the ruling and middle classes maintained their own separate schools for a long period.) In it, children learnt the basic cultural capabilities which were becoming increasingly necessary for all wage workers: reading, writing and arithmetic. The material used to teach these cultural capabilities was in no way related to the interests of working-class children or to their future position in the production process; on the contrary, its content was usually religious or nationalistic. It was designed to instil the ideology of the ruling class and to hide the reality of the economic structure. All later changes in state schooling (creation of different types of schools, longer school attendance, new subjects, etc.) maintained the abstract nature of learning and the division between school and production.

The abstractness and irrelevance of learning at school does not mean that it plays no function in preparing children for wage labour. Quite the contrary. At school, working-class children learn to arrive punctually and to sit still for hours; they learn to accept commands – the logic of which escapes them – from teachers and from the educational bureaucracy, and to carry out activities which are useless for themselves. They absorb abstract knowledge, motivated not by interest, but by rewards and punishment. It is the very uselessness of school learning which makes it a suitable preparation for wage labour, for subjection to the authority of foremen and factory-hierarchy, for the life-long drudgery of alienated work in the interest of the employer.

It is certainly no coincidence that the consequence of this type of education is apathy and failure at school for many working-class children. This corresponds with another important function of the school system in capitalism: that of selection for various positions in the social hierarchy. The apparent increase in equality of opportunity through the democratisation of entry to educational establishments in the twentieth century serves to hide the fact that the system is designed to classify a large proportion of children as failures. There is no question of every individual developing his or her true potential. Selection through the schools has the function of giving a minority an elite consciousness and the majority the feeling of having failed through their own inability. This helps to divide the working class and therefore to safeguard class domination. As André Gorz has written:

> This result is achieved by a conceptual and abstract form of teaching, which makes it particularly difficult for the children of less well-educated parents to obtain intellectual qualifications, and which equates good school achievements with the right to a privileged position in society. The school system is therefore the key instrument for the creation of social hierarchies: it pretends to discover differences in innate ability and achievement which it in fact itself creates.[3]

The Hierarchy Within the Working Class

There has never been a completely homogenous working class with equality of income and social position. Early industry took over certain hierarchical forms from handicraft and manufacture production. But during the industrial revolution there were levelling tendencies, connected with the destruction of skilled trades and the deskilling of labour. The first technological revolution was the beginning of a new tendency towards diffentiation and hierarchy. Later, the extreme division of labour introduced by the new production and management methods of Henry Ford and Frederick Winslow Taylor sharpened the difference between the unskilled or semiskilled mass production workers on the one hand, and the skilled workers, foremen, technicians and engineers on the other. At the same time, a new differentiation appeared in the form of the increasing numbers of non-manual wage workers, both inside and outside industry. Particularly important was the rapid growth of public service employment. Civil servants were granted special privileges with regard to security of employment, working conditions and social status. In return, a high degree of loyalty to the prevailing system was demanded of them.

An ever larger proportion of the population had become wage workers, but this did not lead to a unified 'proletarian consciousness'. Within the working class a complicated stratification developed: unskilled, semiskilled, skilled workers, then supervisory staff, technicians and middle management, in the sphere of production; hierarchies of white-collar workers and civil servants in the services sector and administration. Wage workers only form a single class in the sense that they all – directly or indirectly – serve the interests of, and are exploited by, capital. They are divided from each other by different types and levels of payment, by varying working conditions, and by differences in job security. One very important factor in determining class consciousness is that manual workers generally reach an early peak in status and earning ability, while non-manual workers and civil servants usually follow a career with regular promotions throughout their working lives. Also important in hindering unified class consciousness, is the fact that the performance of technicians and supervisory staff is often measured according to how much they help to increase the exploitation of manual workers. Technicians, foremen, non-manual workers and civil servants often appear to manual workers (and to themselves) not as members of the same class, but as part of the ruling class apparatus for exploitation and control. This does not mean that these groups never come into conflict with their employers, but their demands often concern special privileges compared with other workers. To the extent that new forms of production and organisation threaten hitherto privileged groups with deskilling, they are forced to carry out defensive struggles against worsening of working conditions and payment. Such struggles offer the best opportunity for them gaining consciousness of belonging to the working class, and for their integration into the labour movement.

To match the hierarchy in employment, a hierarchical system of education and vocational training was developed. The British system of secondary modern schools for future workers, technical school for technicians and middle level non-manual workers, and grammar school for management and the professions represented a trio of school types to be found in most European countries. Each one provides the basic capabilities, behavioural patterns and ideologies appropriate to the particular stratum. The recent trend towards comprehensive schools in some countries means more efficient veiling of the hierarchy, rather than its abolition. The new form of school looks more egalitarian and encourages the ideology of equal opportunity, but at the same time streaming inside the comprehensive maintains selectivity. Vocational training builds on these foundations: apprenticeship or on-the-job training for manual workers, technical colleges, sandwich courses, business schools, staff colleges for technicians, middle level non-manual workers and civil servants; universities for future bosses, managers and members of the professions.

Changes in production and education in the last hundred years have done nothing to abolish the distinction between manual and mental work. The right to general education for everybody has been achieved, but only in the perverted form of pumping children's heads full of useless and boring knowledge, while keeping them ignorant of what they need to know to transform production and society to meet their own interests. The skills necessary for new technological processes have been created not by means of a general and all-sided education for the whole working class, but through a narrow and highly specialised training of certain sections. Capitalist education does not produce the 'totally developed individual', but the 'expert' – highly specialised in one field but a total idiot in every other. The educational system plays an important part in the ideological legitimation of the capitalist system, claiming to offer equal opportunity to everybody. But in reality it defines most working-class children as inferior and condemns them to a lifetime of boring low-skilled work; a few are given a chance of upward mobility, but at the price of taking on the forms of behaviour and social consciousness required by the employers.

Recent Changes and the 'Great Debate' in Britain

Socialists have always questioned the function of education in capitalism and the division between schooling and work. But in recent years there has been a growing tendency for employers and state policy makers to realise that the present form of schooling does not provide an adequate preparation for the changing demands of the production process and of social life. A dramatic expression of this trend was the 'great debate' on education in Britain connected with the publication in 1977 of a government Green Paper, 'Education in Schools'.

The 'sputnik shock' of the late 1950s led most capitalist countries to re-examine their education policies. But concern was mainly with raising expenditure to improve the teaching of scientific and technical subjects, in order to provide highly qualified personnel to take part in world economic and military competition. The debates and changes of the mid-1970s have had a new quality: they have been concerned with the content and form of teaching at all levels of education, and the way it prepares young people for working and social life. More efficient ways of inculcating formal knowledge are no longer the main issue. It is a question of purveying the ideologies, attitudes and behaviour patterns necessary for providing loyal and disciplined wage workers during a period of crisis and restructuring of capitalist social and economic relations.

In Britain the new education strategies are also concerned with cutting expenditure. One function of the 'great debate' was to sugar the pill of such cuts by providing new and seemingly better content and forms for education. The dual aim of making education more relevant to production while at the same time cutting expenditure is summarised by the Green Paper as follows:

> It is vital to Britain's economic recovery and standard of living that the performance of manufacturing industry is improved and that the whole range of Government policies, including education, contribute as much as possible to improving industrial performance and thereby increasing national wealth.[4]

There is still some emphasis in this debate on the raising of 'standards', that is improving levels of formal achievement in absorbing cultural capabilities (like reading and writing) and knowledge. But the main point is inculcating 'general skills' – and the most general skill in capitalism is submission to the discipline of alienated work and to the authority of the state apparatus. As John Holloway and Sol Picciotto put it:

> What capital wants out of the education system is not so much workers trained for industry as adaptable *individuals* 'who are willing and have a cooperative attitude to work', who take their civic duties seriously and do not regard themselves as part of a class standing in hostile opposition to their exploiters.[5]

In the context of current changes in the labour process, such aims have to be related not only to work itself but also to maintaining mass loyalty in the face of the process of deskilling of labour power and of growing and persistent youth unemployment. Future workers are to be trained in schools and further education institutions not only to be disciplined and submissive at work, but also to accept the necessity of mobility and down-grading in response to 'technological necessity' and to cope with unemployment without posing a threat to law and order.

It is in the light of these changing aims that the Green Paper and other new developments in British education must be examined. Such developments include:

1. The setting up of the Manpower Services Commission to provide courses for unemployed youth, with the dual aim of getting them off the streets and providing 'general skills'.

2. The considerable growth in further education in recent years. The increasing realisation that a large proportion of young people are just not going to find work at school-leaving age has made it necessary to find a new way of keeping them under control. Since staying on at school is obviously irrelevant to most of them, further education with its doubtful promises of useful training provides a way out. The Holland Report, with its emphasis on 'social and life skills', appears as an attempt to make this new sector of education function more systematically in accordance with the interests of employers.

3. The upgrading of careers teaching at schools and the improvement of co-ordination with the Youth Employment Service. The latter now actually has sub-offices of the 'Jobs Centres' within many schools. Careers teachers also organise 'work experience' schemes, in which school students spend some weeks working in local factories and offices. The main purpose of such appears to be

to destroy 'unrealistic expectations' about the type of work available, and to create a smooth flow of labour power from school to work, by allowing firms to 'try out' young people before actually employing them.

4. Pilot schemes designed to test and introduce new school subjects aimed at helping young people to orientate themselves with regard to changing work and social patterns. The furthest advanced of these appears to be the 'Understanding Industrial Society' course now being used in Coventry schools. This is co-ordinated with work experience schemes and with 'work simulation' courses in which pupils make saleable products.[6]

5. New forms of assessment of pupil achievement, to provide employers with 'objective' information about potential workers. The main feature of this tendency has been the setting up of the Assessment of Performance Unit (APU) to monitor secondary schools. The Coventry scheme mentioned above also contains plans for 'diagnostic tests' for all pupils. In addition, there is talk of a 'five-plus' test for all children before admission to primary school.

6. New forms of management and control of schools. The Taylor Report on school management and government has proposed the inclusion of 'representatives of the community' – meaning, among other things, industrialists – on school governors boards. Obviously, one purpose of this is to make school more relevant to the needs of industry.

The reaction of teachers, students and parents to these tendencies has been very mixed. 'Progressivists' have emphasised that school should develop the creativity and the emotional qualities of children, and have fought against attempts to relate learning to work. The response of the National Union of Teachers (NUT) has been to insist on 'professionalism' – the government should provide the resources and leave the teachers to get on with the job. Socialists are in principle in favour of breaking down the barrier between learning and work, but see that the present tendencies are a far cry from the marxist theory of polytechnic education.

Capital's need for a new relationship between school and work does provide important possibilities for transforming the educational system. The precondition for seizing these opportunities is understanding how educational change originates from the changing nature of the labour process and the new problems of maintaining social and political stability in a crisis situation. Rather than going into this further on a global, theoretical level, we will now describe the changes in the relationship between production and education which led up to the introduction of the new school subject *Arbeitslehre/Polytechnik* in West Germany at the end of the 1960s. Although these developments are little known outside Germany, they do foreshadow current developments elsewhere to a surprising extent. The analysis of the new school subject in West Germany may be regarded as a case study for the way in which the state is trying to make education meet new economic and social conditions throughout advanced capitalist countries.[7] Although, as we shall show below, the new subject *Arbeitslehre/ Polytechnik* only makes up a relatively small part of schooling in West Germany (a few hours per week in secondary modern and comprehensive schools), it is indicative of an important trend: a first step towards eroding the division between school and society.

2. New Tendencies in West Germany Since the Mid-Sixties

The so-called West German 'economic miracle' after the military and economic collapse of 1945 was based mainly on the availability of a large industrial reserve army.[8] There were millions of unemployed workers, and millions more came in from the parts of the Reich which had been lost to Poland, the Soviet Union and Czechoslovakia. A little later, no less than three million persons, mainly of working age, left East Germany for the West. Once Marshall Aid and the 1948 Currency Reform had given the economy an initial boost, the vast reserves of labour kept wages down and profits up, allowing a labour-intensive expansion. Production was expanded by bringing existing plants back into use, or by building new plants with the same type of technology. The main aim of investments was the creation of new jobs, rather than raising productivity.[9] In this period, the education and vocational training of workers was no problem: the existing reserves of skilled labour were adequate (not to mention those from East Germany). The federal government could neglect the educational system and keep educational expenditure below the level in other comparable countries – in 1965, West Germany spent 4.5 per cent of its national income on education, compared with 5.6

per cent in France, 6.4 per cent in Britain and 6.5 per cent in the USA.[10]

The situation changed after 1960. By then the labour reserves had been absorbed. Between 1950 and 1960 the number of economically active persons had risen from 20 million to 26 million, while unemployment had fallen from 1,600,000 to 235,000. By 1960 there were twice as many vacant jobs as unemployed persons.[11] The employers tried to fill the gap with immigrant workers, but this only worked to a limited extent: due to lack of training and language difficulties, foreigners could not be employed for certain jobs, and in addition, employers and government were not willing to meet the social costs necessary for long term integration of a very large immigrant labour force.[12] The labour shortage led to wage increases, which began to cut into profits. Increasing international competition made it difficult to pass rising costs on to the consumers in the form of higher prices. The 'economic miracle' came to an end and the normal capitalist economic cycle became evident once more with the recession of 1966–67.

The free-market oriented Christian Democratic (CDU) government proved incapable of dealing with the new situation and was replaced, first by a CDU-SPD (Social Democrats) coalition, and then by an SPD-FDP (liberal 'Free Democrats') coalition. The strategy adopted for dealing with the economic situation was modernisation of production, increased state planning and intervention, and reforms in the social and education sectors. The main aim was to replace growth through increased employment by growth through higher productivity. In principle, higher productivity may be produced in two ways: 1. by increased capital investment per job, which means that each worker has, on average, more or better machinery at his disposal; 2. through speeding up production by means of better organisation, time and motion studies, faster assembly lines, piece-rates, productivity deals, so that the worker does more work in a given period. In practice, West German employers tried to combine both methods: the introduction of new machinery or plants was used to speed up work.

Such changes in the production process made new demands upon the workers. The 'Committee of Experts to advise on the Development of the Economy', a standing committee set up in 1963 soon pointed this out:

The introduction of new methods of production may meet with obstacles if vocational skills are required which are not available, or which are available to an insufficient extent, and which can only be acquired through a long training period ... This makes it evident to what degree the productivity of investments in material capital depends on whether enough resources have been put into training, research and technical development.[13]

On this there was agreement. The differences of opinion among educational experts, politicians and employers concerned what new skills were required and how they could be obtained quickly and cheaply through the educational system.

The earliest critics of the West German 'educational catastrophe' declared that the poor quality of the education system was a danger to further economic growth, and therefore a threat to the existing social order.[14] They regarded education and training as a vital investment in 'human capital', and called for a general raising of the skill level of employees through more and better schools and vocational training. The 'Committee of Experts' took a somewhat different view: they demanded a new attitude on the part of workers, above all 'mobility' – that is, a willingness to change jobs, occupations and homes as dictated by the needs of industry. Workers should give up the 'craft-guild notion' of a trade which a man does for his whole working life. They must be prepared to learn a new job and to be retrained.[15] The 'Committee of Experts' was thus not demanding higher skill-levels for all workers, in the sense of more technological knowledge, but rather new personal characteristics and forms of behaviour. These required a new form of education, but not necessarily a qualitatively better or costlier one.

An important empirical study carried out by Kern and Schumann on behalf of the 'Rationalisation Board of the German Economy' (*Rationalisierungskuratorium der deutschen Wirtschaft*) helped to settle the question of whether what was needed was 'more skill' or a 'different type of skill'. They found that technical changes in the production process were changing the job structure both qualitatively and quantitatively, leading to corresponding changes in the skills required of workers. However, this did not mean a general raising of the skill level. A high degree of mechanisation and automation did lead to a greater need for highly skilled employees, but repetitive, simple, specialised production jobs and monotonous control tasks were not eliminated. Rather than a general raising of skill levels, Kern and Schumann observed a 'polarisation': a growing but still relatively small number of technicians, maintenance workers and so on required a very high level of education and training, while the majority of workers required very little skill for their new tasks. They came to the conclusion that the existing system of vocational training (based mainly on training in the factory in three year apprenticeships) was, on the whole, adequate for future needs. The main changes required were an increase in general knowledge, which should be provided by improved school education, and a more positive attitude of workers towards technological change and the ever more frequent necessity of changing job and occupation. 'Mobility' and 'flexibility' were the vital abilities for future workers.[16]

The 'educational reform' started by the SPD-FDP coalition in the late 1960s therefore had two main aims with regard to preparation for the production process: first, the enlargement and improvement of educational institutions concerned with the training of scientists, technicians, engineers and other experts; and, second, alterations in the structure and content of the educational establishments responsible for socialisation of the masses of manual and non-manual workers. This latter aim was less a question of qualitative improvement than of a change in function: nurseries and schools were to create the personal characteristics and behaviour patterns necessary for the mobility and flexibility of the future workers. Kern and Schumann had emphasised the importance of so-called 'non-process-dependent capabilities' (*prozessunabhängige Fähigkeiten*), meaning transferable skills necessary for most types of work, rather than for a particular occupation. They mention: intellectual adaptability, ability to grasp things rapidly, powers of observation, technical sensitivity, technical intelligence. Future workers obtain their general education in nursery schools, primary schools, secondary modern schools (*Hauptschule*) and, of late, though only to a small degree, in comprehensive schools (*Gesamtschule*). Changes in the form and content of teaching in these establishments is connected with the aim of creating these 'non-process-dependent capabilities'. This is – as we shall show below – the real reason for the introduction of the new subject *Arbeitslehre/Polytechnik*.

But mobility and flexibility are related not just to work – people who change jobs because of technological change often also have to change place of residence, way of living and social status (upwards or downwards). Changes in the educational system can therefore not be explained adequately by the requirements of the production process alone: the sphere of reproduction of labour power (housing, consumption, recreation, social services) is equally important. Here too, increasing bureaucracy and complexity require new capabilities of the workers. To function adequately in a modern capitalist society, they must be familiar with bureaucratic communication forms, know how to consume properly and how to fulfil their duties as state-citizens. This often makes greater demands on workers in terms of knowledge and capabilities than does the job itself. What use is it to an employer if workers are capable of adapting to a new machine in a new factory, but become unfit for work because their cannot cope with being forced to move house and having this social life completely disorganised? According to a government report, the number of persons suffering from alcoholism in West Germany rose from 600,000 in 1969 to between 1·2 and 1·8 millions in the mid-1970s. Two to three per cent of the population are alcoholics. The incidence of other forms of mental illness has risen correspondingly. This shows the real price to be paid for technological change based solely on the criterion of profitability, rather than human need.[17]

The man or woman who has to seek refuge in alcohol or illness because of changes in the production process or the environment, which his or her socialisation has not prepared him for, may be a serious loss for capital. And since the beginning of the long-term economic crisis in Germany in 1974, a new problem has arisen: the future worker must be psychologically prepared to accept a long period of unemployment or deskilling, without degenerating physically and mentally. This is another new task for the school: *Arbeitslehre/Polytechnik* is as much related to preparing people for future problems outside work as for their occupational role.

Finally, it is important to realise that the 'educational reform' was due not only to economic factors but also had important political causes. The 'student movement' of the mid-1960s had drawn public attention to the unthinking materialism and crass inequality of West German society, in particular the discrimination against working-class children in the educational system. Here they gained the support of apprentices and school pupils, and, to some extent, even of the usually very passive German labour unions. This movement threatened the ideological legitimacy of the prevailing system, so that even liberal reformers like Ralf Dahrendorf (later a member of the Commission of the European Community and currently Director of the London School of Economics) began to call for an educational reform to achieve equality of opportunity, under the slogan 'education is a civil right'.[18] Changes in schools and universities thus also had the function of improving selection mechanisms within the educational system through granting apparently equal chances for social mobility. The call for 'compensatory education' for working-class children, the plan to introduce comprehensive schools (which has so far not been carried out, except for a few experimental schools) and the introduction of *Arbeitslehre/Polytechnik* were all measures aimed at creating welfare-state illusions of equal opportunities. Those who remained without adequate skills or qualifications were to learn to regard this as the result of their own inadequacy, rather than a product of class discrimination. At the same time, many of the students who had become politicised by the student movement themselves became teachers, lecturers or educational planners. A large number tried to work for greater equality and for social change from within the educational system. That is why, despite the intentions of government and employers, there were attempts to make schooling serve the interests of the working class. And that is also why the West German authorities started vetting the political views of teachers and other civil servants, and throwing them out through the *Berufsverbot* (denial of employment on political grounds) which was introduced in 1972.

3. The New School Subject *Arbeitslehre/Polytechnik*

Before turning to the introduction of the new school subject it is necessary to look briefly at the structure of the West German education system. The German Federal Republic consists of ten states (*Länder*). Each has its own state government, including a ministry of education. Education policies, institutions and curricula vary somewhat from state to state, although they are coordinated through regular meetings of the Federal and Länder education ministers. The recommendations of the *Kultusminister-konferenz* (Conference of Education Ministers) have a binding character, but they are implemented in differing forms in the various states. The CDU-controlled state governments (Bavaria, Baden-Wörttemberg, Rheinland-Pfalz, Lower Saxony, Schleswig) tend towards conservative education policies; SPD ruled states (Hesse, Rheinland-Westfalia, Berlin, Bremen, Hamburg) favour technocratic modernisation measures. Although all states have introduced the new subject, it has taken different forms. The CDU states have generally called it *Arbeitslehre* ('learning about work') to emphasise the link with employers' interests, while the SPD states have sometimes (though not always) used the term *Polytechnik* to link the subject with traditional demands of the labour movement. It is sometimes difficult therefore to make accurate generalisations about education in West Germany as a whole, although basic trends do seem to follow a common pattern.

The general introduction of the subject *Arbeitslehre* in all secondary modern schools (*Hauptschule*) was first recommended by the German Committee for the Educational System in 1964.[19] Its aim was to ease the transition from school to work, by giving pupils a basic understanding of the rationalisation and technology of modern working life. A combination of practical work in school workshops, visits to factories and explanations by teachers was to provide 'pre-occupational basic training'. School was to become the first stage of vocational training. This plan did not suit the employers at all – they saw a threat to their monopoly of vocational training for manual workers, and feared that they would have no control over this new 'basic training'. In addition, they were worried that workers might become 'over-skilled', which would lead to low job-satisfaction. The employers protested against the proposal and set up working groups with the aim of influencing teaching and educational planning.[20]

The employers got their way: the plans for the introduction of *Arbeitslehre* passed by the Conference of Education Ministers in 1969 left out all reference to 'pre-occupational basic training'. Instead, the tasks of the new subject were to be: first, to provide a general orientation to the economic and working world; second, to teach a positive attitude towards work; and third, to help with the choice of an occupation. There was a clear emphasis on the creation of personal characteristics and behaviour patterns necessary for mobile, well-adapted workers:

> The choice of subject-matter to be used should be made mainly according to the criterion that it should allow young people to develop and practise fundamental working qualities, like concentration, adaptability, co-operativeness, thinking economically, acting according to a plan. The learning of fundamental work

qualities has priority over the development of specific work capabilities.[21]

These aims were taken over in the plans made for *Arbeitslehre* by the educational authorities of the various *Länder*:

> Training in tenacity of purpose, reliability, endurance, conscientiousness, exactness and cleanliness, but also readiness to give information, adaptability, acting according to a plan, ability to work in a team. (Baden-Württemberg)

> Getting used to working exactly, responsible treatment of machines and tools, training in economic use of working time. (Bavaria)

> Preparation of pupils for the modern working world, which requires an adaptable, independent skilled worker with general technical intelligence and great adaptability; learning to judge the contribution of each employee towards the development of the whole factory, in particular with regard to responsibility, ability and the personal involvement which is daily required. (Hamburg)[22]

These objectives are concerned mainly with the second task mentioned above for *Arbeitslehre*: Learning a positive attitude towards work. But the 'general orientation to the economic and working world' and 'helping with the choice of an occupation' were also concerned with attitude and behaviour patterns useful to employers. In order to prepare pupils for adaptation to their future job, they were to be given an idea of the complexity of the economy and to be informed about possible occupations. This did not, of course, mean learning about the history of capitalism and the inherent contradiction between the owners of the means of production and the wage workers. The industrial system was to be described in terms of technical efficiency, rational organisation and inter-dependence between workers and employers, following the prevailing ideology of 'social partnership'. Suggested teaching topics were: 'the structure of a large corporation', 'individual firm – national economy – world economy', 'the economic importance of savings – from saving to property', 'the role of the social partners in society'. It was suggested that the employer should be portrayed as being 'dependent on the consumers' as all production has the final aim of satisfying the needs of the private households. Pupils were to be helped in making a 'sensible choice' of occupation: in other words, they were to be disabused of the idea that they would be able to do what they wanted and persuaded to take up an occupation for which industry had a use.[23]

Exactly how these basic aims of the new subject were to be translated into school lessons was not laid down by the Conference or Education Ministers in 1969. They vaguely mentioned the importance of learning through using tools and machines, drawings and tables, and suggested topics like structure of a factory, rationalisation, automation, hierarchy in a factory, competition, interest groups, legal problems, working hours. Since neither the teachers nor the school structures were prepared for the new subject, a considerable number of research programmes were set up in the various states to work out exact teaching plans for *Arbeitslehre*. The results of these programmes varied very widely, both in the political intention of the suggested teaching plans, and in the methods to be used. Some of the research programmes led to official, general guidelines (or curricula) for *Arbeitslehre* in the various Länder; others were published in the form of projects, either as books or audio-visual teaching kits, which could be used at the discretion of teachers. It is impossible to go into detail here on the great variety of *Arbeitslehre* methods now in use, but we will try to show some important features.

It should be noted that although the subject has been introduced in all parts of West Germany, it is in fact confined to secondary modern schools and to comprehensive schools. In the latter *Arbeitslehre* is often a voluntary option as an alternative to learning a second foreign language, which means that it is done more by working-class than middle-class children. In grammar schools the subject is not taught. The age-group concerned is generally thirteen to sixteen year olds. *Arbeitslehre* is rarely taught using traditional classroom methods. Most common is the project-teaching approach, in which a class or group sets itself the task of making a certain product or of investigating a certain phenomenon, and then carries out over a long period all the theoretical and practical tasks needed to achieve this aim. A typical project might combine practical work in school workshops with theoretical instruction on the scientific principles involved, and be rounded off by a visit to a factory where similar work is done on an industrial scale. Some attempts have been made to combine such projects with the work-experience schemes which exist in all states, but this has proved difficult: although virtually all secondary modern school children do a three to four week *Betriebspraktikum* (i.e. work in a factory or office), usually during the last year of school; exactly what work is done depends mainly on what is available in the area concerned, and to some extent on the wishes of the child. It is virtually impossible to ensure that all children in a class do jobs which relate to the *Arbeitslehre* projects.

The aims and methods of the projects vary widely. Roughly, the projects may be divided into three main categories, which we shall look at briefly in turn.[24]

Elementary Technical Training

It is important to realise that most of the teachers entrusted with teaching the new subject of *Arbeitslehre* were trained as teachers of woodwork, handicrafts or domestic science. They lacked the knowledge necessary for the integration of productive work, and technological and socio-economic instruction, which is the real basis of polytechnic education. Such teachers tended to use projects aimed at making pupils understand technical systems, but excluded most questions of changing production technology and the accompanying social and economic problems. A typical example is a project on internal combustion engines, which aims to give pupils 'a basic understanding of the relationships of the mechanical movement-processes as well as of the electrical and chemical-physical processes in a vehicle motor.'[25] The programme for the project is as follows:

> Dismantling of a moped motor; analysis of the movement-processes; analysis of the gas-exchange-processes; reading standard values in prospectuses.
>
> Additional tasks: measurement and calculation of standard values; making a working model; information on piston-engines. Extension: Getting information on fuel mixtures at a service station; visit to a moped sales firm; visit to a moped factory; dismantling and analysing other vehicle parts, driving instruction.[26]

Using a moped motor as teaching matter is a plausible way of raising pupil motivation, for it relates to the interests of this age-group. The merit of the project is that it sets out to demonstrate scientific principles through an object of daily use. But the perspective of the course is merely that of the consumer – it does nothing to show the methods and conditions of production. Both the relevance of natural science and technology for human social life, and problems of the social relationships of production play no part. Technical processes are shown as objective results of scientific laws and not as products of specific historical structures.

This type of purely technical project has declined in recent years. Official guidelines for *Arbeitslehre* increasingly emphasise economic and political aspects, and newer projects correspond with this policy.[27] One reason for this is no doubt that in the meantime special courses for teachers of *Arbeitslehre* have been set up at many training colleges and universities. Another reason is probably that the increasing unemployment caused by technological change makes it impossible to deal with technical processess as if they had no effect on workers and society.

Technology and Industrial Management

This type of project is concerned with the technology of the production process, and the way in which this changes, as well as with problems of organising a factory and selling its products. In a typical project the pupils start by developing a small-scale method of producing pottery in the school workshop. They then visit a brick works and a porcelain factory. Before the visits the pupils are asked to voice their expectations with regard to methods of production, degree of mechanisation, structure of the labour force, etc. The teacher informs them about the products and about marketing problems, as well as on production technology and automation. In the factory the pupils learn the importance of research and development and production planning, and they see the complicated structure of the commercial side of the firm (cost and price calculation, advertising, market research).

> The pupils learn that the use of new machines and automatically controlled devices eliminates jobs, but that on the other hand increasing production requires new activities, above all in the sectors: purchasing, and planning and design.[28]

The pupils' interest in automation is aroused by the visits, so that the next phase of the project is to make simple electronic control devices in the school workshop. These are then used to control the school pottery oven. The pupils thus learn to introduce automation themselves.

The obvious purpose of this type of project is to give young people a positive attitude towards automation. They learn to see automation through the employers' eyes – purely in terms of technological rationality and reduced costs. Devising automatic control mechanisms by themselves, they learn to identify with the

F

engineers who rationalise production, rather than with the workers who become redundant. This is a very inappropriate perspective, in that most of them are far more likely to become unskilled workers than engineers. The project makes no provision for pupils to talk to workers when they visit factories, or to investigate the social results of automation. Such projects propagate a techno-cratic ideology: technological change is an inescapable objective necessity, workers must accept this and adapt to it through personal mobility and flexibility. The rationality of decision-making by management in the industrial firm is not questioned, for all questions relating to the development of the whole economy and the social situation of the workers are excluded. This technocratic ideology is shown clearly in the assessment of automation in another project:

> Automation continues to advance in our economy. It changes the living and working conditions of our time, through making possible new products which raise the standard of living for many people; through reducing working hours, costs and prices; and through replacing manual work by machine work, which means trans-ferring labour from the production sector to the planning and administrative sectors.[29]

This technocratic type of project is by far the most common in *Arbeitslehre* and *Polytechnik* courses in West German schools.[30]

Economic, Social and Political Education

Various attempts have been made – particularly in Berlin, Bremen and Hesse – to develop *Arbeitslehre* models which can give working-class children a critical understanding of their future position in the occupational world, and of the effects which tech-nological change is likely to have on their lives. The starting point for such models is the contradiction between the increasing feeling of helplessness and dependence experienced by working people in the face of large technically rationalised production and administrative units, and the potential for increased personal autonomy implicit in improved means of production.[31] There are 'tensions' between economic growth and rationality, and human-isation of working conditions; increase in self-determination and co-determination and the general improvement of the quality of life. A teachers' guide published by the Education Ministry of Hesse describes the task of *Arbeitslehre* as follows:

It has the task of preparing young people for life in the world of work. That includes making them capable of reacting productively to its contradictions through critical examination aimed at a qualitative improvement. The precondition for this is that economic processes and their interlocking with social and political relationships must be made transparent for young people.[32]

Technical processes, technological developments, economic organisation and social change are all analysed in relation to the effect on the worker's job, and, since work has the purpose of satisfying material and mental needs, in relation to effects on family, recreation and public affairs. Understood in this way, *Arbeitslehre* becomes a combination of economics, technology and socio-ecology[33] (the latter meaning the study of the effects of economic and technological processes on human living conditions). Teaching future workers to understand production and society, so that they can change prevailing conditions, obviously implies that the educational process is expressly designed to serve the emancipation of the worker. Certain proposals for *Arbeitslehre* actually state this as their aim.[34]

All this sounds very like the marxist theory of polytechnic education, and curiously out of place in official publications of a West German Education Ministry. Why should the authorities of a capitalist state suddenly have an interest in politically aware workers? Or could it be that this stated intention is ideological window-dressing, and that the real content of the projects in the schools have different aims? These questions could only be answered by an analysis of the projects actually based on these progressive guiding lines, and of the subject matter actually taught in the schools. All we can do here is give a few pointers.

The basic problem is how an abstract political aim, however progressive, is to be translated into the reality of everyday school life, where *Arbeitslehre* is merely one subject among others? It is easy to show children how a technical process works, in experimental form at school and in reality by visiting a factory, but how can children experience a social conflict situation between labour and capital? Various solutions have been suggested. As an example, we describe briefly the 'Berlin concept', a project worked out by educationalists in Berlin which has done much to shape the new subject in the schools of that city.[35]

The general 'emancipatory' aims are to be achieved through projects which represent the working world in the form of models.

A project has four phases: decision (as to what to do), planning, execution and control. The contents of these phases are decided upon by the pupils themselves. The 'didactic framework' (which has in the meantime become part of the official *Arbeitslehre* teaching plan for Berlin schools) includes the three interrelated aspects: technical processes, economics, and politics. Each of these is studied in the context of three stages of development of production: first, working for a purpose decided upon by the pupil himself; second, working for an easily understandable market; third, working for an anonymous market. In the first stage pupils learn working techniques through producing simple objects for themselves (e.g. optical instruments). In the second they produce commodities using handicraft methods and division of labour, working in groups; the commodities are produced on contract for a known purchaser, so that the purpose of the work is clear. The third stage corresponds with industrial conditions of production: using scientific and technological principles, the pupils produce commodities for sale on an anonymous market. The three stages are linked through an analysis of the problems of industrial management: in the first stage, pupils learn 'preliminary forms of management thinking' like household planning and saving; in the second, they become familiar with business accounting; and in the third, pupils are confronted with 'the striving for maximum productiveness of the various factors of production, in terms of value and volume'.

However, it is not possible for pupils to really experience industrial production within the school, so the third stage of the project is in fact limited to explanations about the problems involved by the teacher, using various teaching aids. The teacher uses theories of industrial management to explain models of the structure of industrial production processes, paying special attention to theories of accounting and organisation. In other words, the pupil learns about the working world in terms of the rationality of management, and not the social situation of the worker. This is regarded as being in the future workers' interest – through learning management thinking they are supposed to be best able to understand their own interests at work and be able to use their labour power optimally. The 'Berlin concept' pays particular attention to the relation between industrial management and the running of a private household. Pupils learn that industry is run in a rational way, through planning, accounting and optimal use of technology.

They are then supposed to learn to use these principles for organising their own needs and activities outside school, and, later, for work. The same principles are applied to helping pupils choose a future occupation and planning how to get the appropriate training.

This example makes it clear that 'emancipation of workers' can mean very different things. The result of the 'Berlin concept' is not likely to be workers who understand the class structure of society and who are equipped to fight for their own interests. More probably, it would be workers who accept the technological rationality of modern capitalism without questioning the class structures on which it is based. The 'Berlin concept' does serve the interests of such workers to the extent that it helps them to learn to plan rationally, organise consumption and household optimally, and sell their labour power effectively. But the end product is an illusion: namely that the worker possesses the autonomy to plan his or her life, as if it were not shaped by the decision-making of powerful economic groups, which decide on rationalisation, redundancy, and transfer of production to other places.

To avoid misunderstandings: there can be no doubt that the attempt to link technical instruction with economic and political knowledge made in various guidelines and projects for *Arbeitslehre* is in essence a progressive tendency. This does not, however, mean that it is automatically a form of socialist education. Even in this form *Arbeitslehre* can be used to give pupils an affirmative attitude towards the capitalist system, through emphasising technological rationality and ignoring class relationships. But this need not be the case: there are many examples of projects in which teachers have taken the class position of pupils and their parents as a starting point, and have tried to make the real contradictions of industrial work and class domination clear to them. In one project, for instance, a school class visited a chain factory, which was the main local employer, analysed the repressive nature of the work in the factory (where many of the children's fathers worked), and tried to relate this to their situation at home: 'Why is Father always tired and irritable after work?' An attempt was made to simulate industrial work at school through making small objects on a conveyor line, with a high degree of division of labour.[36] The project must have been effective, for the factory owner felt it necessary to complain to the education authorities, who stopped it and threatened the teacher with dismissal. In other projects, attempts have been made to help children understand the historical development of the means of production, through working with various forms of division of labour in well-equipped school workshops, and visiting factories to examine the form of division of labour there. In such projects, teachers have set out to give the work the character of socially-necessary productive labour, by arranging the sale of products for use in school common rooms and the like. Whatever the limitations of such attempts – and we will look at these below – they are a modest step on the way to raising pupils' consciousness of production and society. They are an important political contrbution made by progressive teachers.

4. The Difficulties of Polytechnic Education in the Capitalist School

We have seen how the new school subject *Arbeitslehre/Polytechnik* has been developed in West Germany as a reaction to problems of labour qualification, social integration and political legitimacy, which have resulted from economic and technological changes. The overwhelming majority of plans and projects for the new subject aim to convince pupils of the technological rationality of the capitalist form of production, to hide class conflicts, and to help pupils to become mobile, flexible and well-adapted workers. On the other hand, some progressive teachers and educational planners have attempted to use the opportunity presented by the introduction of the new subject to help future workers develop a real understanding of the relationship between the mode of production and the structure of society, and to comprehend their own class position. Such teachers have generally received their own political socialisation through the student movement of the late 1960s, and are usually orientated towards the trade union movement and left-wing political groups. Their educational models are the marxist theory of polytechnic education, and the educational systems of countries like China and Cuba. In addition the educational demands of the pre-1933 German labour movement have had some influence. But progressive teachers meet enormous difficulties in trying to introduce polytechnic education in the schools of a modern capitalist state like West Germany.

First, *Arbeitslehre* is taught as one subject among others. It is hardly ever co-ordinated with the contents of other subjects like natural science, languages or mathematics, to make a general analysis of all aspects of an important social or economic problem. *Arbeitslehre* is simply an isolated part of the school timetable – perhaps two hours per week. By the time working-class pupils get to the *Arbeitslehre* class, which is generally only in the last few years before leaving school, they almost always have a resigned and alienated attitude towards school. Even the best and most committed teacher has little chance of changing this in the few hours at his or her disposal. To make matters worse, s/he has to give marks at the end of the term, which makes a spontaneous and co-operative relationship between teacher and pupils very difficult. Things are particularly bad where *Arbeitslehre* is not compulsory but an option usually taken by 'intellectually less capable' children instead of a second language. Then the subject has a discrimina- tory character, which tends to make pupils aggressive. It is very hard for a teacher to take the problems and interest of children as the starting point: they do not come to the teacher when they feel a need to discuss a problem but when the timetable dictates it. And when the school-bell rings discussions have to be broken off – a week later it is necessary to start anew. The *Arbeitslehre* teacher generally has many different classes each week; s/he therefore does not know the children, their family situation, and their parents' jobs well enough to give these aspects their essential place in project-teaching. Instead, pressure of work usually forces the teacher to use a pre-structured course or teaching-kit, which may have little to do with the real interests and problems of the children.

Second, most teachers lack the training and experience necessary for genuine polytechnic education. They have had a middle-class education, going straight from school to training college. Few have worked in factories before studying. Older teachers were probably trained as handicraft or domestic science instructors, and know little of economics or social science. Younger teachers may have had an *Arbeitslehre* option in their training, or even have attended one of the new teaching courses concerned primarily with the new subjects.[37] But they too generally lack real experience of the situation of the manual worker in the factory, and of the problems of working-class children. Genuine poly- technic education would require teachers who have themselves been brought up in such a way as to allow an all-sided personality development. Of course, this demand cannot be realised in the existing situation, but there is little doubt that the most successful

Arbeitslehre teachers have been those who started off as workers and then completed their education through night-school and the like.

Third, the existence of one subject concerned with helping young people to find their way into the world of work does not abolish the basic division between school and work in capitalist society. The great bulk of school learning remains abstract and irrelevant to later occupational and social life. This affects the attitude of pupils towards *Arbeitslehre* as well – how can they be highly motivated and involved for two hours a week, when the rest of their school life is boring and frustrating? Polytechnic education means learning through socially necessary productive work. But capitalists are not interested in integrating children into a production process in such a way as to allow them to learn about the technology and the social relations of production. The factory is there to make a profit and not to educate children, and, above all, employers have no interest in having future workers understand these matters. This means that the manual work which forms an important part of nearly all *Arbeitslehre* courses is not real productive work, but rather handicraft work at school, and therefore not under factory conditions. Attempts to simulate conveyor line work and the like at school cannot change this fact: children are required to learn about work through an artificial school situation, and then to make an intellectual transfer of this experience to their later work situation. Most children will probably think – and rightly so – that these experiments at school have relatively little connection with the daily life of their fathers and mothers in office and factory. It is questionable whether experience gained in this way has much effect on later behaviour at work.

Fourth, West German employers and state have no interest in workers' gaining a real understanding of production and society. As long as *Arbeitslehre* courses purvey a technocratic ideology and help to make future workers mobile and adaptable, things are fine. But teachers who try to make class relationships clear are likely to find themselves in very serious trouble. Since the decision of the Ministers of the Interior to investigate the political views and behaviour of civil servants in 1972, well over half a million have been vetted, many of them teachers or applicants for teaching jobs. At least three thousand persons have received the *Berufsverbot* – either dismissed or refused employment for political reasons.[38] Since teachers who want to develop polytechnic education in the interests of working-class children are generally politically active persons, they are always threatened by the *Berufsverbot*. Any reference to class interests or to capitalist exploitation in a school lesson may lead to the suspension and dismissal of the teacher as an 'enemy of the Constitution' or a 'communist sympathiser'.

Fifth, the current economic and political crisis in West Germany is reducing the leeway for any form of progressive changes in education. As we have pointed out, the 'educational reform' of the late 1960s was a result both of problems of economic and technological change in a growing economy, and of the need of the state and the ruling class for new ways of securing mass loyalty. The student movement played a dual role, exposing the deficiencies of the educational system, and providing enthusiastic young teachers and planners committed to developing new structures. Since 1974, economic expansion has slowed drastically. Unemployment has averaged one million for three years, and automation is leading to a steady decline in jobs. Researchers forecast continuing stagnation with two million unemployed by the mid-1980s. Falling state revenues have been the death-knell for many projects and reforms in education. The introduction of the comprehensive school has been stopped, pre-school education has stopped growing, and new, experimental models are being wound up. Employment in education and the social services is stagnating, and thousands of graduates have little prospect of finding work. For working-class school leavers, job prospects are very poor. The number of apprenticeships for training as skilled workers has fallen steadily. Young people count themselves lucky if they can even find an unskilled job. This situation has two effects on attempts at developing genuine polytechnic education: it is very hard to motivate young people to learn through productive work and to get to know about their future as workers, when they know that it is likely that they will not find employment at all, or at best in dead-end jobs; and fear of social conflicts arising from the economic situation has led to a further tightening up of political control over educators. *Arbeitslehre* continues to be taught at schools, but the innovative impulse has been destroyed. The new emphasis is on special courses designed to take unemployed youth out of the labour market and off the streets. Apart from teaching young people supposedly useful skills, such courses also have the advantage (for the state) of taking unemployed teachers and social workers off the streets too. This development is rather similar to the growth of further education in Britain, although the organisational form is somewhat different.

To sum up: polytechnic education in the sense meant by Marx is not possible in a capitalist school system; genuine polytechnic education means linking school with production, so that schools cease to be separate institutions, cut off from the real life of society. Instead of learning abstract compartmentalised subjects, children take productive work and their own social situation as the starting point of self-determined processes of study, observation and experimentation. Factories, offices, shops and other economic and social institutions become places of learning, and all adults become educators. In doing so, they themselves participate in a process of life-long learning. Polytechnic education implies a different form of society. To regard it as one school subject among others is a contradiction in terms. Polytechnic education can refer only to the basic principle of the whole education system, and its relationship with production and society. Naming one subject *Polytechnik*, as in parts of West Germany, proves only that polytechnic education is not practised there.

Does that mean that progressive teachers can learn nothing from the theory of polytechnic education and from attempts to apply it in countries like China, Cuba and the Soviet Union? Does that mean that they should sit back and wait for socialism, or even work to change society in their spare time, but not relate this to their profession? These are the questions we shall examine in the final chapter.

7.
A Revolutionary Ferment

In this final chapter we shall summarise our main findings and examine some implications for the educational practice of progressive parents, teachers, youth workers and other educators. To avoid abstraction, we shall describe two models which have made important steps towards applying polytechnic principles in capitalist countries: the Tvind schools in Denmark and the Freinet movement in France.

1. Main Findings

The Theory of Polytechnic Education

New forms of education are not the product of the thoughts of great educationalists. They are a reaction to changing demands made on education by the production process and by the social and political structures of society. Education is always 'class-specific': members of different social classes receive different forms of education to fit them for their place in the production process and in social life. The transition from one mode of production to another (from feudalism to capitalism, from capitalism to socialism) means changes in the educational patterns of all classes.

However, the relationship between mode of production and education is dialectical: a transition from one mode of production to another necessitates changes in education; but the new form taken by society can be consciously influenced by means of new patterns of education. Most theories which call for a new type of society emphasise the importance of education in changing consciousness to make people capable of transforming economic, social and political relationships. The foremost principle of education for social transformation is that it must help people to understand the world they live in. This refers to the natural world – the material conditions and scientific laws which form the basis of production – and to the social world – the economic, social and political structures of society. Conversely, conservative education means preventing people from understanding the world, either by denying them education, or by training them as narrow specialists whose knowledge is restricted to their immediate field of work.

We have seen how the principles of polytechnic education developed by socialist thinkers in the nineteenth century were foreshadowed by the discussions on the need for mass education resulting from the social crisis which marked the breakdown of feudal society. Two traditions emerged from these discussions. One – first found in More's *Utopia* – advocated education linked with productive work as a means of securing efficient production and distribution and maintaining social order within a 'meritocracy' in which wise rulers make the decisions. The other – epitomised by the ideas of Winstanley – viewed education as a vital political instrument of working people.

This same dichotomy between theories which decide what is good for the masses and theories which aim at making workers the subjects of the learning process is to be found once more when looking at the next main turning point in the development of society and of educational theory: the industrial revolution. Owen's New Lanark schools were an enormous step forward in the practice of mass education. For the first time, working-class children received a high level of general education designed to make them understand the real mechanisms of the natural and social world. In addition, Owen made an extremely important contribution towards working out the new teaching methods necessary for the liberation of education. He understood that learning-by-rote and teaching according to rigid curricula suppress children's natural curiosity and creativity. Owen introduced methods based on the free development of children's interests and abilities. But his educational ideas remained paternalistic for all that. Parents, teachers and children were not permitted to take an active part in planning and running the schools: only the wise educationalist (Owen himself) was competent in such matters.

Marx regarded Owen's schools as an important model for education in an industrial society, but dismissed his utopian ideas on changing society. Marx showed that only conscious action by the working class could supercede capitalist exploitation and bring about socialism. Education had a vital role to play, both in the struggle against capitalism and in the construction of a new society. Marx's theory of polytechnic education has two main foundations. The first is his aim of overcoming the extreme form of division of labour which alienates work from real human needs and abilities: the historical division between mental and manual labour is the chief basis of class domination. Hence the task of education in the struggle for liberation is that of creating the conditions for overcoming this distinction. The second foundation is Marx's analysis of the forces of production. He shows how modern technology has the potential of providing the material basis for the liberation of workers from the drudgery of over-specialised, degrading and monotonous work. These two factors led Marx to formulate a new aim for education: the totally-developed individual, a person with a full practical and theoretical grasp of the technology of production, and of the economic, social and political relationships which correspond to this. Clearly, the achievement of these aims is above all a question of political struggle. But Marx regards the fight for a new type of education as a vital part of working-class politics. That is why he refers to polytechnic education as a 'revolutionary ferment' for capitalist society.

What are the principles of education aimed at producing totally-developed individuals? To start with, it is necessary to overcome the gulf between school and the real problems of economic and social life. The most important way of doing this is to combine learning with productive work. Taking part in socially necessary production from an early age would help children to understand the real basis of society. A further principle is that all children should receive a high level of general education designed to make them understand the scientific foundations of the production process and the mechanisms which determine economic and social life. This is political education, in the sense that it is meant to prepare all workers to take an active part in planning and decision-making. In addition everybody should have a broadly-based vocational training which qualifies them for various types of work, so that they can no longer become the victims of unpredictable changes in production methods. Physical development is a further essential aspect of the totally-developed individual: gymnastics, sports and participation in manual work prevent one-sided mental development. Taken to its logical conclusion polytechnic education means overcoming the division between a period of life in which learning is the main occupation, and a subsequent period in which work is the main activity. People should learn and work all their lives. And since children would learn through work, all adult workers would become educators. That does not mean that there would be no place for schools and teachers in socialist society. Schools would still have the vital role of organising the work processes through which children learn; they would be places for exchanging experience and for systematic theoretical work on the problems which children encounter in society.

Marx mapped out the principles for a polytechnic education system, but said nothing about the teaching methods and the forms of school organisation necessary to realise his aims. It was in this field that Krupskaya made her main theoretical contribution. Krupskaya was not only a revolutionary, but also a teacher with a deep understanding of the way children think and learn. She studied the most progressive bourgeois teaching methods, and adapted them for use in socialist education based on marxist principles. She showed how vital it is to get away from abstract, rigid subject teaching. Socialist teachers must start by understanding their own position in society, and studying the living conditions and the social and economic situation of the children. This knowledge is the precondition for helping children to find forms of work and study which correspond with their real needs and interests. Grown-ups, whose horizon is restricted by their own rigid education and by the stupefying division of labour in capitalism, are not competent to dictate to children what they need to know, and what political and ethical characteristics they require. Krupskaya demanded the abolition of rigid curricula and their replacement with 'complex' or 'project' methods which examined all aspects of a particular problem, rather than dividing up reality into the neat compartments of academic disciplines. The children were to become the subject of the education process so that they would later be capable of becoming the subjects of social transformation.

Education in Transitional Societies

After the Russian revolution the bolsheviks attempted to create a polytechnic education system as envisaged by Marx. Lenin emphasised the importance of a cultural revolution as a precondition for building socialism in a backward country. Krupskaya took a leading part in planning the new education system. The policy pursued by the People's Commissariat for Education between 1917 and 1931 concentrated on linking learning with productive work and on guaranteeing a high level of general education for all children. But there was considerable controversy about these aims: many bolsheviks argued that the material backwardness of the country and the urgency of developing the forces of production made it vital to rapidly train large numbers of specialists using 'monotechnic' methods. Lenin, Krupskaya, and Lunacharsky (the Commissar for Education), regarded it as more important to fit people to run society consciously through polytechnic education. However, by the end of the 1920s they had only been able to achieve their aims to a very limited extent. Lack of schools, equipment and teachers, as well as disputes on the aims of education, meant that a high level of polytechnic education for all children was never achieved. But great advances were made in some schools and experimental projects, so that it is possible to get an idea of what polytechnic education could really be like under socialism.

The victory of the stalinist bureaucracy put a stop to all such efforts. Stalin had no use for totally-developed individuals; he needed large numbers of skilled workers and technicians, trained to unquestioning conformity. The re-introduction of the rigid and abstract methods of traditional schooling was the best way of achieving this aim. Even where productive work and collective education continued, as in Makareno's Dzerzhinsky Commune, strict discipline, authoritarian hierarchies and division of labour ensured that the young workers did not learn to fight for their own interests.

However by the 1950s the gulf between soviet education and the problems of work and social life was becoming a serious problem. After Stalin's death Khrushchev launched an attack on the education system, and called for the re-introduction of polytechnic principles. This led to important changes in education throughout the Soviet bloc. We examined the new tendencies in the case of the German Democratic Republic, which may be regarded as representative for other East European countries. In 1958 the ruling SED proclaimed the aim of constructing a system of polytechnic education based on marxist principles and designed to produce 'socialist personalities'. The underlying reason for this change in policy was economic difficulties: first, the old system of rigid centralised planning was an obstacle to further growth; second, competition with the capitalist system made the introduction of advanced technologies vital. Both these factors demanded new skills from workers: a higher level of technical training, greater flexibility, the ability to work without continual supervision – these were the new requirements which shaped educational policies.

Closer examination showed that 'polytechnic education' in the GDR is limited to the linking of learning with productive work, and to giving everybody a high level of general education and vocational training. No attempt is made to use education as a lever to overcome the distinction between manual and mental work. Nor is political education aimed at developing the abilities necessary for workers' control. Instead we find a form of moral education designed to guarantee political conformity and obedience to the orders of the ruling party. Again, we meet up with the problem of teaching methods: rigid curricula, systematic subject-learning and the commanding role of the teacher are basic principles of education in the GDR. They are just not compatible with the marxist concept of polytechnic education. The official concept of 'socialist personality' is an ideological veil for the real aim of education in the GDR: the well-trained, flexible, obedient wage worker.

In China, there has been even more emphasis on education as a means of changing society than in the Soviet Union and Eastern Europe. The Chinese Communists gained power through a long drawn-out guerilla war, which could only be won by educating the peasants to take an active and conscious part in the struggle for liberation. The 'Yenan Spirit' – based on principles of self-reliance, improvisation and the leading role of political consciousness – was firmly established before the CCP came to power in 1949. Mao Tse-tung tried to revive this tradition during the period of the Great Leap Forward (1958–60). Faced with the problem of building socialism in an extremely backward peasant society, Mao argued that political consciousness and mass initiative could compensate for lack of capital, modern technology and trained specialists. This has been one of the main issues in the 'struggle between two roads' which has shaped Chinese politics since 1949. The group led by Liu Shao-chi, which had the upper hand in the early 1960s, regarded mass education and political consciousness as secondary factors in development strategy. Their main priorities were the training of highly qualified specialists, import of modern technology, efficient centralised planning and material incentives.

The cultural revolution of 1966 was a new attempt by the Maoists to make revolutionary consciousness the leading factor of economic and social development. Proletarian culture was to transform every sector of society. Criticism and re-education of bourgeois specialists was to remove obstacles to Mao's policy of basing development on mass initiative. But the cultural revolution was quickly stopped, because it looked like turning into a genuine workers' revolution against the ruling CCP bureaucracy. Nevertheless, the cultural revolution did have profound effects on education. Important principles of polytechnic education like linking learning with productive work were implemented. But one vital factor was missing: political education designed to make working people the real masters of production and society. Instead, Chinese children were subjected to continual indoctrination with moral principles calculated to make them loyal and efficient tools of the party and state bureaucracy. Similarly, teaching methods were rigid and teacher-centred. Since 1976 the new CCP leadership has repudiated most of the changes brought about by the cultural revolution and a return to stalinist methods is taking place, both in economic and educational strategies.

New Trends in Capitalist Education

Finally, we looked at attempts to link learning with productive work in capitalist education systems, in particular at *Arbeitslehre/ Polytechnik* in the German Federal Republic. The basic cause for the introduction of this new subject is current technological changes in the production process, which make qualities like flexibility and mobility vital for workers. The old abstract form of general education, and the highly specialised forms of vocational training no longer meet the interests of capital. A further cause for such educational innovations is the political crisis of the last decade, which has made educational reforms which promise greater equality of opportunity necessary for securing political stability.

Although some of the curricula and teaching projects for the new subject actually refer to the marxist theory of polytechnic education and claim to serve the interests of working people, our analysis shows that the real purpose of *Arbeitslehre/Polytechnik* is technocratic integration of workers. There is a striking similarity between the sort of character aimed at by *Arbeitslehre/Polytechnik* plans, and the GDR concept of 'socialist personality'. However, educational reforms in West Germany, and *Arbeitslehre/Polytechnik* in particular have been responses to the critique of West German society made by the student movement of the late 1960s. Many of the young people who received their political socialisation in this movement have become teachers and have tried to carry out real changes in order to make school serve the interests of working-class children. One way of doing this has been the attempt to carry out *Arbeitslehre/Polytechnik* projects which reveal the real class antagonisms underlying the production process. As we have seen, the West German state has made great efforts to suppress subversive activities of this kind.

The Relevance of Polytechnic Education

Nowhere in the world is there an education system that realises the principles of polytechnic education as propounded by Marx and Krupskaya. There have been and continue to be attempts to develop this form of education in transitional societies, but they have all failed or stopped half-way. The reasons for this have been connected on the one hand with the economic and cultural backwardness of the countries concerned, on the other hand with the political interests of the new bureaucratic ruling classes, who have no use for workers capable of running production and society. Attempts to link learning with productive work in capitalist school systems can only be very restricted in scope: employers and state have no interest in subversive education.

So why is polytechnic education relevant for socialist parents, teachers, social workers, etc? We argue that the attempt to introduce polytechnic principles and methods in educational work can be a 'revolutionary ferment' in capitalist society, as Marx put it. Even though such attempts can only be partially successful, they may still make an important contribution to the struggle against capitalist exploitation and for a new form of society. To illustrate this let us look at two models which exemplify the potential of polytechnic education in capitalist countries.

2. The Tvind Schools

The Tvind Schools in Denmark were started up in 1970 by a group of teachers who were dissatisfied with the abstraction and irrelevance of teaching in the state school system. Tvind runs general courses for young people, a teachers' training seminar and a school for 14- to 18-year-olds. The quickest way of grasping the special character of the Tvind schools is to look at a plan of the main complex in Ulfborg, West Jutland (see p. 176). Here we see not only school buildings and living accommodation, but also a motor workshop, a building depot, a farm with barns and livestock houses, greenhouses and meeting halls. Most surprising is a huge propeller – Europe's largest wind power station, and if we looked more closely we would find solar energy collectors, bio-gas installations and many similar objects. When we realise that virtually everything has been designed and constructed by the students and teachers, then we understand one of the main principles of Tvind: learning is based on necessary, productive work.

The self-sufficiency of the schools does not mean that they form an inward-looking educational island. They are a base from which students go out and study work and life in Denmark and in other countries. A lot of time, effort and finance at Tvind goes into providing transport and making journeys of exploration. 'In the Tvind schools, the classrooms are buses and ships. The group rooms are animal houses and workshops and the place of learning is the world.'[1] The function of the school buildings is to serve as a place for comparing, exchanging and systemising experience. The students make their reports here and discuss them with the teachers. Theoretical work arising from outside experience can be organised and carried out here. We will look briefly at three main sectors of the Tvind schools.

The Travelling High School

Transport plays a particularly important part in the 'travelling high school' which was Tvind's first project. A typical nine month course includes four months bus travel through Asia. The course begins with a two month preparatory period. The participants meet and are divided up into groups of ten, with one teacher. They discuss what they want to do and how to organise and finance the

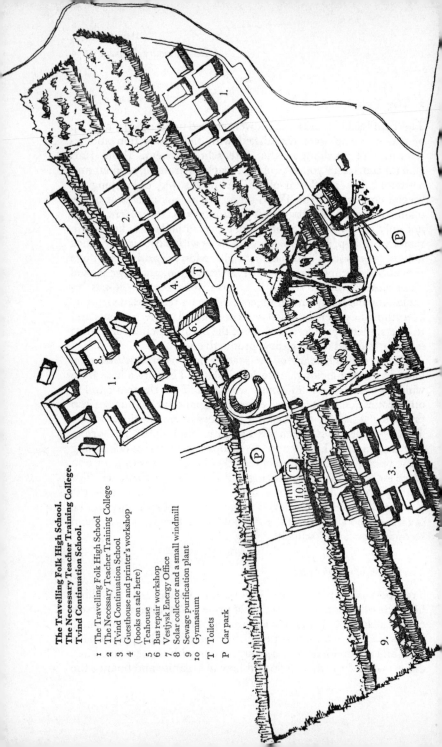

The Travelling Folk High School.
The Necessary Teacher Training College.
Tvind Continuation School.

1 The Travelling Folk High School
2 The Necessary Teacher Training College
3 Tvind Continuation School
4 Guesthouse and printer's workshop
   (books on sale here)
5 Teahouse
6 Bus repair workshop
7 Vestjysk Energy Office
8 Solar collector and a small windmill
9 Sewage purification plant
10 Gymnasium

T Toilets

P Car park

project. In Denmark, everybody has a right to study at a 'people's high school'. The grants available for this cover part of the costs of Tvind course for the period spent in Denmark, but they do not meet the expenses of travel abroad. Students therefore have to raise a certain amount of money before starting a course. The students buy an old bus which they overhaul and fit out for living and learning. Since no professional mechanics are employed, this means that students have to learn technical skills. Some take the driving test for public service vehicles. At the same time, the students read about the countries which they wish to visit, practise the languages (mainly English, in the case of Asia), and work out a research programme. The main emphasis is on understanding the problems of the third world and the history and structure of imperialism. On the journey the following topics might be examined: a Turkish village; the position of women in Afghanistan; Islam; land reform; class barriers in Pakistan; the relationship of Turkey to the European Community; the peasants' movement in India; education in India; Zionism. The method is always to learn not only through books but through observation: by talking to people, visiting their homes, observing work and daily life, carrying out interviews with officials and ordinary people. Sometimes students split up to do different things, like living with Indian building workers for a few weeks, and then report the findings to each other.

Upon returning to Denmark, the participants of the various bus-groups (there might be 10 at one time) discuss what they have learnt and pass on results to each other. They also go out and report their findings to interested groups, like trade-union branches. Usually, students find that seeing undeveloped countries leads to a wealth of questions about their own society and its relationship with the third world. They therefore do a two week political economy course and then split up to study one of the following topics: working conditions of manual workers; trade unions; vocational training; the history of revolutions; public services; housing policies. After the nine months course there is an option of continuing for another eight months. The first five are spent living in small groups in various Danish towns and working in factories. Students and teachers meet twice a week to discuss what they learn about the working and living conditions of the population. They also talk about their own future occupations. The last three months are spent at Tvind, where theoretical analysis and re-

flection is possible. Throughout the course, Tvind students organise their own daily life, looking after the household, cooking,
cleaning, etc. Their factory work helps to pay their expenses.

The Necessary Seminar

The course of the 'necessary seminar' (the teachers training
course) lasts four years, and starts in much the same way as the
'travelling high school' with a journey to Asia, Africa or Latin
America. This is called the 'international field of practice'. It is
followed by the 'national field of practice', which starts with three
months of factory work to earn money for the down payments on
houses in various towns. Here the students live in groups of eight to
twelve, together with a teacher. The next nine months are spent
working in factories. In the evenings the students discuss what they
learn at work, and study wage systems, labour law, class structure
and the situation of working people. They take part in the political
and social life of the town, learning about housing problems, town
planning and local government. Then comes the 'school field of
practice' which lasts two years: the students remain in the town
where they have been working. They spend the mornings as
teaching assistants in local schools, and the afternoons studying the
subjects required for qualification as teachers. Their practical experience helps them to learn quickly and critically. Although
Tvind students spend only two years studying the required subjects, compared with four years theoretical work in normal teachers
training colleges, they have proved highly successful in the state
teachers' exams. Of the 90 who started the first course, only 10
dropped out. The rest passed the exams in 1976 with above-
average marks. Clearly, an important factor is the tolerance of the
Danish education authorities for such experiments. They have not
only recognised the 'necessary seminar', but even helped to finance
it, in accordance with a law that requires the state to meet 85 per
cent of the costs of private schools, providing that a need can be
shown for them. Teachers trained at Tvind are much sought after
in state schools.

The Efterskole

The *efterskole* is a secondary school for young people aged fourteen
to eighteen. Again it has received a certain amount of state
support, probably because the authorities hope that it will provide

new methods for dealing with unemployment among school-leavers. At the beginning of the course, the pupils are divided (usually by lot) into groups of three, which are the basic learning units. These small groups are linked together in 'occupational groups' embracing nine to eighteen pupils and one teacher. These are responsible for organising and carrying out daily chores like cooking, cleaning and washing clothes. There are no classes divided up according to age: the occupational groups include pupils of varying ages. The school year is divided into four 50-day periods, and a one-month travel period. For 50 days an occupational group is responsible for one of the following tasks: printing, food preparation, motor maintenance, journalism, building work, energy technology, farming, office work. The work is not just a trick for motivating pupils – it has a serious character: nobody can travel if the motor mechanics do not repair the buses; there are no eggs if the farmers do not feed the hens; life is uncomfortable if the builders do not keep the accommodation in repair; financial chaos results if the office workers do not keep the books in order. So young people learn not only how to carry out practical work, but also the importance of each task. Each occupational group is responsible for deciding what needs doing and how to do it and they learn to organise their own working and learning processes. The printers produce the school books and works on education which have come out of the Tvind projects. The journalists are concerned with giving information to the outside world, receiving guests, etc.

About half the time is spent on practical work and half on theoretical work. As far as possible, the topics for theoretical work are derived from practice. For instance, the motor mechanics visit a motor factory and a repair workshop. This leads to questions like: why do cars wear out so quickly? To find an answer requires studying both technological and economic problems. The office workers have to improve their reading and writing abilities to do their job properly. They also learn how to organise the administration and economy of a large institution. They do the accounts, using a computer, and provide information in such a way as to allow collective decision-making. The journalists start to wonder why youth problems are dealt with so inadequately by the press, and start learning about the political economy of the mass media. The building workers learn about materials, costs, mathematics and technical draughtsmanship. However, it has been found that certain subjects and capabilities, like reading, writing, mathematics and languages, do require regular, systematic practice. So there are special learning periods called 'fixed doses'. Contact with the outside world plays a big part in the *efterskole*. The journalists follow the mass media and make regular reports on important events. The occupational groups go out and visit people who carry out similar work in everyday life. For instance, those concerned with agricultural work visit farmers, perhaps helping with the work, and learn about methods of production and their economic and historical backgrounds. The energy technicians visit factories, power stations, oil refineries. The knowledge they gain encourages them to carry out experiments in saving energy through insulation or in producing energy with sun-collectors, through bio-gas or with wind power. The travel period might consist of a visit to England which includes going down a mine and staying in the home of a miner.

At the end of every school year, pupils can take state exams for various school-leaving certificates or for technical qualifications. The collective efforts of pupils and teachers ensure that the success rate is very high.[2]

Principles and Problems

The three sectors of the Tvind schools are based on certain common principles. The first is that education has a political character. School is an important part of society and it should give children the knowledge and capabilities they need to understand reality. School must therefore deal with real things – with the problems of society and of the pupils. Teachers have to understand society and the background of the children. They must take a clear position against domination and exploitation, against nationalism and imperialism. By learning how ordinary people live and work in various countries, the teachers and pupils of Tvind take their side and try to change oppressive social relationships. One example of this is the important role played by Tvind in the ecology movement: through studying the technology and economy of energy production and use, Tvind has provided important material for the struggle against atomic power and other wasteful and dangerous technologies. This is not just a question of theoretical work: Tvind has proved the possibility of cheap decentralised power with its wind-power station, sun-collectors, and the like.[3]

The second principle is that of learning through useful productive work. Technical learning at Tvind is never a purpose in itself, but a means to an end. Working methods are learnt and work carried out because it is necessary for daily life, for travel and for meeting school expenses. This means that pupils learn to respect work, to see its importance and to understand its relevance to social relationships. A third principle is closely related to this: learning through concrete experience rather than just from books. At Tvind, young people learn through work, travel and observation. They also learn through talking to people of all kinds about their life, work and problems. This direct experience helps people to realise the need for systematic theoretical study, which therefore takes on a new relevance.

Fourth, pupils learn to work and to solve problems collectively. Competitiveness is reduced with the realisation that an objective can only be achieved through the ideas and efforts of all participants. Solidarity is regarded as the best precondition for the development of the individual personality. This is only possible if everybody takes part in planning and decision-making. The work groups decide on their own methods and objectives. In the event of difficulties, general assemblies are held. Decisions are not made by majority votes, but by discussing a matter until everybody agrees on a solution, however long that may take – one assembly actually lasted five days before general agreement was reached.

Fifth, knowledge should not be collected for its own sake, but because it is useful to pupils in their present and future situation. Knowledge should be passed on to other people and made into a tool for improving society.

All in all, the Tvind schools have shown that it is possible to achieve many principles of polytechnic education within capitalism. Of course, the Tvind model has certain limitations and problems. To start with it is a boarding school, which means that some of its methods are inappropriate to normal day schools. Second, outside pressure has led to certain restrictive rules which are hard to reconcile with free education: for instance, sexual relationships, drinking alcohol and taking any sorts of drugs are forbidden. Transgressions have led to expulsions, although these have been decided upon by general assemblies and not by the teachers alone. Anyone wanting to learn from Tvind must look closely at this kind of problem. A further question is the extent to which the success of Tvind depends on special conditions in

Denmark. It is highly unlikely that the West German or the British states would be willing to follow the example of the Danish authorities in recognising and subsidising the Tvind schools, and even paying some of the teachers' salaries. Tvind has also received considerable support from the labour movement. In 1976, a second *efterskole* was set up with support from the SID (a trade union for unskilled workers). One third of the pupils are to come from the families of SID members, and there is to be close co-operation between pupils, teachers, parents and other SID members.

3. The Freinet Movement

Unlike Tvind which is concerned mainly with young adults and the last years before leaving school, Freinet teaching techniques are used mainly with younger children. The movement's name derives from its founder, Célestin Freinet (1896–1966), who started developing the methods of the *école moderne* (modern school) in a little village school in the 1920s. Today, Freinet methods are used by 25,000 teachers in France and by thousands more in other countries, mainly in primary schools but also in grammar, comprehensive and educationally sub-normal schools, and in youth work. The Freinet methods are not the product of educational theorists or of state planners, but of rank and file teachers. They have sought ways of escaping from the abstraction and pointlessness of traditional school learning, which make it a torture for both pupils and teachers. Freinet teaching (despite the fact that it bears the name of its first exponent) is the collective product of many teachers, who have set up organisations to co-ordinate their work and to produce the special material which is so vital for transforming the school.[4]

The classroom of a Freinet teacher looks more like a workshop than the classroom of a normal school: it is full of working material, tools, machines, models, pictures and all sorts of natural objects used for biology teaching. Usually, a hand printing press takes a prominent position. Seats and desks are not in rows facing the teacher's dais – in fact there is no dais, and the desks are probably used to support apparatus for experiments. The seats are grouped around whatever objects are being worked upon by the children. And this varies considerably – the class is split up into groups, doing quite different tasks. At the same time some children may be working completely on their own, using work sheets. The teacher goes from group to group, helping and giving advice as required.

'Free Texts', Printing and 'Free Expression'

Writing is just a big drag for many school children – especially for those from working-class homes. It has no useful function for them, it is not a form of communication. They do it because the teacher forces them to write what s/he requires of them, and know that nobody else will read it. In Freinet classes, children do not have to write essays or dictations; they write what and when they want – 'free texts'. They describe their experiences, their feelings, their dreams – what is important to them, not to the grown-ups. And why do they write? Because it is a means to an end – communication. The children print their texts on the little hand presses devised by Freinet, and produced by the *Cooperative de l'Enseignement Laic* (Co-operative for Lay Education). The texts are read by the class, discussed and published in the class newspaper, which is sold outside school to parents, neighbours and friends. Or they are sent to another school class: most Freinet classes correspond regularly with another class, usually in quite a different area. For instance, a class in a fishing village in Brittany might correspond with a class in Paris. The children have a thousand things to ask and tell each other: about their parents' work, the way they live, about differences between town and country. Through free texts, children learn to read and write correctly – the teacher and other children help in correcting a text before it is printed. In addition, the free texts have other important functions: the teacher learns a lot about his pupils, their problems, what they know and what they think. Pupils learn to express themselves and lose their fear of the written word. The 'free text', printing, the class newspaper and correspondence help to make the children the subject of their own education. They are the first steps on the way to creativity.

Some teachers outside France who have taken up Freinet teaching have had a tendency to concentrate only on printing. The press is attractive, easy to use, and great fun for the children. But if printing is the only new technique introduced it will eventually become boring. Freinet methods include many other forms of free expression; free painting plays an important part: in many Freinet classes paper and paints are always readily available, and children may use them whenever they feel like it. Linoleum printing and the use of a machine known as the limograph (a sort of simple duplicator) allow the illustration of class newspapers. In some classes children take and develop photographs and make cine films, although this is restricted by the high costs involved. Musical instruments are available and the children are encouraged to compose their own tunes and texts. Dancing, theatre and artistic work with all sorts of materials play an important part in Freinet teaching. By creating their own art, children gain a new relationship to culture. It becomes possible for them to appreciate and criticise what they see on school visits to theatres, art galleries and museums, for they understand the conditions of their production.[5]

Practical Work and Experiments

In the traditional school nearly all learning takes place through verbalisation – by means of the written and spoken word. Manual abilities are regarded as inferior; they are eliminated from normal classes and restricted to a few woodwork or domestic science lessons. This corresponds with the division between mental and manual work in society, and the domination of hand workers by brain workers. Teaching through verbalisation helps maintain class privilege, for middle-class socialisation, due to the parents' work situation, is always more orientated towards verbal communication than that of the working class. Freinet teachers do not divide between practical work and intellectual learning: the questions and curiosity of the children lead continually to construction projects, experiments and practical tasks. These in turn raise problems which make it necessary to learn intellectual capabilities and to examine theoretical questions.

A Freinet classroom is full of tools and working material. Since Freinet classes do not get more money than other classes, such material has to be obtained through the joint efforts of teacher, children and parents. This is not a bad but a good thing, for it gives children a new relationship to consumption and, often, a new form of self-reliance. This is what Freinet meant when he wrote: 'It is a question of transforming our whole educational system from the material basis'.[6] The introduction of the objects of everyday life as teaching material makes a new form and content of learning possible.[7]

Children carry out experiments with electricity, look at plants and insects under the microscope, make useful objects, toys or technical models. Their daily experience provides the topics for their research: a boy has helped his father repair the car – how does a car-motor work? Children have seen a demonstration against a nuclear power station – how can energy be produced, what is it needed for? To carry out their projects, children have to weigh, measure, calculate, write down results, read instructions – they learn these intellectual techniques because they are useful and necessary, and therefore they learn more quickly and easily than children for whom these things are an abstract compulsion. This is all possible because Freinet teachers work together and exchange results. When children have a problem, the teacher can help them to find a practical solution by using the index of experiments, building instructions, etc., compiled over the years by teachers and children using Freinet methods, and printed and distributed by the *Cooperative de l'Enseignement Laic* (CEL).

Individual Learning with Work Sheets and Brochures

Children in Freinet classes have to meet the same learning targets and to take the same examinations as other children. This makes the systematisation of the knowledge they gain through printing, free expression and experimentation a necessity. The teachers prepare a collection of 'work sheets for self-correction' (*fichiers auto-correctifs*) for various subjects like spelling, grammar, arithmetic. Children work individually with these sheets as and when they want to, but they must go through a certain number within a given period. The sheets are so designed that pupils can see for themselves whether they have mastered the topic. If not they continue to practise. When they have reached the necessary proficiency in one they can go on to the next.

A further teaching aid is the 'working library' (*bibliothèque de travail*), which consists of over nine hundred brochures about a wide range of subjects. These have been compiled over the years by Freinet teachers and can be ordered as required. Most classes have several hundred brochures. When a pupil is interested in a particular topic, the teacher recommends the appropriate brochure. For instance, a pupil who has visited Verdun with his parents wants to know more about the first world war. Another has seen a film on Mexico on television and seeks further information. A third has visited the zoo and wants to know more about monkeys.[8] After reading the brochure, a pupil may give the whole class or an interested group a talk on the matter.

In addition, teachers and pupils collect newspaper articles, pictures, and other interesting documents on various subjects. These can be used as a source of information whenever required. In a similar way, reports on visits or experiments carried out by the class are kept in albums which can be consulted whenever the topic comes up again. Freinet classes may have normal school books in their libraries, but they do not use them in the normal way – all children doing the same lessons from the same book – for this stultifies curiosity and takes no account of varying interests and ways of learning.

Excursions

One aim of Freinet teachers is to abolish the isolation of the school from the rest of society and, in particular, to introduce children to the world of work. Teachers and pupils regularly leave the school to visit local farmers, artisans, factories or building sites. They interview people about their work and the way they live. These excursions are also used to learn about nature by looking at plants and animals. The curiosity and interest of the children is aroused and problems found for further study at school. Correspondence with other classes, as mentioned above, often has a similar function.

The Organisation of Work

A Freinet classroom is a busy place, and children have lots of choice as to what activities to carry out any one time. Planning and organisation is necessary to prevent chaos and to make sure that all children meet the educational targets. Certain formal rules are necessary. These are made, developed, and changed as need arises, through discussions within the class. A typical rule is that once a group of children have started a task they must finish it before starting another. Other rules prohibit children from disturbing each other while working, and the like.[9] Regular class meetings play a vital part in the life of the Freinet school.

Each Monday the class discusses what is to be done during the coming week and makes a large poster listing the tasks. At the end of each school day the class members report to each other on the findings of the day's work. Printed texts are given out and discussed. At the end of the week all important problems which have arisen are dealt with. Often a large poster is hung on the wall and children write down complaints, conflicts with other pupils, criticism of the teacher, and so on, as they occur. This poster is then discussed at the final meeting of the week and solutions sought for the problems which have arisen. Teachers try to avoid dominating these meetings. One method is for the class to elect pupils to carry out various tasks, like chairing the meeting, writing down decisions, or acting as class treasurer. Other jobs are also done in rotation: cleaning the board, writing a poster with tasks to be done, etc.

Planning is based on work plans for certain periods: the teacher prepares a work plan for the whole year, laying down roughly what each child needs to learn to meet official requirements, and breaks this down into plans for each month. These give the children an idea of what and how much they need to do in this period. This is the basis for the individual work plans which each child makes at the beginning of the week.[10] A pupil might, for instance, decide to carry out two experiments, print a text, work through four maths work sheets and hold a talk.[11] The teacher and other pupils help to make sure that the plan is realistic. Once the pupil has decided on his plan, it is compulsory to carry it out. Self-discipline is thus demanded of the children. The whole class decides upon weekly or daily plans for certain joint actions, like an excursion, or discusses when group work is to be done and at what times the whole class is to work together. In this type of planning the principle is once again to make the children the subjects of the education process. Joint planning and discussion makes the life of the class 'the personal concern of every child. The school becomes his school, and that is indeed already a first decisive success.'[12]

The Freinet Movement

The educational principles of the Freinet teachers are not particularly new – readers will recognise many of the principles of polytechnic education as proposed by Marx and applied in various ways in the Soviet Union and China. What is important about the Freinet methods is that they are actually applied by thousands of teachers in ordinary state school classes. Our brief description is of necessity superficial: of course there are problems and conflicts in Freinet classes. Overcrowding, the stress of marks and exams, language difficulties of immigrant children – these are daily reality for Freinet teachers, just as they are for their colleagues. But 50 years of experience have proved that the Freinet methods can transform the school situation. Nor do the new methods require a super-competent and dedicated teacher. It is more difficult for a teacher to maintain discipline and motivation in a class where children are forced to carry out completely useless rituals, than in a class where children learn through useful and fascinating work. Children in Freinet classes do at least as well in state exams as other children, and what they learn in addition is quite immeasurable.

No individual teacher could transform his or her school class in the face of sceptical hostility from educational bureaucrats and traditionally minded colleagues and parents. Freinet teachers have thus joined together in 97 regional groups which meet regularly to exchange experience and discuss problems. The groups are linked nationally in the ICEM (*Institut Coopératif de l'École Moderne*), which organises an annual congress, regular working groups on special problems (sport, sexuality, mathematics, and so on), and one week training and discussion seminars for teachers. Teaching material and publications are produced and distributed by the CEL.[13] All organs are democratically run and controlled by the teachers themselves. On the international level, teachers from forty countries have combined in the FIMEM (*Féderation Internationale des Mouvements de l'École Moderne*), which organises regular international meetings of teachers interested in Freinet methods.

A movement concerned with the transformation of mass education cannot be unpolitical. Freinet himself met with opposition from privileged groups from the outset. He wanted to make education serve the interests of workers and peasants, and saw that this could not be divorced from political and economic questions. In the village where he taught his first class, he helped the peasants to organise production and marketing co-operatives. A few years later, after moving to another village, he was attacked by right-wing extremists led by the local big landowners. Freinet was forced to defend his school with a revolver, backed by supporters armed with iron bars. He got the sack, and had to set up a private school to continue his work. The rise of the popular front in the mid-1930s led to an upsurge of interest in progressive education:

the Freinet movement soon numbered 1,500 teachers. In revolutionary Spain, Freinet's methods were introduced in elementary schools in Aragon and Catalonia.[14] The fascist Vichy government put Freinet in a concentration camp. Upon release he became a leader of the resistance in the Briançon area.

After the War, the Freinet movement grew once again, but by the mid-1960s it was showing tendencies towards stagnation and bureaucratisation. Then the movement of May 1968 led to an upsurge of interest in the problems of working-class education. The new left rediscovered Freinet. Thousands of teachers joined the movement and reintroduced democratic structures. The 'Charter of the Modern School', adopted at a conference in Pau in 1968, was a clear statement of the political aims of education.[15] 'We reject the illusion of an education which is an end in itself, and which stands outside the great social and political currents, which are its preconditions', stated the charter. It also declared that: 'The school of tomorrow will be the school of work'. Freinet teachers regard their work as part of the struggle for a juster and better society, and side with the working class in this struggle. The 1973 Congress of Freinet teachers reiterated this point of view:

> The educational struggle of our movement for an authentic culture of the people is related to the economic, social and political struggles. We can only partially achieve Freinet education in this society, which is based on exploitation and profit.[16]

Freinet teachers come very close, perhaps as close as is possible in a capitalist society, to using polytechnic educational methods in their daily work. It is their clear intention to make education a revolutionary ferment for capitalist society. As Jean-Claude Girardin says of Freinet teaching: 'It can be characterised quite simply as the education of transition.'[17]

4. Working Subversively in Capitalist Schools

What Can We Learn from Tvind and Freinet?

The real value of these models for progressive educators is that they demonstrate ways of introducing some of the principles of polytechnic education in a modern capitalist society. Of course both the Tvind schools and Freinet methods have their limitations. The Tvind schools are not part of the state education system. They

G

are run privately by progressive teachers. Moreover they are boarding schools. Both these factors make it difficult to apply their methods in normal schools. The tolerant educational policy of the Danish Government is another special factor. Teachers who have tried to introduce the methods of Tvind in the repressive atmosphere of West Germany have met with almost insurmountable obstacles.

Freinet methods, on the other hand, are the work of ordinary teachers in state schools. But Freinet teachers have rarely managed to bring real productive work into the school. Children learn through work, but it is not part of the social production process. The political character of Freinet teaching is not always clear, even though the need for teachers to take a stand against exploitation and repression is emphasised in theory. There is a danger that some teachers may simply regard attractive methods, like the printing presses, as useful techniques for arousing children's interest, and forget the basic aim of helping children to become aware of the real problems of society.

Despite these quibbles, we think that the Tvind schools and the Freinet teachers have made great advances, and that there is a lot to be learnt from them. People concerned with higher education, adult education, and youth work are more likely to be able to learn from Tvind. School teachers are more likely to find useful ideas in the Freinet methods.

Reform and Subversion

Reforms in the state education systems of capitalist countries give socialist educators (by which we mean parents, teachers, youth workers and everybody concerned with education) the chance of working for real changes in the form and content of learning. The ruling class does not carry out reforms because it wants working-class children to understand production and society better. On the contrary – it would like to keep them ignorant. But, as we have tried to show in the case of the German Federal Republic, technological changes in the production process and problems of maintaining political legitimacy force the capitalist state to accept changes in education. The real aim of such changes is more effective integration, control and manipulation of the working population, but representatives of the state claim that the goal of educational reform is increasing equality of opportunity. This contradiction between the real and the declared aim of capitalist educational reforms give progressive educators the chance of working within the system, exposing the structures of class privilege, and demanding changes which really serve the interests of working-class children. To achieve this, teachers must work together with parents and pupils, and make the struggle for better education part of the struggle against capitalist exploitation.

For reasons which we described in chapter 6 it is becoming increasingly necessary to link learning with productive work. This gives socialists the opportunity of fighting for polytechnic education. Clearly, this can only be partially achieved in capitalism, but every step in the right direction helps to create the political awareness necessary for changing society. And even the defeats can help to raise the consciousness of pupils and educators, and make them understand the real nature of education in the present form of society. In this struggle, we can learn a lot from attempts to introduce polytechnic education in countries like the Soviet Union and China, even if we do not think that they are socialist countries, or that they have realised the marxist principles of education.

Principles for Changing Education

There is no general blueprint for transforming education. The correct way of going about this task depends on varying local conditions, and on the needs and interests of pupils, parents and teachers, youth workers, etc., is to analyse their own social position. and how to go about it. But to conclude, here are a few ideas which may prove useful in working out strategies.

1. The starting point for education must be the real situation and interests of pupils, teachers and parents. The first task of teachers, youth workers, etc., is to analyse their own social position. Teachers have a contradictory role in society. On the one hand they are servants of the capitalist state. As such they have the task of implementing policies designed to prevent working people becoming aware of their situation and changing it. On the other hand teachers are wage-earners who have an interest in struggling against exploitation and for a better form of society. When teachers try to bring this interest into their professional work they run up against a disciplinary system designed to make them loyal instruments of the state. Teachers have to decide where they stand and

work out political and trade union strategies to fight for their own interests as wage workers.

2. The second task of teachers and other educators is to study the living conditions of pupils, the work situation of parents, the structure of the neighbourhood and the problems of the community. These factors help to determine the way a teacher works with children, the choice of content matter, the material and methods to be used.

3. If a teacher really wants his or her professional work to help change society, the worst way of going about it is to try to indoctrinate children with the ideas of a particular party, however right it may be. Constant moral lessons are just as bad. The main aim of education for transformation must be that of helping children to understand the material and social world around them. Children should not be educated for the future, but so as to be able to organise their own lives collectively here and now. If children learn to recognise their needs and interests, and to find their own ways of working to realise them, then they will be well prepared for fighting for a share in controlling production and society as grown-ups.

4. The aims and methods of teaching are closely connected. Rigid and abstract teaching methods cannot fit children for running their own lives, however correct the contents of the subjects taught. Education for transformation means that children become the subjects of the learning process and not its passive objects. Learning takes on the character of a collectively determined research process, based on children's needs and interests. The function of the teacher is to help children to organise their work and research.

5. Parents and other working people must be brought into education. A lot of progressive teachers regard parents as reactionary – a stumbling block for the introduction of non-authoritarian methods. But one does children no favour by forcing them into a permanent conflict situation through different types of education at home and at school. In investigating the background of his pupils, a teacher should try to find out what special abilities various parents have, and attempt to bring these into the school. Parents can be asked to help make things the class needs for its work, or to come and tell the children about their jobs, or to take children to visit their place of work. Once productive work becomes part of education parents will more easily be able to see the

value of school and the part they can play in it. Similarly, people whose work is concerned with the school can be made conscious of their role as educators. There is no need for the janitor to be the children's worst enemy. He could be brought into the class to explain his work, and children could learn to help him. Nursery school teachers may discover that the only person who does work which is recognisable as such by smaller children is the cleaning lady. She may already be the main educator in the nursery, without knowing it. It is essential to make her a conscious part of the teaching team.

6. All educators should try to bring questions of production and of social, economic and political relationships into their work. State curricula certainly do not permit polytechnic education in the full sense, but they are rarely so rigid as to preclude all mention of productive work and class structure. This possibility exists in virtually every subject.

7. Education is not confined to school. Children learn a lot at home, in the street and in the community. But they learn in an unplanned and unreflective way. Educators should try to help children become more aware and critical of what they learn, by exchanging information and discussing information at school. Excursions, school travel and work experience schemes can help in this.

8. Educators should help children to take part in community life and local political struggles. This is only possible if the educator becomes aware of what is going on in the community and the extent to which it affects children. Activities and disputes which really concern children's interests and living conditions can be an important instrument of political education. Examples of struggles which may be relevant for children are: slum-clearance and housing schemes, traffic planning, school closures, health service restrictions, playgrounds and cultural facilities, industrial disputes (if their parents are involved).

9. New contents and forms of education cannot be worked out and introduced by a single teacher, in isolation from his or her colleagues. The task is too big for one person, the political vulnerability too great. Teachers must get together and organise themselves if they want to work for change. Teachers' co-operatives on the pattern of the Freinet movement are one possibility. Another is to try to make existing organisations like trade unions into instruments for the transformation of education.

10. One of the most important struggles in which children, parents and teachers can participate is the struggle to change school itself. If teachers get into trouble for using progressive methods, this may help to raise awareness of the class character of education. The support of pupils and parents can be crucial in preventing disciplinary measures and in pressing for teaching which corresponds to the interests of working-class children. Teachers who introduce new methods without securing the understanding and co-operation of pupils and parents will not get their support in a conflict situation. It is vital to develop and introduce new methods in co-operation with children and parents.

Appendix
The Relationship Between Form of Production, Division of Labour, Social Conditions of Workers, Skill Level, and Education

The purpose of this appendix is to make clearer the relationship between production and education. It relates mainly to chapters two, three and six, and should be read in conjunction with these. The table is concerned only with Western capitalist countries (although some aspects of the relationships described would also apply in transitional societies). Agricultural production is excluded.

The first five forms of production are based on terminology and definitions used by Marx in *Capital*. The 'first, second and third technological revolutions' are terms used by Ernest Mandel in his *Late Capitalism*. Generalisations applied to a whole historical period are always problematic. The reduction of the complexity of whole societies to a few basic concepts is inevitably superficial. It is always possible to find cases for which these generalisations are wrong. But we think that the schematic representation is useful and that it does help to make important historical relationships more easily understandable.

This is not an historical chronology. The various forms of production exist at different times in different countries and overlap in time. This applies particularly to the early forms: handicraft production, domestic industry, co-operation and manufacture all existed side by side in seventeenth century Britain, though there was a tendency towards dominance of the last form. Later the emergence of the capitalist world economy led to an international synchronisation of form of production.

1. Pre-Capitalist Handicraft Production

Form of Production/Historical Period/Technology and Energy Sources: From the late middle ages until the industrial revolution.

Work done with hand-tools and a few simple machines (e.g. smith's bellows worked by water-wheel). Energy provided mainly by muscle power of human beings and animals, some wind and water power.

Division of Labour: Each craftsman produces the whole commodity, possessing the necessary tools, materials and capabilities for a particular trade. Guilds control each craft. A long drawn-out struggle for power within the guilds usually ended in the dominance of the richer masters and reduction of upward mobility.

Social Conditions (of workers): Workers still generally own the means of production (tools and workshop). Their social position is relatively secure.

Skill Level: High skill level, as each craftsman must be capable of carrying out all tasks necessary to produce all commodities which belong to a particular craft.

Education (for workers): Virtually no general education. Highly developed vocational training system controlled by the craft guilds, which lay down conditions of entry, regulations on training and examinations. Apprenticeship generally lasted seven years (partly to exploit cheap labour). After passing the exams, workers often had to spend a period working elsewhere – hence the name journeyman.

2. Domestic Industry or 'Putting-Out' System

Form of Production, etc.: From the period of primitive accumulation until the industrial revolution (still used today in certain branches). England sixteenth to eighteenth century, Germany seventeenth to nineteenth century.

    Production technology and energy sources as in handicraft production.

Division of Labour: The capitalist orders commodities from the domestic worker and provides the necessary raw materials. The worker has his or her own workshop and tools. The finished product belongs to the capitalist, who pays the worker a piece-rate. The main advantage for the capitalist is that he can encourage new production in rural areas, where there are no guilds, forcing prices down.

Social Conditions: Many urban craftsmen are ruined by the competition of cheap commodities produced by domestic industry. Domestic workers are completely dependent on the capitalist. Isolation from one another makes any form of organisation difficult. Piece-rates are generally so low that the whole family has to work. However, many domestic workers still have some agricultural land, which somewhat reduces dependence on the capitalist.

Skill Level: Still fairly high, as the domestic worker must be capable of carrying out all operations necessary to produce a particular commodity, but is probably not able to produce all commodities which belong to a traditional guild craft. Beginning of the *historical tendency of deskilling*.

Education: Virtually no general education. Sometimes the domestic worker gets a rudimentary training from the employer. More frequently knowledge of the trade is passed on from generation to generation within the family. The formal training system of the guilds begins to break down.

3. Co-operation

Form of Production, etc: From the period of primitive accumulation until the industrial revolution, usually as a brief transitional phase to manufacture. Energy sources and technology as in handicraft production, but with a tendency to increased use of animal, wind and water power.

Division of Labour: Several workers employed in one workshop, but each worker still takes part in all work operations. The means of production (workshop, tools, materials) as well as the finished product belongs to the capitalist. The workers are paid wages.

Social Conditions: This also forces down commodity prices, to the ruin of many guild craftsmen. Workers in the workshops where co-operation is applied are completely dependent on the capitalist and have no security of employment. Forced labour in workhouses plays an important part in the development of this form of production.

Skill Level: The same as for craftsmen, as each worker must be able to carry out the whole production process.

Education: Virtually no general education. Vocational training often still within the guild system, as the workers were often ruined guild craftsmen.

4. Manufacture

Form of Production, etc: An obvious further development of co-operation from the period of primitive accumulation until the industrial revolution. Production technology and energy sources as in handicraft production, with a continuation of the tendency towards increased use of animal, wind and water power.

Division of Labour: Work is divided up within the workshop – each worker carries out only one of the operations needed to make a commodity. The advantages for the capitalist are:
1. Fewer tools needed
2. Workers become faster and more proficient through the constant repetition of one operation
3. Wages can be reduced as workers require no qualification.

Social Conditions: High degree of specialisation of work leads to the physical and mental degeneration of the workers, who are highly dependent on the capitalist. Low wages, bad working conditions, no security. Forced labour in workhouses plays a big part here too.

Skill Level: Workers no longer need craft skills. Only strength and endurance are important. *Deskilling.* Only overseers and foremen still require craft skills.

Education: Virtually no general education, except perhaps religious indoctrination in workhouse schools. Vocational training no longer necessary for workers. Overseers may receive craft training.

5. Large-Scale Industry

Form of Production, etc: The industrial revolution, from about 1760 in England, about 1830 in Germany. The new technology starts with textile working machines like the spinning jenny and the power loom. Initially, these are turned by muscle power, then by water power. Later the introduction of the steam engine as source of energy allows the working machines to unleash their full potential. The development of the new technology is possible only because of capital accumulation in the preceding forms of production.

Division of Labour: Each worker operates machinery which carries out one of the operations needed to make a commodity. The various stages of production are linked together within the factory system. The worker becomes a living appendage, a servant of the machine. Rapid increase in productivity. Competition between capitalists necessitates the optimal utilisation of machinery, leading to a very long working day.

Social Conditions: The competition of the factory system destroys other forms of production and forces hitherto independent craftsmen to become wage workers. As physical strength is no longer important, women and children are employed instead of men. Low wages, long working hours, unplanned urbanisation, very poor housing and social conditions. The working-class family virtually collapses and is incapable of bringing up children adequately.

Skill Level: Even physical strength is no longer required for most factory jobs. Obedience, discipline and 'nimble hands' are the necessary qualities. Women and very young children are employed. *Deskilling.*

Education: Most children still receive no general education, but first attempts are made to develop schools for working-class children, mainly to keep them under control: Bell and Lancaster's monitorial schools. Owen's experiments in New Lanark. Introduction of the *Volksschule* in Prussia as a compulsory form of ideological indoctrination. General education becomes an important demand of the working-class movement. Vocational training is not necessary for most workers.

6. First Technological Revolution

Form of Production, etc: From the economic crisis of 1847 until the 1890s. Steam engines and working machines are no longer produced by artisans, but by a new industry: engineering. Important developments in mining, metallurgy and chemistry. Steam power revolutionises transport – railways and steamships.

Division of Labour: The industrial form of the division of labour becomes increasingly widespread. Improvements in machinery make the intensification of work (increase in relative surplus value) more important than the lengthening of working hours (absolute surplus value).

Social Conditions: The new industries lead to differentiation within the working class. Development of new privileged strata ('labour aristocracy'): skilled workers, supervisory staff, technicians, managers, research workers. The growing labour movement, combined with bourgeois fears of destroying labour potential through appalling living conditions, lead to the first Factory Acts: restriction of working hours for women and children.

Skill Level: The emergence of new strata of skilled workers, technicians, managers, etc, leads to an increase and differentiation of occupational qualification. *Reversal of the historical tendency of deskilling.*

Education: General education becomes necessary, partly in order to qualify workers for new production processes, partly as a means of ideological control – to combat the self-education measures of the working class. Compulsory elementary education is introduced in Britain and most other industrial capitalist countries. Growth of higher education, especially science faculties. Beginnings of technical education. Vocational training for skilled workers mainly within industry.

7. Second Technological Revolution

Form of Production, etc: From the 1890s until the second world war.
    The introduction of electric and internal-combustion engines transform production and transport in all sectors. The chemical, electrical and vehicle building industries grow in size and importance.

Division of Labour: New forms of production organisation: taylorism, assembly lines, time and motion study, piece work. For a large section of the working class, work is split up into ever-shorter repetitive single operations, which are repeated endlessly. On the other hand, other sections get highly skilled jobs as technicians, machine setters, etc.

Social Conditions: Further differentiation within the working class: the new strata of skilled workers, technicians, etc., grow. Their living and working conditions improve, while other strata – unskilled workers, migrant workers – remain impoverished. The explosive growth of the capitalist system leads to economic crisis and wars, causing great misery and suffering, particularly for the working class.

Skill Level: Continuation of the tendency to increase and differentiation in skills. Further new occupations emerge with high requirements in terms of education and training.

Education: Further growth and improvement in general education. Differentiation of school types. More technical and scientific education. Growth of vocational training schemes within industry. Day release schemes combine practical training at work with theoretical training in technical colleges.

8. Third Technological Revolution

Form of Production, etc: Since the second world war. Electronic control mechanisms and electronic data processing lead to enormous changes in factories, services and administration. Electricity becomes one of the main forms of productive energy. Input of energy in production grows rapidly, encouraged by cheap oil at first, then by atomic power. It becomes evident that there are physical limits to growth. The traditional periodic economic crises are joined by a long-term ecological crisis.

Division of Labour: Automation: many jobs are eliminated by electronic-controlled machines. Not only repetitive tasks, but even complicated small-batch production can be done by programmed machine tools. The new technology also changes the character of the products (e.g. quartz watches, electronic office machines), which in turn change working conditions in other branches. Jobs which are not completely eliminated often change in character, generally requiring reduced qualification (e.g. printing).

Social Conditions: Initially, improvements in wages, living and working conditions. Material living standards are, for many workers, higher than ever before, though at the price of long-term destruction of the environment through urbanisation, traffic, air and water pollution. Capitalist-controlled mass media tend to destroy working-class culture, just as technocratic planning destroys working-class communities. Later, a tendency towards structural unemployment again reduces living standards for many workers. Perspectives for young people are poor, but state welfare projects attempt to prevent social conflicts.

Skill Level: New reversal of the historical tendency: *deskilling again predominant.* Most workers require relatively little specialised training, while a small minority of technicians, scientists, planners, etc., need a very high level of education and training: polarisation of the labour market. Non-job-specific abilities become increasingly important, for instance: mobility, flexibility, ability to work in a team, technical sensitivity.

Education: At first: improvements in general and technical education; 'educational emergency' and educational reform in West Germany. Later: reversal of this tendency, end of the educational reform, educational opportunities are closed. The new priority of the educational system is the creation of non-job-specific abilities. In addition, general education increasingly emphasises abilities and characteristics not related to production: ability to consume, to manage in a bureaucratic society, mobility, social behaviour. There is tendency to reduction of the quality and quantity of vocational training. Short training courses in industry instead of apprenticeships. Training for highly qualified workers is increasingly a task of the state.

References

1. Introduction

1 The term was not invented by Mao Tse-tung, as is sometimes supposed. As far as we can make out, it was first used by Lenin in 1923; but the concept of a cultural revolution is implicit in the whole of marxist thought.
2 Again, terms first used by Lenin, in this case in his famous speech to the youth organisations in 1920. See: Lenin, 'The tasks of the youth leagues' in *Collected Works*, vol. 31, London: Lawrence and Wishart, pp. 283–99; (also in *Selected Works*, London: Lawrence and Wishart 1909, pp. 607–20).
3 *ibid.* p. 296.
4 We shall try to show how this has happened in later chapters. We do not wish to enter the discussion of which label may be most appropriately used to designate the systems of the Soviet Union, China, etc. (e.g. revisionism, state capitalism). Readers may draw their own conclusions from the analysis.
5 Lenin, 'The achievements and difficulties of the Soviet Government', *Collected Works*, vol. 29, p. 61.
6 The terminology varies: in the 'Critique of the Gotha Programme' Marx spoke of a lower and higher stage of communism, while Lenin and most other marxists speak of socialism and communism.
7 Karl Marx, 'Critique of the Gotha Programme', in *The First International and After*, Harmondsworth: Penguin 1974, p. 346.
8 See: Lenin, *The State and Revolution*, in *Selected Works*, *op. cit.* pp. 264–351.
9 Marx, *op. cit.* p. 347.
10 Karl Marx, *Capital*, vol. 1, Harmondsworth: Penguin 1976, p. 614.
11 *ibid.* p. 619.

2. Owen and Marx: Polytechnic Education During the Ascendancy of British Industrial Capitalism

1 See: Karl Marx, *Capital*, vol. 1, Harmondsworth: Penguin 1976, part eight, for a detailed account of 'So-called primitive accumulation'.
2 Sir Thomas More, *Utopia* (translated by Paul Turner), Harmondsworth: Penguin 1977.
3 Gerrard Winstanley, 'The Law of Freedom in a Platform', in Christopher Hill (ed.), *Winstanley: The Law of Freedom and Other Writings*, Harmondsworth: Pelican Classics 1973.
4 Johne Locke, *Some Thoughts Concerning Education*, 1693. A brief summary of

Locke's ideas is to be found in John Lawson and Harold Silver, *A Social History of Education in England*, Methuen, London 1973, pp. 174–76.

5 John Bellers, *Proposals for Raising a College of Industry of All Useful Trades and Husbandry*, London 1696.

6 *Capital*, vol. 1, *op. cit.* chapters 13, 14 and 15.

7 Adam Smith, *The Wealth of Nations*, Harmondsworth: Penguin 1970, p. 110.

8 *Capital*, vol. 1, *op. cit.* p. 494.

9 *ibid.* p. 503. Marx takes pains to show that the industrial revolution was not the result of inventions, but rather that such inventions can only be applied when social and economic conditions are ripe. He gives examples for inventions made 'before their time', which were therefore suppressed, sometimes even leading to the execution of the inventor: *ibid.* pp. 553 ff.

10 *ibid.* p. 589.

11 The classic description of early industrial Britain is Friedrich Engels's *The Condition of the Working Class in England*, first published in 1845. A good contemporary description by a doctor, who was later to become the first Secretary of the Committee of the Privy Council on Education is Sir James Kay-Shuttleworth, *The Moral and Physical Condition of the Working Classes Employed in the Cotton Manufacture in Manchester*, 1832.

12 See Stephen Castles and Godula Kosack, *Immigrant Workers and Class Structure in Western Europe*, London: Oxford University Press 1973, pp. 15 ff. A century later, the Ruhr industrialists did the same, fetching their miners from Poland.

13 In Prussia, characteristically, the discussion which led to the first restrictions in child labour in 1839 was concerned mainly with the fact that recruits from factory districts were too weak and sickly for military service.

14 In the terminology 'industrial revolution', 'first technological revolution' and so on, we follow the usage of Ernest Mandel, *Late Capitalism*, London: New Left Books 1975.

See our Appendix on the Relationship between Form of Production, Division of Labour, Skill Levels and Education, pp. 195–201 below.

15 *Capital*, vol. 1, *op. cit.* p. 613.

16 Lawson and Silver, *op. cit.* p. 188.

17 Marx, *Capital*, vol. 1, *op. cit.* p. 388.

18 Charles Dickens's *Oliver Twist* describes the workhouse régime.

19 Marx, *Capital*, vol. 1, *op. cit.* p. 382.

20 Lawson and Silver, *op. cit.* p. 239.

21 See: Nadeshda Konstaninowna Krupskaya, 'Volksbildung und Demokratie', in *Krupskaya Sozialistische Pädagogik*, vol. 1, East Berlin: Volk und Wissen 1972, p. 271.

22 Lawson and Silver, *op. cit.* p. 243.

23 Marx gives details of the various tricks thought up by the employers to get round the Factory Acts. See *Capital*, vol. 1, *op. cit.* pp. 389–411.

24 See Lawson and Silver, *op. cit.* p. 273.

25 *ibid.* p. 271.

26 *ibid.* pp. 260–61.

27 *ibid.* p. 318.

28 See: G. D. H. Cole, *Socialist Thought – The Forerunners 1789–1850*, London: MacMillan 1962, pp. 87–90.

29 See also: Krupskaya, *op. cit.* p. 280.
30 Robert Owen, 'A New View of Society', in Harold Silver, ed. *Robert Owen on Education*, Cambridge: Cambridge University Press 1969, p. 71.
31 'A New View of Society', in *ibid.* p. 73.
32 *ibid.* pp. 76–77.
33 'The Life of Robert Owen by Himself', in *ibid.* p. 50.
34 'A New View of Society' in *ibid.* p. 86.
35 *ibid.* p. 88.
36 *ibid.* p. 95.
37 'The Life of Robert Owen by Himself', in *ibid.* p. 55.
38 *ibid.* p. 65.
39 *ibid.* p. 64.
40 *ibid.* p. 64.
41 *ibid.* p. 63.
42 *ibid.* p. 64.
43 See: Krupskaya, *op. cit.* p. 283.
44 The schoolroom was originally modelled on the type used in monitorial schools, but proved unsuitable for good work. Owen's son, Robert Dale Owen, was to write that smaller classrooms, for twenty to thirty children would have been better. Robert Dale Owen, 'An Outline of the System at New Lanark', in Silver, ed. *op. cit.* p. 150.
45 *ibid.* p. 152–53.
46 *ibid.* p. 154.
47 *ibid.* p. 158.
48 *ibid.* pp. 161–62.
49 'A New View of Society', in *ibid.* p. 120.
50 Robert Dale Owen, in *ibid.* p. 164.
51 'A Life of Robert Owen by Himself', in *ibid.* p. 62.
52 See: 'Six Lectures delivered in Manchester (1837)', in *ibid.* pp. 206–8.
53 See 'Report to the County of Lanark (1820)', in *ibid.* pp. 165–89, for details of the 'Villages of Co-operation'.
54 Quoted in E. P. Thompson, *The Making of the English Working Class*, Harmondsworth: Penguin 1968, p. 861.
55 Quoted in *ibid.* p. 861. Thompson gives a summary of contemporary criticism of Owen.
56 See G. D. H. Cole, *op. cit.* for further details.
57 Karl Marx, 'Theses on Feuerbach' (as edited by Engels), third thesis, in Marx and Engels, *Selected Works*, London: Lawrence and Wishart 1970, p. 28.
58 See Alfred Schmidt, *The Concept of Nature in Marx*, London: New Left Books 1971, p. 145.
59 Marx, *Capital*, vol. 3, quoted in T. B. Bottomore and M. Rubel (eds.), *Karl Marx, Selected Writings in Sociology and Social Philosophy*, Harmondsworth: Penguin 1969, pp. 259–60; see *Capital*, vol. 3, London: Lawrence and Wishart 1962, pp. 799–800 for a different translation.
60 *Capital*, vol. 1, *op. cit.* pp. 616–18.
61 *Capital*, vol. 1, *op. cit.* p. 614.
62 See above, p. 21.
63 *Capital*, vol. 1, *op. cit.* p. 613.
64 See: *ibid.* pp. 523 ff.

65 See Appendix, pp. 195–201 below.
66 *Capital*, vol. 1, *op. cit.* p. 619.
67 Marx, *The First International and After*, Harmondsworth: Penguin 1974, pp. 88–89.
68 Marx, 'Critique of the Gotha Programme', *op. cit.* p. 358. Emphasis in original.
69 Marx wrote the draft of the Geneva Resolution in English. The German translator translated 'technological training' as 'polytechnische Erziehung' (polytechnic education). This term has since been used by marxists to refer not only to the technological part of Marx's proposed educational system, but to the system as a whole. Both the Soviet Union and the German Democratic Republic have used the term to refer to their school systems. We follow this practise in the present work, as 'polytechnic education' seems the best term to characterise what Marx had in mind.

3. The First Attempt to Build a Socialist Education System: the Soviet Union 1917–31

1 We have worked mainly from sources available in German. Since the publishers of documents on the Russian revolution generally follow their own political motives in choosing what to publish, this makes it hard to give a full picture. During the 1930s and 1940s, the stalinist bureaucracy made great efforts to suppress the educational ideas of the early years. After the Twentieth Congress of the Communist Party of the Soviet Union polytechnic education was reintroduced in the Soviet Union and in Eastern Europe (see chapter five). This led, for example, to the publication of an eleven volume collection of the works of Krupskaya in the GDR. This was soon allowed to go out of print and replaced by a four volume collection, leaving out many important items. There is a risk that such omissions are meant to support the interpretations favoured by the bureaucracy at a given time. The works of Schatzky, one of the most important educationalists of the Russian revolution, were completely suppressed during the stalinist period, and have only become available since 1958. Even today, only a restricted selection has been published. The best known of Soviet educationalists is Makarenko, whose ideas were favoured by Stalin. His works have always been readily available.
2 See Maurice Dobb, *Soviet Economic Development Since 1917*, London: Routledge and Kegan Paul 1966, chapter two, for a detailed description of economic and social conditions prior to 1917.
3 See R. Lorenz's introduction to: Leo Trotzki, *Ergebnisse und Perspektiven*, Frankfurt: Europäische Verlagsanstalt 1971, p. 19.
4 Oskar Anweiler and Klaus Meyer, *Die sowjetische Bildungspolitik seit 1917*, Heidelberg: Quelle und Meyer Verlag, 1961, p. 21.
5 Lenin, 'The question of Ministry of Education policy' (1913), *Collected Works*, vol. 19, p. 139.
6 See: Tony Cliff, *Lenin*, vol. 1, London: Pluto Press 1975, pp. 54–55.
7 See: Krupskaya, 'Volksbildung und Demokratie' (1915), in: *Sozialistische Pädagogik*, vol. 1, East Berlin: Volk und Wissen 1972. This is an excellent short history of mass education.

8 See: Krupskaya, 'Zwei Typen der Organisierung des Schulwesens' (1911), and 'Die Frage der Arbeitsschule auf der Deutschen Lehrerversammlung zu Berlin' (1912), both in *ibid.*

9 Reprinted in Anweiler and Meyer, *op. cit.* pp. 55–60.

10 *ibid.* pp. 60–66.

11 *ibid.* pp. 66–73.

12 Quoted from: Anweiler and Meyer, p. 69.

13 Krupskaya, 'Die Verbindung des Unterrichts mit produktiverArbeit in der Einheitsarbeitsschule', in *op. cit.* vol. 2, pp. 163–4.

14 Quoted in Anweiler and Meyer, *op. cit.* p. 71.

15 See: Krupskaya, 'Schülerselbstverwaltung und Arbeitsorganisation', in *op. cit.* vol. 2, pp. 66–71.

16 P. Blonsky, 'Axiome des pädagogischen Dilettantismus', reprinted in Krupskaya, *op. cit.* vol. 1, pp. 366 ff.

17 See: Krupskaya, 'Ein interessanter Artikel', in *op. cit.* vol. 1, pp. 366–69.

18 See 'Programme of the Communist Party of Russia' (adopted at the Eighth Party Congress, March 1919), in N. Bukharin and E. Preobrazhensky, *The ABC of Communism*, Harmondsworth: Penguin 1970, pp. 443–45; see also *ibid.* chapter 10.

19 Lenin, 'The tasks of the youth leagues' (1920), in *Collected Works*, vol. 31, p. 296.

20 Lenin, 'The achievements and difficulties of the Soviet Government' (1919), in *Collected Works*, vol. 29, pp. 69–70.

21 *ibid.* p. 71.

22 'Speech delivered at the Third All-Russia Congress of Water Transport Workers' (1920), in *Collected Works*, vol. 30, p. 430.

23 Lenin, 'Report on the party programme' (speech made at the Eighth Congress of the RCP (B), March 1919), in *Collected Works*, vol. 29, pp. 178–80.

24 *ibid.* p. 183 (emphasis in original).

25 Victor Serge, *From Lenin to Stalin*, New York: Monad Press, 1974, p. 119.

26 'On cooperation' (1923), in *Collected Works*, vol. 33, p. 475.

27 'The tasks of the youth leagues', *op. cit.* p. 287.

28 *ibid.*

29 *ibid.* p. 293.

30 *ibid.* p. 289.

31 Karl-Heinz Günther and Helmut König, 'Einführung' to Lenin, *Uber Bildungspolitik und Pädagogik*, vol. 1, East Berlin: Volk und Wissen, 1975 p. 41.

32 'On Cooperation', *op. cit.* p. 475.

33 Victor Serge, *op. cit.* p. 119.

34 Krupskaya, 'Über den Zustand der Kinderheime', in *op. cit.* vol. 2, p. 119.

35 *ibid.* p. 368, note.

36 See: Dobb, *op. cit.* chapter six.

37 See Victor Serge, *op. cit.* pp. 39–40 for a vivid description of how 'classes were reborn under our very eyes'.

38 See Anweiler and Meyer, *op. cit.* pp. 30–31.

39 See *ibid.* p. 31.

40 Krupskaya, 'Das Volksbildungssystem in der RSFSR', in *op. cit.* vol. 2, p. 76.

41 'Rede auf einer Beratung der Leiter der Regionalabteilungen für Volksbildung' (1929), in *op. cit.* vol. 2, p. 99.

42 'Über die Mittelschule', in *ibid.* p. 109.

43 'Anlässlich der Thesen zu B. G. Koseljow's Referat über "beruflichtechnische Ausbildung"' (1920) in *ibid.* p. 170.

44 'Allgemeinbildung und Berufsbildung' (1923) in *ibid.* p. 174.

45 *ibid.* p. 176.

46 'Gutachten für den Entwurf des Lehrplans für den Arbeitsunterricht in den Schulen der zweiten Stufe' (1927) in *ibid.* pp. 192–93.

47 'Zur Frage der Ausbildung der Arbeitskraft', in *ibid.* p. 196.

48 *ibid.* p. 197.

49 See Georg von Rauch, *History of Soviet Russia,* 5th ed., New York: Praeger 1967, p. 182.

50 See: Tony Cliff, *State Capitalism in Russia,* London: Pluto Press 1974.

51 See: Agnes Katzenbach, 'Zu einigen Problemen der Aufhebung der Schule als abgesonderte Institution der Gesellschaft' (Unpublished Dissertation, Frankfurt, 1974).

52 Bubnov, Speech of 23 April 1931, quoted from Anweiler and Meyer, *op. cit.* p. 178.

53 Decision of 3 September 1931, in *ibid.* pp. 178–86.

54 Decision of 25 August 1932, in *ibid.* pp. 188–94.

55 Decree of 4 March 1937, in *ibid.* pp. 232–33.

56 See for instance Krupskaya's letter of 9 February 1937 to Zhdanov, in Krupskaya, *op. cit.* vol. 2, pp. 138–40.

57 This account of Schatzky's ideas and his work in the experimental station is based on the following articles by him: 'Munteres Leben' (1914), 'Die Schule der Zukunft' (1921), 'Ist die Schule für die Kinder da?' (1922), 'Mein pädagogischer Weg' (1928), 'Das Studium des Lebens und die Teilnahme an ihm' (1925), all reprinted in German in: Stanislaw Teofilowitsch Schazki, *Ausgewählte pädagogische Schriften,* ausgewählt, übersetzt und kommentiert von Isabella Rüttenauer und Bernhard Schiff, Berlin: Osteuropa-Institut an der freien Universität Berlin 1970.

58 See Oskar Anweiler, 'Leben und Wirksamkeit des russischen Pädagogen Stanislaw Teofilowitsch Schazki', in *Internationale Zeitschrift für Erziehungswissenschaft* 1964.

59 See: 'Ordnung der Ersten Versuchsstation für Volksbildung', in Schazki, *op. cit.* pp. 425–31.

60 See in particular: 'Auf dem Wege zur Arbeitsschule' (1918), in *ibid.* p. 251.

61 Our account is based mainly on the following writings of Makarenko: 'Der Marsch des Jahres Dreissig', 'Aus der Geschichte der Dzierzynski-Kommune', 'Umgeblätterte Seiten', all in Makarenko, *Werke,* vol. 2, East Berlin: Volk und Wissen, 1964; and: 'Flaggen auf den Türmen', in Makarenko, *Werke,* vol. 3, East Berlin: Volk und Wissen 1964.

62 Makarenko, *Werke, op. cit.* vol. 5.

63 Makarenko, 'Pädagogen zucken die Achseln', in *Werke, op. cit.* vol. 2, p. 447.

64 Makarenko, *ibid.* p. 443.

4. Education in Eastern Europe Since Stalin: the German Democratic Republic

1 Werner Fuchs, 'Schule und Produktion im polytechnischen Unterricht der DDR', Marburger Forschungsstelle für vergleichende Erzeihungswissenschaft 1977, p. 7.

2 The *Sozialistische Einheitspartei* (SED – Socialist Unity Party) is the ruling party of the GDR. It was founded in 1946 by merging the Communist Party (KPD) and the Social Democratic Party (SPD). The SED has always closely supported the policies of the Soviet Union.

3 Decision of the Central Committee of the SED of 29 July 1952, quoted from: *Quellen zur Geschichte der Erziehung*, East Berlin: Volk und Wissen 1975, p. 499.

4 See *Geschichte der Erziehung*, East Berlin: Volk und Wissen 1973, p. 640.

5 A short account of Soviet education policy is to be found in: Oskar Anweiler and others, *Bildungssysteme in Europa*, Weinheim and Basel: Beltz 1976.

6 'Das Gesetz über die sozialistische Entwicklung des Schulwesens in der DDR', quoted from: *Quellen zur Geschichte der Erziehung, op cit.* pp. 507 ff.

7 See Fuchs, *op. cit.* pp. 15–18.

8 Quoted in Helmut Klein, *Bildung in der DDR*, Reinbek bei Hamburg: Rowolt 1974, p. 63. This is an interesting account of education in the GDR by an East German professor of education.

9 See S. G. Sapovalenko, 'Noch einmal zur polytechnischen Bildung', in Oskar Anweiler (ed.), *Polytechnische Bildung und technische Elementarerziehung*, Bad Heilbrunn: Klinkhardt 1969, p. 47.

10 See Oskar Anweiler and others, *op. cit.* pp. 150–51.

11 Klein, *op. cit.* p. 89.

12 An important East German account of these changes and their causes is Heinz Frankiewicz. *Zur Theorie der polytechnischen Bildung und zu ihrer Anwendung auf die Überarbeitung der Lehrpläne für den polytechnischen Unterricht*, East Berlin 1968; reprinted West Berlin: Rossa 1972.

13 'Gesetz über das einheitliche sozialistische Bildungswesen von 1965' (Law on the Unitary Socialist Education System of 1965), quoted from: *Quellen zur Geschichte der Erziehung, op. cit.* p. 533.

14 Preamble to the Law of 1965, *ibid.*

15 'Verordnung über die Sicherung einer festen Ordnung an den allgemeinbildenden Schulen vom Oktober 1967' (Regulation on the Establishment of secure Order at general Schools), quoted from Oskar Anweiler and others, *op. cit.* p. 63.

16 *ibid.* p. 64.

17 *ibid.* p. 65, and Klein, *op. cit.* p. 206.

18 *Bildungs- und Erziehungsplan für den Kindergarten*, East Berlin: Volk und Wissen 1967.

19 Irmgard Launer, *Persönlichkeitsentwicklung im Vorschulalter bei Spiel und Arbeit*, East Berlin: Volk und Wissen 1970. This is an extremely interesting study on methods of achieving desired personality characteristics in pre-school education.

20 In 1972 there were 562 such schools, with about six thousand pupils. Klein, *op. cit.* p. 210.

21 The figures in this paragraph are from Anweiler and others, *op. cit.* p. 66.

22 See Frankiewicz, *op. cit.* pp. 54–84.

23 The theoretical basis and a summary of these teaching instructions is given in *Allgemeinbildung, Lehrplanwerk, Unterricht*, East Berlin: Volk und Wissen 1973.

24 Quotations from *Einführung in die sozialistische Produktion – Lehrbuch für Klasse 9*, East Berlin: Volk und Wissen 1972, pp. 119 ff.

25 *ibid.* p. 126.

26 Klein, *op. cit.* p. 120.

27 *ibid.* p. 121.

28 Erika Runge, 'Schüler, Lehrer, Schulen – Tonbänder aus dem Bezirk Rostock', in: *Kursbuch* (West Berlin) 24, 1971, p. 96.

29 See Klein, *op. cit.* pp. 128–31.

30 See pp. 148–50 below.

31 See Anweiler and others, *op. cit.* p. 69.

32 Figures from *ibid.* p. 70.

33 Klein, *op. cit.* p. 138.

34 *ibid.* p. 135.

35 See pp. 96–97 below.

36 Artur Meier, *Soziologie des Bildungswesens*, Cologne: Pahl-Rugenstein, 1974, p. 187. This study, although published in West Germany, is by an East German sociologist.

37 See Anweiler and others, *op. cit.* pp. 70–71.

38 See Meier, *op. cit.* p. 185.

39 See Introduction, pp. 1–9 above.

40 See pp. 5–6 above.

41 See Philip Neumann, 'Der Sozialismus als eigenständige Gesellschaftsformation', *Kursbuch* 23, 1971, for an analysis of this theory.

42 Quoted from *Quellen zur Geschichte der Erziehung*, *op. cit.* p. 506.

43 In 1965, an engineer in the chemical industry earned about twice as much as a normal worker. See: Udo Freier and Paul Lieber, *Politische Ökonomie des Sozialismus in der DDR*, Frankfurt: Makol Verlag 1972, pp. 244–45. Unfortunately, we have been unable to obtain new figures, but there is absolutely no reason to think that there has been a trend towards greater equality.

44 For a description of the planning system see: Renate Damus, 'Planungssysteme und gesellschaftliche Implikationen – am Beispiel der Planungssysteme in der DDR', in Peter Hennicke (ed.), *Probleme des Sozialismus und der Übergangsgesellschaft*, Frankfurt: Suhrkamp 1973.

45 See below, pp. 130–31 ff.

5. Education and Cultural Revolution in China

1 An example was the glowing report on the situation of women and children in China written by Claudie Broyelle: *La Moitié du Ciel*, Paris: Editions Denoel/Gonthier 1973 (translated as *Women's Liberation in China*,

London: Harvester Press 1977). After a further visit to China, Claudie Broyelle (together with Jacques Broyelle and Eveline Tschirhart), wrote a further book showing that most of the information in the first one was wrong or misleading, and trying to explain why Western visitors in China often misunderstand what they see. She argues that the motivation of the visitors sometimes leads to self-deception. See *Zweite Rückkehr aus China*, Berlin: Wagenbuch 1977 (translated as *China: A Second Look*, London: Harvester Press 1979).

2 We cannot describe here this economic and social order, which remained basically unchanged for two thousand years. A good brief account is to be found in C. P. Fitzgerald, *The Birth of Communist China*, Harmondsworth: Penguin 1964.

3 The classic description of this period is Edgar Snow, *Red Star over China* (1938), Harmondsworth: Penguin 1977. A contemporary analysis of the role of the Comintern in the disaster of 1927 is to be found in the articles of Victor Serge in the French journal Clarté, which have been republished in German as *Die Klassenkämpfe in der chinesischen Revolution von 1927*, Frankfurt: Verlag Neue Kritik 1975.

4 See: Edgar Snow, *op. cit.* p. 273.

5 See *ibid.* pp. 270–72.

6 See: Harry Magdoff, 'China: Contrasts with the USSR', in *Monthly Review*, vol. 27 no. 3, July–August 1975, pp. 12 ff., and Die Volksrepublik China, *Informationen zur politischen Bildung* Nr. 166, Bonn: Bundeszentrale für politische Bildung, 1976.

7 The educational clauses are to be found in Peter Mauger and others, *Education in China*, London: Anglo-Chinese Educational Institute 1974, p. 9.

8 Figures from *ibid.* p. 14.

9 *ibid.* p. 11.

10 Quoted from *ibid.* p. 14.

11 Mao Tse-tung, *On the Correct Handling of Contradictions Among the People*, Peking: Foreign Languages Press 1960.

12 Magdoff, *op. cit.* p. 36.

13 *Education Must Be Combined With Productive Labour*, Peking: Foreign Languages Press 1958, quoted here from Mauger, *op. cit.* p. 18.

14 See: Mauger, *op. cit.* p. 18.

15 See: Magdoff *op. cit.* pp. 38 ff.

16 Adrian Hsia, *The Chinese Cultural Revolution*, London: Orbach and Chambers 1972

17 See: Victor Nee and Don Layman, *The Cultural Revolution at Peking University*, New York and London: Monthly Review Press 1969.

18 Jerome Ch'en (ed.), *Mao Papers*, London: Oxford University Press 1970, pp. 21–22.

19 The 'Sixteen Points' were published in full in *Peking Review*, 12 August 1966; they are reprinted in Jerome Ch'en (ed.), *op. cit.*

20 See: Jaap van Ginneken, *The Rise and Fall of Lin Piao*, Harmondsworth: Penguin 1976, for a blow-by-blow description of events.

21 See *ibid.* pp. 86 ff, and Charles Reeve, *Le Tigre de Papier – sur le Développement du Capitalisme en Chine 1949–71*, Paris: Editions Spartacus 1972 (In German *Der Papiertiger*, Hamburg: Verlag Association 1975, pp. 139 ff.)

22 See: Hsia, *op. cit.* p. 136.
23 See: Jürgen Domes, 'The Role of the Military in the Formation of Revolutionary Committees 1967–68', in *The China Quarterly*, no. 44, October–December 1970, pp. 112 ff.
24 See: Hsia, *op. cit.* p. 168.
25 An interesting assessment, first published in *Il Manifesto*, is Rossana Rossanda, *Der Marxismus von Mao Tse-tung*, West Berlin: Merve Verlag 1971.
26 The fullest description of the affair is given by Ginneken, *op. cit.* pp. 11 ff.
27 *ibid.* pp. 283 ff.
28 See above, p. 24 and p. 32.
29 These principles are not laid down in this form at any one place. They are our summary of the main points in: 1. Mao's directive of 7 May 1966, reprinted in Jerome Ch'en *op. cit.*; 2. The 'Sixteen Points', see above, p. 115, also reprinted in Ch'en; 3. The 'Kirin Programme', a widely publicised plan for organising education on the local level (1969), reprinted in Mauger, *op. cit.* pp. 77 ff.
30 Hsia, *op. cit.* pp. 167 ff.
31 *Frankfurter Rundschau*, 2 September 1977. Chou came to a sticky end in the upheavals of Summer 1976. He was forced to resign and to take part in numerous self-criticism sessions. During one such session, he died of a heart attack.
32 According to: Peter Kuntze, *China – Revolution in der Seele*, Frankfurt: Fischer 1977, pp. 94–95.
33 An interesting description of family education is to be found in William Kessen (ed.), *Childhood in China*, New Haven and London: Yale University Press 1975. We have drawn on this report of a visit to China by a team of US American educationalists and psychologists extensively for the present and following sections.
34 Timetables are to be found in Kessen, *op. cit.* pp. 98–99 and Mauger, *op. cit.* p. 38.
35 Kessen, *op. cit.* p. ix.
36 According to an article by Ch'ün P'u in *Peking Rundschau*, 29/1975, quoted by Carlos Castillo Rios and Joachim Schickel, *Erziehung in China*, Reinbek bei Hamburg: Rowolt 1977, p. 252.
37 A timetable is to be found in: Mauger, *op. cit.* p. 42. Descriptions of lessons in various subjects are given in: Kessen, *op. cit.* pp. 121–27.
38 Kessen, *op. cit.* p. 115.
39 See Mauger, *op. cit.* p. 42 and Kessen, *op. cit.* p. 130.
40 Rios and Schickel, *op. cit.* p. 253. Since there were 145 million primary school pupils in the same year, and both primary and middle school last five years, it is obvious that there are not enough places for all children in the age group in secondary education. However, to calculate the exact deficit, it would be necessary to know the age-structure of the Chinese population.
41 Mauger, *op. cit.* p. 46.
42 Kessen, *op. cit.* p. 154.
43 Quoted from Mauger, *op. cit.* p. 81.
44 Figures from *China – Gesellschaft, Politik, Staat, Wirtschaft*, Düsseldorf: Bertelsmann Universitätsverlag 1973, p. 82.
45 During this campaign, the newspaper *Renmin Ribao* reprinted an

'Application to leave the university', by a student whose father had got him a place through influence. *Renmin Ribao*, 18 January 1974.

46 *Peking Rundschau*, no. 3 1973, reprinted in *Wer Erzieht Wen – Revolution im chinesischen Erziehungswesen*, Berlin: Oberbaumverlag 1976, p. 184.

47 Example from Mauger, *op. cit.* p. 57.

48 See above, p. 127.

49 For a description of such a school, see: Alexander Casella, 'The Nanniwan 7 May Cadre School', in *The China Quarterly*, no. 53, January/March 1973, pp. 151–57.

50 Mao Tse-tung, *On the Correct Handling of Contradictions among the People*, Peking: Foreign Languages Press 1960.

51 Rios and Schickel, *op. cit.* pp. 69–70.

52 See Claudie Broyelle and others, *Zweite Rückkehr aus China, op. cit.* p. 20.

53 In her book on everyday life in China, Claudie Broyelle describes many cases of this kind of repressive social control. *ibid.*

54 The poster, with the title 'Democracy and the Legal System in Socialism' by Li Yi Zhe was duplicated and circulated all over China. It contains a detailed analysis and is over seventy book pages long. Reprinted in Li Yi Zhe, Helmut Opletal and Peter Schier, *China: Wer gegen wen?* West Berlin: Rotbuch 1977.

55 *ibid.* p. 114.

56 Mao Tse-tung, 'Where do correct ideas come from?' (May 1963), in *Quotations from Chairman Mao Tse-tung*, Peking: Foreign Languages Press 1967, p. 206.

6. Polytechnic Education and the Transition from School to Work in Modern Capitalism

1 Trades Union Congress, 'Note of Comment on the Government's Consultative Paper "Education in Schools" ' London: TUC 1977.

2 See Appendix pp. 195–201 below.

3 André Gorz, 'Technologie, Techniker und Klassenkampf', in André Gorz, ed., *Schule und Fabrik*, West Berlin: Merve Verlag 1972, p. 40, our translation; for English version see André Gorz, 'Technology, technicians, and class struggle', in A. Gorz, ed., *The Division of Labour*, Brighton: Harvester Press 1978.

4 'Education in Schools', Government Green Paper, London 1977.

5 John Holloway and Sol Picciotto, 'Education and the Crisis of Social Relations', paper from the Conference of Socialist Economists, Bradford, 1978, emphasis in original.

6 See Simon Frith, 'Youth Employment and Education – the Message from Coventry', in *Socialist Teacher* 5, Summer 1978.

7 See the important analysis of the US education system to be found in: Samuel Bowles and Herbert Ginits, *Schooling in Capitalist America*, London and Henley: Routledge and Kegan Paul 1976.

8 The availability of plentiful cheap labour is regarded by many experts as the main cause of the 'economic miracle'. See Ernst-Ulrich Hüster and others. *Determinanten der westdeutschen Restauration 1945–49*, Frankfurt am Main: Suhrkamp 1973, and Charles P. Kindleberger, *Europe's Postwar*

Growth – the Role of Labour Supply, Cambridge, Mass: Harvard University Press, 1967.

9 Which does not mean that no productivity increase took place – the introduction of new machinery increases the proportion of highly productive plants in the economy, even if that is not the primary aim of investment. Between 1950 and 1956, productivity in West Germany increased by 40 per cent, of which only 4 per cent was due to greater capital intensity. See Stephen Castles and Godula Kosack, *Immigrant Workers and Class Structure in Western Europe*, London: Oxford University Press 1973, p. 404.

10 Martin Baethge, 'Abschied von Reformillusionen', in *Betrifft Erziehung* 11, 1972.

11 Friedrich Gerstenberger, Produktion und Qualifikation, in *Leviathan*, 2/1975, p. 259.

12 See Castles and Kosack, *op. cit.* chapter 9, 'The political economy of migration'.

13 Der Sachverständigenrat zur Begutachtung der gesamtwirtschaftlichen Entwicklung – also known as 'the five wise men'. Set up in 1963 as a reaction to increasing economic difficulties, it has the task of making annual reports to the Government, with the main aim of persuading the unions to keep their demands moderate. Here we quote their *Jahresgutachten 1965–66*, Stuttgart and Mainz, 1965, p. 175, from Freerk Huisken, *Zur Kritik bürgerlicher Didaktik und Bildungsökonomie*, List: München 1972, p. 309.

14 The debate started in 1964 with the publication of G. Picht's *Die Deutsche Bildungskatastrophe* (The German Educational Catastrophe) Freiburg, 1964; see also F. Edding, *Ökonomie des Bildungswesens* Freiburg, 1963.

15 Der Sachverständigenrat . . ., *Jahresgutachten 1965–66*, *op. cit.* p. 178, quoted here from Huisken, *op. cit.* p. 310.

16 H. Kern and M. Schumann, *Industriearbeit und Arbeiterbewusstsein*, part 1, Frankfurt am Main 1970.

17 'Bericht über die Lage der Psychiatrie in der Bundesrepublik Deutschland', Bundestagdrucksache 1/4200.

18 Ralf Dahrendorf, *Plädoyer für eine aktive Bildungspolitik*, Hamburg 1965.

19 Der Deutsche Ausschuss für das Erziehungs- und Bildungswesen – a consultative committee of educational experts set up by the Government in 1953; its recommendations were not binding.

20 See *Projektgruppe Arbeitslehre Marburg, Schule, Produktion, Gewerkschaften*, Reinbek bei Hamburg: Rowolt 1974, chapter 4.

21 'Empfehlungen zur Hauptschule, Beschluss der Kultusministerkonferenz vom 3. Juli 1969'.

22 Quoted from W. Voelmy and others, *Arbeitslehre – Bilanz '72*, Weinheim and Basel: Beltz Verlag 1973, p. 16.

23 Most of these examples are taken from a research paper by a Frankfurt teacher, Inge Lehnert, on which we have drawn extensively for this section: 'Arbeitserziehung als "Hinführung zur Arbeitswelt" ', unpublished paper, Frankfurt 1977.

24 See W. Christian, F. Heinisch and W. Markert, 'Arbeitslehre und polytechnische Bildung', in J. Beck and others, *Erziehung in der*

Klassengesellschaft, Munich: List 1972, p. 195.

25 'Sachthema 3: Verbrennungs-Kolbenmotoren', in H.-J. Stührmann and
   B. Wessels, *Lehrerhandbuch für den technischen Werkunterricht*, Band 1,
   Weinheim 1970, quoted here according to *Projektgruppe Arbeitslehre
   Marburg, op. cit.* p. 105.

26 *ibid.* p. 106.

27 See Peter Karasek and Jürgen Pyschik, 'Arbeitslehre – Lehre vom
   Sachzwang', in Wolfgang Christian and others, *Polytechnik in der
   Bundesrepublik?* Frankfurt: Suhrkamp 1972, pp. 13–81. This comparison
   of most published projects shows a clear tendency towards more
   socio-economic content, and away from purely technical aspects.

28 Wolgang Biester, 'Technisches Werken und Betriebserkundungen im
   Aufgabenfeld "Automation" ', quoted here from *Projektgruppe
   Arbeitslehre Marburg, op. cit.* p. 109.

29 Das Fahrrad, in *Praxis der Arbeitslehre*, Wuppertal 1968, quoted here from
   Karasek and Pyschik, *op. cit.* p. 64.

30 As the survey carried out by Karasek and Pyschik showed, *op. cit.* pp. 74–5.

31 *Polytechnik-Arbeitslehre, Handreichungen für die Sekundarstufe*, 1, published for
   the Education Ministry of Hesse by Diesterweg 1974, p. 6.

32 *ibid.* pp. 6–7.

33 *ibid.* p. 7.

34 For instance the so-called 'Berlin Concept' of H. Blankertz, G. Groth,
   J. Kledzig, P. Werner and others, published in 1970. This concept played
   a very important part in the discussion on the development of
   Arbeitslehre/Polytechnik of this type.

35 Our account here is based on the unpublished paper of Inge Lehnert, *op. cit.*

36 Helmut Böttiger, Wulfgar von Koerber and Jutta Kühn, *Unterrichtseinheit
   Arbeit, Beispiel einer Unterrichtseinheit im Unterricht Gesellschaft/Politik an der
   Gesamtschule Fröndenberg*, Offenbach: Verlag 2000, 1972.

37 In recent years, special courses for teachers of Arbeitslehre have been set
   up at the universities of Bremen and Frankfurt.

38 See Georg Zinner, 'Berufsverbote in der Bundesrepublik –
   Auslandsreaktionen', in *Neue Praxis*, 4/1976.

7. A Revolutionary Ferment

1 *Die Tvind Schule in Dänemark*, West Berlin: Arbeitsgemeinschaft
   sozialpolitischer Arbeitskreise 1977, p. 19. This is the German version of
   a brochure produced by the Tvind schools. We have used it extensively for
   this section. Our account is also based on discussion with colleagues who
   have visited Tvind.

2 *ibid.* p. 86.

3 See *Wir bringens in Gang – Energiebuch*, West Berlin:
   Arbeitsgemeinschaft sozialpolitischer Arbeitskreise 1977.

4 A brief account of the development of the Freinet movement is to be found
   in Jean-Claude Girardin, 'Célestin Freinet – ein revolutionäre Pädagoge',
   in André Gorz (ed.), *Schule and Fabrik*, Berlin: Merve Verlag 1972. Freinet
   himself wrote many books on his work. See for instance: *Pour l'école du
   peuple*, Paris: Maspero 1969.

5 See Christoph Hennig, 'Freinet-Pädagogik: Eine konkrete Alternative für die Schule', in Aida Vasquez and Fernand Oury, *Vorschläge für die Arbeit im Klassenzimmer*, Reinbek bei Hamburg: Rowolt 1976.

6 Freinet, *Die Moderne Französiche Schule*, Paderborn: Schöningh 1965 (German translation of *Pour l'école du peuple*), p. 99.

7 Freinet gives lists of the tools and equipment which are necessary and desirable for the classroom, in *ibid.* pp. 68–72.

8 Examples from Hennig, *op. cit.* p. 21.

9 For a list of the 'laws' decided upon by one class, see Aida Vasquez and Fernand Oury, *op. cit.* p. 56. These authors emphasise that it is essential that each class should discuss and make its own rules.

10 See Freinet, *op. cit.* pp. 82–3.

11 Examples from Hennig, *op. cit.* p. 26.

12 Freinet, *op. cit.* p. 78.

13 Details of publications, and of national and international meetings may be obtained from the CEL (Coopérative de l'Enseignement Laic), B.P. 282, Place Bergis, F 06403 Cannes, France.

14 See: Girardin, *op. cit.* p. 142.

15 Reprinted in Girardin, *op. cit.* pp. 151–54.

16 'Déclaration ICEM' in *L'Educateur* 15–16/1973, quoted from Hennig, *op. cit.* p. 34.

17 Girardin, *op. cit.* p. 150.

Index

Note: To avoid undue repetition, the term 'education' does not appear in this index, as it would refer to nearly every page. Entries for the countries dealt with are also omitted, as they may easily be found in the table of contents. The German Democratic Republic is referred to as GDR, the German Federal Republic as GFR.